W9-CSL-615

The Truth About

URI GELLER

The Truth About

URI GELLER

By James Randi
(The Amazing Randi)

PB *Prometheus Books*

700 East Amherst Street
Buffalo. N.Y. 14215

"How Does Uri Do It?" by Donald Singleton, © 1973 by New York Daily News, Incorporated. Reprinted by permission of the New York *Daily News*.

"Investigating the Paranormal," from *Nature,* vol. 251, October 18, 1974. Reprinted by permission.

"Uri Geller and Science," by Dr. Joseph Hanlon, © *New Scientist* magazine, October 17, 1974. Reprinted by permission.

"Andrew Weil's Search for the True Uri Geller," reprinted from *Psychology Today* magazine June and July 1974. © 1974 Ziff-Davis Publishing Company. All rights reserved.

Extracts from *Uri: The Journal of the Mystery of Uri Geller* are reprinted by permission of the publisher, Anchor Books, New York.

"Uri through the Lens Cap," by Yale Joel © *Popular Photography*, June 1974. Reprinted by permission.

"Uri Geller Twirls the Entire World on His Little Finger," © 1974, by *Haolam Haze* (Tel Aviv) for February 20, 1974. Reprinted by permission.

Revised edition of *The Magic of Uri Geller,* by James Randi,
published in 1975
Published 1982 by Prometheus Books
700 East Amherst Street, Buffalo, New York 14215

Copyright 1982 © by James Randi
All Rights Reserved

Library of Congress Card Catalog No.: 82-60951
ISBN: 0-87975-199-1

Dedicated to Uri Geller and Shipi Shtrang,
two men who fooled the world—almost

"I'll have you hanged," said a cruel and ignorant king, who had heard of The Psychic's powers, "if you don't prove that you are a mystic."

"I see strange things," said The Psychic at once. "A golden bird in the sky, and demons under the earth."

"How can you see through solid objects? How can you see far in the sky?"

"Fear is all you need."

Contents

Author's Note

Since this book was first published in 1975 under the title *The Magic of Uri Geller*, much has occurred in the Geller saga. I will attempt to bring the reader up to date.

I have not revealed this previously, but it is surely time to do so. In May of 1975, just before the book was committed to the hands of the printer, I sent Uri Geller a registered, carefully composed letter. It was received by him personally at his apartment in New York City.

The letter offered Geller a way to ward off the dilemma that my book was sure to bring about. I told him that I would meet with him at a time and place of his choosing to discuss what we might work out so that I would not have to proceed with publication. It was something I was willing to forgo if a better solution could be arrived at, but I was convinced that the truth had to be told, one way or another. Though I did not say in the letter what offer I would make, I was prepared to accept a statement from Uri to the effect that he had performed his deceptions in order to show that scientists are easily fooled and that the media are inclined to snap up every paranormal claim they can find, uncritically. In other words, I was offering him a way out that would not only make him a hero and a prince of hoaxers, but also pave the way for him to step into legitimate show-business as an established conjuror. He could have avoided the albatross I was about to hang about his neck, the book would be the official announcement of his revelation to the world, and we'd all be a lot happier.

Knowing the business as I do, I have no doubt that this man could have rescued himself and become a huge success in the theater had he chosen to accept my offer of that private talk. He chose not to, and the manuscript went to the printer.

Weeks before the book was released, I received two letters, both from the same lawyer, on behalf of Geller and two scientists who had tested and validated his powers. The letters stated that, if I made any untrue statements about these individuals, I would be sued for libel. Fair enough. In order to prove libel, a plaintiff has to prove that an untrue statement was made. Obviously, every statement in this book was carefully read and considered by that lawyer. I was never sued.

In March of 1977, I received a letter from Yascha Katz, Geller's former manager, offering to "discuss" the matter with me. I had referred to him as a "dupee" rather than as a "duper," and he found that to be a suitable premise upon which he might approach me. Enlisting the interest of the Italian RAI television folks, who had just completed a lengthy and very negative study of paranormal claims through journalist Piero Angela, I flew to Israel to interview Katz. What he told me was the single greatest indictment of Uri Geller I'd ever heard. This former colleague claimed that Geller owed him upwards of $30,000 in unpaid commissions and that he (Katz) had been dumped after Geller got his start in the United States. He described the scene at the airport in Tel Aviv when he and Geller were boarding the plane to America. Katz had asked, one final time, if his apparent powers were the real thing or a deception. Uri had looked into his eyes and sworn it was all kosher, and the two had walked hand-in-hand up the ramp.

Katz described how he had then been dragooned into serving as a confederate in the Geller vaudeville act, peeking into sealed envelopes, tossing objects over his shoulder as "materializations" credited to Geller, and listening in on conversations to obtain needed information for the deceptions. He had done this when his regular confederates, Shipi Shtrang and others, had been unavailable.

The exposé was broadcast in Italy and published in *New Scientist* magazine in England. Geller then loudly proclaimed that Katz had stolen money from him, and Katz countered by announcing that he was suing Geller. Nothing ever happened.

Ever since, the popularity of this psychic superstar has been waning. Most of the scientists who formerly supported him jumped off his comet as it dimmed. Others have simply lapsed into silence on the subject. The Stanford Research International folks merely grumble that Geller was "only 3 percent of the total work" they carried out in the paranormal field and declined to discuss the matter further—except to insist that they were not fooled in the first place. Harold Puthoff and Russell Targ have contradicted themselves. They said early on in the drama that if they ever even suspected a subject of using trickery, they would throw him/her out on his/her ear. Now they confide that they knew all the time Geller was a trickster but wanted to study his methods!

John Taylor, formerly Geller's most vocal and dedicated supporter, has written a book, *Science and the Supernatural,* in which he does a 180-degree turn at high speed without academic whiplash, reversing himself on the matter in a rather peculiar fashion. He tells us that since only the electromagnetic (EM) spectrum can explain Geller's feats—if they are genuine—and his research shows that EM forces are not involved, therefore the phenomena do not exist. What we look for in vain is a statement from Taylor admitting that he was fooled—completely, thoroughly, and definitively. But the raw courage it took to write the book, preceded as it was by rather tame articles in scientific periodicals that hinted at the reversal to come, can earn only praise from my camp.

John Hasted continues to believe in Geller, the spoon-bending children, and almost everything paranormal, in spite of a plethora of rebuttals, denials, and criticisms of his claims. Charles Crussard, still convinced that he was and is incapable of error, labors on in France to convince the world that he was right in believing in the powers of Geller and of his own Gallic star, Jean-Pierre Girard. Crussard seems not to be aware that Girard long ago declared, as I thought Geller might choose to, that he was playing "psychic" as a hoax on the scientists.

Professor Wilbur Franklin, a metallurgist at Kent State University who had declared strong support of Geller's abilities before meeting me and seeing several demonstrations of psychic tricks—including spoon- and key-bending—reversed his opinion of the famous "platinum ring fracture" and finally decided that it was, as others had known all along, simply a bad brazing job. He died soon after.

In general, Geller can no longer obtain a serious hearing in the scientific community. He has refused to show up in labs where it appeared that he might be subject to genuine observation, and he has refused tests at the last minute because of "negative vibrations." He has walked off numerous radio and television shows when my name has been mentioned, and cancelled out on others where I appeared to challenge him. On one television show in Holland, he stood up and slapped the face of a magician who, unknown to Geller, had been introduced into the panel; he was booed from the stage. On a Baltimore television show (as on others) he was plainly seen to bend a spoon with his two hands surreptitiously, and then to conceal the bend and reveal it slowly to the hosts of the show, who oohed and aahed appropriately. Then he declared that a little girl who had rubbed his hand had performed the apparent miracle. The videotapes make interesting viewing indeed.

There is much more to tell, and some of it is related in my latest book, *Flim-Flam!*, available from this publisher as a companion volume to this one. There are more books in the works as well. The Hydra of the paranormal grows heads faster than one can lop them off. But one tries.

Thank you for your interest in an alternative point of view about these claims. It would be a thankless task to prepare this material were it not for the many letters I receive expressing support and gratitude. These make it well worth doing.

JAMES RANDI

Rumson, N.J.
May, 1982

Acknowledgments

The author wishes to thank sincerely: Villamor Asuncion for typing beyond the call of duty; David Berglas for valuable cooperation; Rose Bonanno, David Davies and Judy-Lynn del Rey; the late Joseph Dunninger for his valued friendship; Dr. Christopher Evans; Dr. Sarah Feinstein, Moses Figueroa, who shared many tense moments with me; Martin Gardner for research materials and other valuable assistance; W. Geissler-Werry; the late Felix Greenfield for caring to fight the good fight; Dr. Joe Hanlon, Farooq Hussain, Dr. Ray Hyman and Leon Jaroff; Norman King for his kindness in many ways; Billy McComb for extensive use of his premises and for his patience while I was in England; Lora Myers; Long John Nebel for his continued camaraderie; Stanley Palm; Fred Pohl, Jr., for patient attendance; Dr. Jack Salz, Marcello Truzzi; Dr. Maurice Wilkens FRS; and especially James Pyczynski.

Air Canada for travel arrangements to the Continent.

The many periodicals that have allowed me to use excerpts from their accounts. They have been most generous.

And the other gentlemen at King's College, London. I am richer for having known them.

To the men such as Targ, Puthoff, Bastin, Hasted, Bohm, Taylor, and others who have lent their scientific acceptance to a chimera, I suggest that it is time to call in their loans.

Foreword

When Psychic Uri Geller first burst into the news in 1973, a naïve America was ripe for the plucking. With consummate showmanship, and leaving a trail of bent and broken silverware behind him, he traveled across the country, making followers—and fools—out of mighty institutions and prominent personalities. Geller convinced executives and researchers at the Stanford Research Institute (SRI), one of the nation's most distinguished "think tanks," that he could read minds, foretell events, and, with sheer psychic energy, distort magnetic fields, streams of electrons, and solid metallic objects. He convinced Apollo-14 Astronaut Ed Mitchell to help finance the research at SRI and persuaded Gerald Fineberg, a well-known physicist, into sponsoring a Columbia University colloquium featuring an amateurish SRI film that "documented" Geller's miracles. Even *Nature* magazine, the world's most prestigious science journal, published a detailed SRI report on Geller's remarkable talents, thus endowing Uri with an aura of respectability that an accompanying editorial disclaimer did little to diminish. *The New York Times, Newsweek,* network commentators including Barbara Walters, and a host of other journalists, both print and electronic, treated Geller seriously and even with awe, utterly failing to exercise the healthy skepticism so important to their professions.

Then, with the U.S. almost under Geller's spell, along came Randi. James (The Amazing) Randi did not have the distinguished credentials of many of the people whom Geller had converted. Born in Toronto in 1928, he was a child prodigy, but never attended college or had any scientific training. Magic was—and has remained—his all-consuming interest, and his prowess at legerdemain has won him invitations to perform before royalty in Europe and Asia, at the White House, on national television, and on college campuses around the world.

Randi first encountered Geller (and I first met Randi) at the offices of *Time* magazine in Manhattan, where Geller had come directly from SRI to convince the editors that his powers were genuine. After Geller had performed and departed, Randi, who had been posing as a *Time* editor, proceeded to duplicate all of Geller's feats, demonstrating that only fast hands and clever psychology were necessary. His revelations contributed to *Time's* first story on Geller, which charged in effect that SRI had been hoodwinked by an Israeli nightclub magician.

From that time on, Randi has relentlessly and gleefully investigated and pursued Geller, determined to put a stop to someone he felt was sullying the good name of magicians and bringing dishonor to their profession. In *The Truth About Uri Geller*, Randi discloses the lengths to which he went and the ingenious snares he devised to expose Geller's methods. After reading Randi's logical and rational explanations of Uri's tricks, only the most fanatic and gullible followers (alas, there are many) will continue to believe in Geller and in the psychic phenomena that he claims to effect. Better yet, Randi's revelations may give pause to the next charismatic "psychic" to appear on the scene. For no matter how clever or deceptive the next Geller is, James Randi will be there, his eyes gleaming, ready to do battle for legitimate magic and magicians everywhere.

LEON JAROFF
Senior Editor, *Time* Magazine

1

Introduction:
Who Is Uri Geller?

I have read with keen curiosity the articles by leading scientists on the subject of psychic phenomena . . . There is no doubt in my mind that some of these scientists are sincere in their belief but unfortunately it is through this very *sincerity* that thousands become converts. The fact that they are *scientists* does not endow them with an especial gift for detecting the particular sort of fraud used by mediums, nor does it bar them from being deceived . . .
— Harry Houdini, *A Magician Among the Spirits*

He is an Israeli citizen, born in Tel Aviv on December 20, 1946, the only child of Itzhaak Geller, a retired Israeli Army sergeant, and Manzy Freud, said to be a very distant relative of Sigmund. Uri attended grade school in Tel Aviv, was sent to a kibbutz at age 9, when his parents divorced, and at age 11 moved to Nicosia, Cyprus, with his mother and new stepfather, who owned a hotel there.

In Nicosia he attended a Catholic high school, where he learned English; there are no records at the Israeli Ministry of Education to show that he graduated. At age 18, he entered the Israeli Army as a matter of course, connected with a paratrooper unit. He did not complete an Officers Training Corps course.

Leaving the Army after minor injuries, he was employed as a fashion model for a time, then was a camp counselor, at which job he met Shimson (Shipi) Shtrang, several years his junior. The two happened upon a book that dealt with magic and magicians, and began working together on the subject. An act developed, and they began working at the kibbutzes, and private parties, and in night clubs, claiming supernatural abilities for what was essentially a two-person "code" routine. Eventually they were brought to court for using the words "psychokinesis," "ESP," and "parapsychology" in their promotion, and from then on they were not allowed to use such terminology, since they were performing conjuring tricks. This, coupled with the exposure that Geller had faked a photograph of himself with Sophia Loren for the Israeli newspapers, led to Geller's decline in his own country.

At this point, he was "discovered" by Dr. Andrija Puharich, an

American parapsychology buff who convinced various persons in the United States that Uri was the real thing. Shortly thereafter, Uri and Shipi came to America, where their rise was meteoric.

Geller made countless appearances on TV and did numerous college and lecture-hall shows. Though the content of his in-person performances seemed rather trivial, the believers—and their ranks grew—marveled at even the most minor effect he produced. He had numerous reverses, too, but they were either ignored or explained away by the media and the faithful.

The major victory of his work in the U.S.A. was the series of "tests" he was put to at the Stanford Research Institute (SRI) in California. This was in late 1972. Though the cautious statement of the results hardly constituted a rave, and strong criticisms of the procedures were soon voiced, Geller claimed that he had been validated, and other labs in Europe and Britain (staffed by believers) hastened to test him.

The rest is checkered history.

This book is not a destructive one. I have been urged for the past two years to produce a manuscript that merely tells the truth behind what has come to be known as the Geller Effect; and in attempting to bring reason and objectiveness to the consideration of the strange events connected with Mr. Uri Geller, I stand the chance of being thought a renegade who is determined to put a fellow-performer out of business. This is hardly the case.

When I first began to investigate Geller, in the offices of *Time* Magazine in New York City, I knew full well what I was up against. I knew that the other conjurors would raise a hue and cry against my statements, believing that Geller was "just another one of the boys," who deserved to be defended by other legitimate entertainers. I was prepared to face the flood of crank letters and calls that were certain to follow and readied myself for the angry protests that the believers were bound to summon up against me.

To be frank, as Charles Reynolds and I sat in the *Time* office posing as reporters for that magazine (details, Chapter 7) and watched the trivial performance that Geller produced, I felt that his star could hardly shine in any prominence on this side of the ocean, though he had arrived with some fair amount of fanfare from European triumphs. Reynolds and I were quick to admire his disarming manner and his total charm. But if what he did at that meeting was to be typical of his future efforts, we were certain Uri could not survive. We were wrong.

One thing I must state in no uncertain terms: I am probably one of Uri Geller's greatest fans. I totally respect his techniques and his quick mind. But I cannot condone his callous disregard for the personal friends and admirers who have given their total allegiance to him, nor can I forgive the damage he has done to respectable men of science and the press who chose to board his comet and who may well have to face, in the end, the ridicule of their colleagues. For it is not impossible that Geller may find the burden of maintaining such a Wizard-of-Oz façade too much for him. With only one or two people who can be admitted into the secret world of his deception, he lives on the brink of exposure every minute. And those who are "in" on the secrets are a Damoclean blade over his head that can not be eliminated until confession time. That time just might arrive, as it did with Margaret Fox, who, as the last surviving sister of the team who started the whole spiritualism thing going many years back, confessed all to a world who largely chose to ignore her when she finally told the truth.

All the above is said with the assumption that Geller is not the psychic superstar he claims he is. This writer is convinced that Geller is a clever magician, nothing more—and certainly nothing less. This opinion is not the result of a previously set mind; it is, rather, a conclusion arrived at after two years of close observation and careful analysis. My first contact with Uri, at *Time* Magazine, showed me a perfectly transparent sleight-of-hand performance. Reynolds and I were watching a conjuror, and we knew it. But we were not ready to say that supernormal phenomena were not possible from him on other occasions. It took a lot of data, and much travel and work, to determine to my satisfaction that Uri's pattern of deception was unmistakable. Clever, yes. Psychic, no.

Magic, in one definition that I prefer, is "an attempt by Man to control Nature by means of spells and incantations." By that definition, I am certainly not a magician. But I *am* a conjuror, "one who gives the impression of performing acts of magic by using deception." And I am proud of my profession. I am even jealous of it and resent any prostitution of the art. In my view, Geller brings disgrace to the craft I practice. Worse than that, he warps the thinking of a young generation of forming minds. And that is unforgivable.

This book is partly in the form of an annotated anthology. Two reasons will become evident to the reader. First, the public view of Geller has been arrived at mainly from press and television accounts and demonstrations. To show the actual facts behind the stories and performances is to write off much of the so-called evidence for his superpowers. Second, since I have been reminded frequently by detractors that I have no academic or scientific standing from which I can properly attack Geller, I will allow those of much firmer grounding to relate their stories and attempt to demonstrate that most of their observations are useless when they are confronted with a clever performer who can beguile them into accepting his conditions and interpretations.

I shall not concern myself very much with the vast amount of silly UFO-divine-origin-save-the-world verbiage which Dr. Andrija Puharich (who "discovered" Geller) throws about when asked for comments on *any* subject. I hardly think anyone takes Puharich seriously, or believes in the planet Hoova, the spacecraft *Spectra,* or the computer "Rhombus 4-D." When Puharich gets into the story of his meeting with the Egyptian god Horus, the mind reels. What I *am* concerned with is the series of purported miracles that Geller has performed, from bending house keys to teleporting himself instantaneously to Brazil. A huge amount of evidence will be brought from behind the scenery that the superpsychic has set up. And I only ask that my readers will consider carefully the new picture that we will see develop here.

There are a number of methods by which the world has allowed itself to be led down this particular garden path. Some of these are contrived by the perpetrators of the myth and others are simply facts of our way of life and business. For example, the press is inclined to ignore "non-stories." By a "non-story" I mean an account which does not present a novel, exciting, or mysterious aspect to the reader. No editor in his right mind would run a story saying that Santa Claus does not exist. But *every* editor would buy a story proving that the old fellow is a real person. Similarly, when stories on Geller show up on editorial desks and are found to be negative toward the wonderful world of things-that-go-bump-in-the-night, they are either quietly discarded or sent back for revision into a more palatable (and salable) form. My investigations have shown this to be very much the case. As an example:

Stanford Research Institute (SRI) managed to talk themselves into some fancy money ($80,000) to build an "ESP Teaching Machine" which was designed to increase the ability of a "sensitive" to perform feats of telepathy. When the results of the experiments with the machine were recorded manually, they appeared to be successful; when, finally, a computerized system of recording was connected up, the results dropped back to chance. Once again, the law of averages was vindicated. But had this kind of "machine" experiment been thought of before? Yes, it had. In 1966, Dr. C. E. M. Hansel referred to it in the conclusion of his book *ESP: A Scientific Evaluation*:

> A great deal of time, effort and money has been expended but an acceptable demonstration of the existence of extrasensory perception has not been given. Critics have themselves been criticized for making the conditions of a satisfactory demonstration impossible to obtain. An acceptable model for future research with which the argument could rapidly be settled one way or the other has now been made available by the investigators at the United States Air Force Research Laboratories. If 12 months' research on VERITAC can establish the existence of ESP, the past research will not have been in vain. If ESP is not established, much further effort could be spared and the energies of many young scientists could be directed to more worthwhile research.

The book was published before the VERITAC experiments had been run. Again, to most investigators' expectation, the law of averages triumphed. But such tests are not too popular with parapsychologists. To them, the experiments "prove nothing," and they set out once more to pursue the Grail of ESP.

Incorrect accounts are responsible for a great deal of the misinformation that gets picked up and reprinted. At the urging of enthusiastic editors, reporters making small semantic changes and liberal applications of hyperbole will transform an account from an accurate description into an impossible enigma. Descriptions of conjuring performances, particularly, always fail to note that the performer did such innocent-appearing things as blowing his nose or perhaps leaving the room to attend a "call of nature." These are too common to seem worth noting, but may be just what is necessary to accomplish the miracle subsequently described as having taken place under tight control circumstances. Observers and recorders cannot really be blamed for omitting these details; but they *are* at fault for assuming they have accurately reported *everything* that might bear upon the matter, having no expertise to support that assumption. One can imagine a person unfamiliar with surgical procedures describing carefully an operation and failing to note that the surgeon washed his hands and sterilized the instruments!

Few of the Geller experiments, especially the famous tests at SRI in which Geller performed apparent miracles of ESP, include in their reports the fact that one Shipi Shtrang, once claimed by Geller as his cousin and his brother, was present. It is significant, you may agree, that when Geller performed the subsequent tests at SRI and *failed* to function clairvoyantly with their one hundred sealed envelopes (the tests were discontinued when the psychologists suspected foul play) Shipi was *not* present. But Shipi *was* present when the cable car stopped in Germany in 1971; and again, in 1972, when a full-grown Labrador retriever was "teleported" in the wink of an eye, Shipi was the only witness. But to the believer, such things are thought to be inconvenient coincidences—nothing more. I know better.

Psychics, those who claim to be able to read minds, to move objects at a distance by "mind power," and to do other "supernatural" things, seem to be more than just gifted people. They also have a very special set of rules by which they operate, and by which they insist on being judged. The "negative success" business is just one special rule. It means that when you win, you win; and when you lose, you win. It will be referred to in Chapter 10, when we discuss Edgar Mitchell. Psychics cannot function when nonbelievers are present, either. Even the presence of a skeptic dooms their experiments to failure, and causes them great distress. By means of such rules, I could safely claim to be the greatest conjuror in history, being able to change myself into an inkwell instantly. Of course, if skeptics were present—

Thus, Geller will not operate with magicians around (except when he doesn't divine that they are there, as in the *Time* Magazine matter and on several other occasions here and in England, or when he is satisfied they are incompetent), and he must be catered to carefully lest he refuse to try tests or throw a temper tantrum. Geller also has, to use his terminology, the option of "passing" on any test he doesn't "feel for." He insists that he be able to refuse any experiment or set of "runs." I do wish that I had that rule written into my book. It would be most convenient.

But the most important fact that I have been trying to get across is this: No matter how well-educated, alert, well-meaning, or astute men of science are, they are certainly no match for a competent magician—fooling people is his stock-in-trade. The only persons the conjuror has difficulty with are the feeble-minded, since they are incapable of following the carefully calculated sensory and psychological cues that make his deceptions possible. Wherever there is any possibility of human intervention, in the form of chicanery, being an element in any experimental process, an experienced conjuror must be called in. And not just any conjuror, but one whose specialty is just that particular brand of chicanery. A common error among laymen is that one who possesses some magical trick apparatus, or who knows a few sleights, is a magician. That is like saying that a man who owns a scalpel and knows where the brain is located is a neurosurgeon.

But scientists are loath to consult magicians. When I called the offices of a science magazine while in London last year to offer my services to them as a consultant on the Geller matter, I was loftily informed that they did not accept papers from those without academic standing in the field concerned. If that is the case, I would suggest that they no longer accept any papers on parapsychology, since it is *not* a science. A science has a repeatable set of experiments to prove its hypotheses; in the business of parapsychology, there are no such experiments.

Is it possible that, when magicians show up, purported miracles suddenly vanish in the dawn of revelation? Could it be that grant money and government funding are abruptly withdrawn when chicanery is exposed? I might point out that in a set of experiments some years back at a prominent parapsychology laboratory in New York, I injected myself into some proceedings involving a little girl who was able to see while wearing a blindfold, and within an hour the weeks of experimentation were terminated and the report to a scientific journal closed with the comment: "It was found useful to have a professional magician as a consultant." I was asked to visit Maimonides Parapsychology Laboratory recently, to look over the experimental conditions for a Geller test series. And when Geller saw the final setup, he suddenly lost interest in being tested. Even while the Stanford Research Institute was involved in testing the Israeli Wonder, I wrote, offering my services, and have never received even the courtesy of a reply. Perhaps they heard about Maimonides.

I opened this introductory chapter saying that this book is not a destructive one; it is not, despite the fact that it attempts to bring a myth to an end. I mean to be as constructive as I can be in suggesting that vast sums of money and countless man-hours can be saved by a careful consideration of the observations within these pages. Some of the revelations to be made are astonishing because they tell the layman what he suspected all along. Some facts are going to surprise with their deceptively simple patterns. The naïveté of learned men in all parts of the world may give you cause to wonder.

As an illustration of the last statement, consider that one of the most facile brains in the field of literature was that of Sir Arthur Conan Doyle. His masterpiece, Sherlock Holmes, will live forever as an example of a carefully constructed character who seemed to almost come to life because of his detailed delineation by Doyle. Yet this same author, knighted and otherwise honored many times over for his cerebral and imaginative creation, wrote these words in 1922: "I would warn the critic, however, not to be led away by the sophistry that because some professional trickster, apt at the game of deception, can produce a somewhat similar effect, therefore the originals were produced in the same way. There are few realities which cannot be imitated, and the ancient argument that because conjurors who on their own prepared plates or stages can produce certain results, therefore similar results obtained by untrained people under natural conditions are also false, is surely discounted by the intelligent public."

He was referring to photographs produced by two girls who told him there were *fairies* in their garden. And he *believed* them!

It becomes increasingly obvious to me that there are many persons who, like Sir Arthur, wish very much to believe, and will go to such extreme lengths to support their belief that they deny all logic and common sense; they cannot reason any longer. They begin to invent all sorts of rationalizations for paradoxes they see before them. No fact is too persistent not to be ignored or ridiculed. No amount of failure or fraud is enough to cause them to halt their eager rush to acceptance of the irrational.

We are taught in philosophy a principle known as Occam's razor. Very briefly, it says that, if a question or a problem has two answers, one of which is exceedingly complex and requires us to rewrite all our carefully reasoned laws of logic, the other of which is simple, direct and to the point, the latter is probably the correct solution, as long as both answer the problem equally well. To accept Geller and his "miracles" requires just such a rejection of logic and science, while the explanation that I expound solves the question and has ample proof, as will be seen in these pages.

Generations of exposure to the so-called "psychic marvels" of this world have allowed us to be talked into certain beliefs that have become firm rules by which it is thought psychics must be judged. Why this should be so, I cannot fathom. But it has become part of the folklore to accept these four assumptions and apply them to psychics:

1. No real psychic can produce phenomena upon command or on a regular basis. Thus the performer who can consistently turn out effects that defy explanation by ordinary means is considered a fraud, and the one who "hits and misses" or who has periods of impotency is judged to be the real goods.

2. Cheating is a compulsion with the psychic, something that he feels he must do if given the opportunity. But he is to be forgiven for this, since he cannot resist the feeling.

3. Unless the detractor is able to explain away *all* the phenomena exhibited by the psychic as done by ordinary means, he has failed to prove his case. Similarly, those who have been exposed as cheats or who have confessed are still assumed to have a margin of real powers that they have been unable to organize effectively.

4. Psychics cannot be expected to produce results when persons of negative attitude are present, nor when controlled so as to inhibit their sense of trusting and being trusted.

To summarize: Psychics exhibit spontaneous, unpredictable phenomena in addition to common tricks that they cannot help using. This small percentage of genuine events cannot be produced except under harmonious conditions and serves as proof of their powers.

Just how seriously have scientists adopted these "Special Rules for Psychics"? In the *Journal for the Society for Psychical Research*, Professor H. C. Berendt of the Israeli Parapsychology Society gives two reasons, among others, for *not* believing in Geller: ". . . the well-known fact of the sporadic occurrence of psi-phenomena and the limited possibility of being 'psychic' all the time. You cannot give one or two performances almost daily for nearly half a year, relying exclusively on psi-information or with psi-forces. Tricks *must* come in, even if part of Geller's power or knowledge *is* paranormal." And he adds, "It should be mentioned that, usually, a *serious medium* gives no stage performances or does not charge for advice, because such a medium thinks of the gift as coming from a higher power, to be used for the benefit of mankind."

Believers observe that all psychics who have passed the test using the "Special Rules" are the *genuine* ones. They have come to a wrong conclusion by poor observations and, observing further, convinced that their conclusions are *correct*, have invented these rules to make their process of reasoning stand up to examination. There is absolutely no reason why these illogical conditions should be accepted. No other discipline would or does allow such gross lapses of logic and procedure. If we were to try applying similar rules to, say, the science of astronomy, we would be laughed out of the running. But the special rules that psychics require are accepted as part and parcel of any investigation with no qualms on the part of the scientists involved. Indeed, even the laymen who get curious about these matters blandly accept the rules as presented them and quite logically decide that, if scientists judge the phenomena and the performers by such silly processes, they must have considered the overall picture and been satisfied.

Referring to the necessity of "repeatability" of experiments designed to prove any postulate, Dr. Hansel, in his valuable *ESP: A Scientific Evaluation*, has said:

> If anyone invents a pseudoscience in which this principle ceases to oper-ate, the result soon becomes apparent for the new "science" fails to have predictive value and leads to more and more findings and theories that are incompatible with orthodox science. This is what has happened in parapsychology. When critics fail to confirm ESP, this is not accepted as a reason for dropping the subject; on the contrary, belief in the reality of ESP is so strong that the principle of repeatability has been rejected or rendered impotent by the invoking of new processes which are claimed as subsidiary characteristics of the phenomenon. Thus, given a high-scoring subject, it would in the normal course of events be only a matter of time before every critic could be silenced, but these subjects cease to score high when tested by critics. Extrasensory perception only manifests itself before uncritical investigators. Again, Rhine and Pratt have observed, "Another major difficulty can be seen in the fact that some experimenters after a period of earlier success in obtaining extra-chance results in psi experiments have proved less effective in their later efforts. In such instances something apparently has been lost that was once a potent fac-tor. The element most likely to change under prolonged testing would seem to be the quality of infectious enthusiasm that accompanies the ini-tial discoveries of the research worker. Those who never succeed at all may, of course, be suspected of not ever having felt such contagious or communicable interest as would help to create a favorable test environ-ment for their subjects." In other words, experimenters fail to confirm their own results. And a further subsidiary characteristic emerges: ESP is affected by the mental state of the person investigating it.

With this set of rules in mind, it becomes less difficult to see why the so-called "science" of parapsychology has found less than wide acceptance among scientists. At least Dr. Joseph Banks Rhine (referred to by Hansel), who was formerly associated with Duke University, had the right idea when he began his ESP experiments to determine statisti-cally whether there was anything to believe in it or not. But Rhine was accident-prone: He kept on bumping into reality. His approach proved only that the law of averages was pretty well intact and that people were out to fool him whenever they had the chance—and were often success-ful. Perhaps he should have borne Rule 2 in mind.

Hansel echoes my thoughts further, touching upon the manner in which the critic is put very much on the spot by scientists in the following way:

> It is often difficult to discuss the possibility of cheating objectively. Parapsychologists tend to present their critics with a "fait accompli." A similar situation would arise in orthodox science if a chemist reported an experimental result that contradicted all the previous research findings and theories of his fellow chemists, together with the statement "Either this finding must be accepted as valid or else you must accuse me of being a cheat and a liar. Do you accept it?" In such circumstances, orthodox chemists might feel diffident about openly expressing their doubts. They might, however, repeat the experiment to see whether they got the same result. If they failed to confirm his result, they would not go into a long discussion as to whether the original investigator was a liar or a cheat. They would just take with a grain of salt any further experimental reports from the same source.
>
> The trickster has often been assisted by the investigator's overwhelming confidence in his ability to detect trickery. Observers, however careful, must be prepared to make mistakes. But in psychical research many of the investigators have considered themselves infallible. Soal claimed that boys of the caliber of Glyn and Ieuan could never hope to deceive him.*
>
> If a trick is used in an experiment, this fact might be expected to make itself apparent in the course of further research. But parapsychologists have erected a system that aids the trickster and at the same time preserves experimental finding.

Then, too, there seems to be developing a public belief that science approves the trend toward parapsychological research and that "most people" believe in psychic marvels. It is a fact that the *vast majority* of scientists today have no interest, or belief, in these things and are content to consider the law of inverse squares, the law of averages, and conservation of energy—among others—quite unassailable and sufficient to depend upon.

In some cases, you will discover that Geller's miracles never occurred. In others, the explanation of what *did* occur is clear and simple. Mind you, I will not be able to explain all of the wonders claimed for the psychic star. I simply wasn't there, and I don't have the information. But, lest the sheep begin roaring that maybe Uri does "a few tricks" and still has the power for the Real Stuff, let me put this proposition before you:

Can you prove to me that Santa Claus does not exist? (I assume that you are disinclined to believe in him, else you have invested your money

---

* The highly touted experiments with these two Welsh schoolboys were discredited when an ordinary dogwhistle was used to perform the trick. Professor Soal never thought of such a simple ruse. The boys went out of business shortly afterward.

poorly in this book.) No, of course you can't. You can indicate that such a belief is juvenile, illogical, and improbable. You can lecture me for a day on how silly such a conviction is, but you can't *prove* it isn't so. All right, suppose we set up a test. Let us examine every gift under every Christmas tree in a certain area said to be visited by Mr. Claus. We cover a lot of the territory, and everywhere we discover gifts labeled "From Santa" but subsequently determine, by questioning, that others have actually signed the tags. So—and we are well on our way to showing that there is no physical evidence for this belief. But, alas, in the last home on our list we come upon several gifts labeled in this fashion, and we cannot determine by the most rigorous interrogation if others are responsible for the deception. Do we then conclude that there is indeed a man named Claus who delivers these gifts? Or that he delivers only to a few selected homes such as this one?

Consider this carefully. Are our observations sufficient to establish the existence of Santa Claus? No, of course not. Because we have not found the deceiver does not mean that the preposterous belief in Santa is true. But when we deal with such a phenomenon as Uri Geller, we are asked to come to just such an irrational conclusion if we cannot explain away every one of the reported events, whether they are substantiated or not.

I have often been asked, "Do you deny the existence of ESP and other paranormal occurrences?" The answer is that I doubt their existence simply because I have never had evidence presented to me that would prove their existence. I cannot choose to believe something because I *want* to. Give me some hard proof, and I will change my mind; until then, I am burdened with Reality. I cannot, of course, deny that such things *might* exist. It would be illogical to do so.

It has taken man thousands of years to establish the concept that we call "science." It has its imperfections, true. But basically the structure of science is quite sound, and those who profess its expertise are legitimate laborers in a trade that demands great restraint and care in its performance. That restraint also demands that no scientist claim he is infallible or that he has expertise in a field outside science, unless such is clearly demonstrable. We shall see in these pages that men of science have not always followed these demands. They have frequently allowed themselves to bring their personal bents into the calculations.

Which only shows, I'm sure you'll agree, that scientists are human.

But is it true that "most people" believe in psychic marvels? My personal observation indicates that this is probably so. In my appearances before many hundreds of thousands of persons in the past thirty years, I have consistently denied any possibility that what I do is done by supernormal means. Yet some of my audience will argue with me at great length that some of the illusions I've presented are impossible of explanation by any other reasoning. Though I should certainly be the one who knows the answer to that, these people are unable to accept the obvious fact that they have not been able to solve a puzzle.

There are several good reasons for their confusion. A magician has a set of premises upon which he designs his performance. For example, he does not say *what* is going to occur, or *when*. This technique will be seen to constitute a good part of the "psychic's" repertoire as well. Also, the magician will reconstruct the event or the preparations for same in great detail — but incorrectly, so that the subject is steered off seemingly small points of procedure and is incapable of coming to the correct conclusion for analysis.

Therefore, a person who has been entertained (we trust) by a conjuror is unable to solve the process by which the illusion is created simply because he has been misdirected — psychologically, sensorially, and physically. I will give you one small example, with misgivings that my fellow-conjurors may object: During the performance of the classic trick of the Levitation of a Living Woman (as I prefer to bill it, though it has been called by many other titles) I pass a steel hoop around the body of the girl as she floats in the air. There is naturally a great deal of suspicion from the audience concerning that hoop, since if there were any "invisible wires" — how I wish such things existed — to hold the lady suspended, small slots in the hoop might conceivably allow it to pass such supports. Now I could quite properly allow my assistant to take that hoop down into the audience for a thorough examination, but that would be a mistake because not only would the atmosphere of the performance be destroyed but *the audience would then be thoroughly* convinced that no wires are used! I do not want that to get through to them — yet. I want those people to wonder about that hoop. I want them to be totally preoccupied with the hoop so they will not be able to spend their attention on other aspects of the presentation. And, as soon as I have passed the hoop over the floating girl, I allow it to just touch the couch from which she rose, and the bell-like ringing that results is a most subtle convincer that this is indeed a solidly constructed hoop! But that kind of "subliminal" clincher is not remembered as such. If you were to ask the spectators afterward how they were convinced of the legitimate nature of that metal hoop, they would not remember. But they are convinced nonetheless. And bear in mind that I have allowed them to doubt the hoop until the last moment. The moments during which they might have picked up the necessary information for a solution are now past. They have been misdirected. (I *must* add that the hoop is *really* solid. Honest!)

As you read on, you may well think back to these last few paragraphs more than once. I hope so, for the very techniques — as well as many others, of course — will be written between the lines when the description of other wonders unfolds.

The articles and conversations that follow are heavily annotated to supply the reader with additional pertinent data that often change considerably the conclusion one might come to. Of necessity, I have to pass up several opportunities to reveal certain principles of the conjuring art, since legitimate folks make their living by these means, as do I. This is no cop-out; it is a legitimate rationale. There is honor even among conjurors.

Uri, if you were one of the happy people who make a living by delighting young and old by a craft as old as man, I would long ago have sought you out as a friend. But that cannot be. You have chosen to become a semi-religious figure with divine pretensions. We could have been good friends, you and I.

2

How Does Uri Do It?

Witchcraft always has a hard time, until it becomes
established and changes its name.
—Charles Fort

I begin with an appropriately titled piece—"How Does Uri Do It?"
by Donald Singleton in the *New York Daily News.* The answer to the
question is not contained solely in the next few pages, but will become
more and more evident in following chapters. In this excellent article
Singleton has troubled to seek out expert help in attempting to assess
the worth of what he has observed and has listened carefully to the advice
offered. He has never made the pompous assumption that he is perfectly
capable of judging a possible trickster without any qualifications for the
task; nor has he concluded that, if he is fooled, it means he lacks any
intellect whatsoever. For one who spent relatively little time with Geller,
he has solved a good number of the basic techniques (with a little help
from his friends), and I regret that he was not present when some of the
heavy money was being voted into use to study Geller. I feel he would
have put in more than his two cents' worth.

I will interrupt Singleton's narrative occasionally to insert a comment I feel is needed to amplify or clarify matters.

Uri Geller and I are sitting in adjacent seats on the Metroliner, heading
toward Philadelphia.

Geller is an Israeli with a fast-growing reputation as a psychic, and I
am going to spend a few days with him, watching what he does and trying to figure out (a) whether he's for real, and (b) if not, how he
manages to achieve his effects.

He asks me if I have a key with me. I don't, having left my heavy
ring of keys at home. He asks if I have some other metal object. I do; a
nail clipper. Geller takes the nail clipper in his hand and examines it. He
swings open the small nail file section, and tells me to hold the file in my
fingers. He strokes it lightly, with one finger. A few seconds later the file
bends upward. A few more seconds and it cracks. A few more seconds and
it breaks in two.

"Isn't it amazing?!!" Geller says with great enthusiasm. (During the
next few days I find no matter how amazed people are by the things he
does, Geller is usually the most amazed.)

I agree that the broken nail file is amazing; but, frankly, I've seen so
many pictures of the keys and silverware he has bent of late that I am not
particularly surprised at this feat.

Geller asks me if I am wearing a watch. I am not. So he asks if I have one at home. Only a pocket watch, I say. He says to pick a time of day, and draw a clock face on a pad with the time indicated. I draw a clock face with the hands pointing to 3 o'clock. Geller looks over and says it wasn't necessary to draw the minute hand, but only the hour hand.

He says he will try to make the hands of my pocket watch point to 3 o'clock by long-distance telekinesis (moving objects without physically touching them). I ask him what about the wind-up alarm clock I have brought with me. He says he usually can only move the hands of wrist-watches, not larger clocks, but he'll give it a try.

Later, when I open my suitcase in the hotel, the alarm clock is staring me in the face. It says 3:03 p.m. It's a strange coincidence—that happens to be the correct time of day.

(When I arrived home three days later, I stuck the alarm clock in the dresser drawer and went to check the pocket watch. The pocket watch said 7:34 p.m. But a few days later, I happened to open the dresser drawer again. The alarm clock, which had been ticking when I put it into the drawer at about 11 p.m., had run down and stopped. The time that was, and still is, showing on the clock was less than 30 seconds after exactly 3 o'clock.)

Here enter two characters in the Geller drama who will be featured in starring parts. Yasha Katz was an elocutionist in Israel who decided to dedicate himself to Geller's cult. He gave up his life in Israel and came with Uri to America. He has said that he believes implicitly in the man he refers to as "Savior" and that he is quite aware that Uri has cheated on a few occasions and has been detected. "But," he says, "that just proves that every time he cheats he gets caught!" The assumption, and an illogical one, is that, when he is *not* caught, he is not cheating. (Refer to Rule 3.)

Incidentally, I feel sure that Katz is an innocent dupe of Uri and Shipi and not in any way involved in the deceptions.

Shipi Shtrang, the second new character Singleton mentions, is a most persistent presence at the successful Geller performances but is seldom mentioned, since he appears to be just a quiet assistant who hangs about to run off and fetch coffee when commanded. We will see Mr. Shtrang in a different light by the end of this book, I trust.

We check into the hotel, Uri Geller, his manager, Yasha Katz, and an assistant, a young man named Shipi. Almost immediately, we start off on a round of television and radio shows, newspaper interviews and special appearances, all of them designed to publicize a public appearance in nearby Cherry Hill, N.J., to be held Nov. 3 in Cherry Hill High School East.

Everywhere we go, Geller leaves people gasping. Skeptics become converts. Geller bends people's car and house keys, apparently by the power of his mind alone. The people hold the keys in their hands, and Geller touches or strokes the keys lightly until they curl up.

Keys and spoons and forks are not the only things to bend when Geller is around. People bend, too — mostly women. Geller is charming, personable. The 26-year-old psychic is tall, slender, graceful. He has glistening black hair and sparkling dark eyes, and he dresses with studied casual elegance. Everywhere we go, some woman or other is trying to press a telephone number into his hand or make a date for dinner, or an interview, or anything. At one point, Geller tells me that during one of his appearances, a survey showed that a number of women in the audience had experienced orgasm during the course of the evening.

One afternoon, Geller tapes a Mike Douglas show. In the three hours we are in the KYW-TV studios, Uri bends keys for Hugh Downs and several people on the production staff. He also bends rings and bracelets for a number of swooning women.

Before the show, Uri sends Shipi running to buy a camera. After the show, Uri has his picture taken with Mike Douglas, Tony Curtis and Kirk Douglas. "My mother gets a big kick out of it," he says.

One evening we all go to Cherry Hill, to a private reception at the home of one of the sponsors of Uri's coming appearance. The house is filled with people wearing name tags. Some are identified as members of the "Psychic Information Exchange" or some other group; others are merely identified as "Psychic."

Enter another character, Dr. Andrija Puharich, whose book *Uri* was to be both a boost and a millstone to Geller. Though Geller-watchers felt he would probably have the good sense to repudiate the book, along with its silly theories (I still haven't recovered from their meeting with the giant hawk-god, Horus, in the desert), Uri decided to go along with Puharich and declare that "every word in the book is true." (Puharich has a long history of strange pursuits.)

Though Geller and Puharich have appeared together many times on television and were almost inseparable in the early days of Uri's meteoric rise, things appear to have fizzled since. Uri is now complaining bitterly about some money Puharich failed to split with him, and I have heard that they only speak about once a month by phone.

Uri tells the rapt gathering what they have come to hear — all about himself: how he discovered he could read minds at the age of three by telling his mother how much she had won or lost at cards; how he learned at the age of seven that he could bend the hands of his wristwatch merely by concentrating on them and willing them to bend; how he became a big entertainment attraction in Israel; how he met Andrija Puharich, a physician/inventor/parapsychological investigator, who brought him to America to be studied by the Stanford Research Institute in California and who has written a book about Uri.

Geller also tells them strange secrets: how he and Andrija saw a flying saucer in an Israeli desert: how the brass cartridge of a pen dematerialized one day and rematerialized in the flying saucer; how various films of unidentified flying objects and eerie tape-recorded messages from unworldly beings dematerialized before the very eyes of Uri, Andrija, and others.

He tells them everything, in fact, except the identity of the source of his powers, and what is the deeper meaning of it all—for that, he says, you'll have to wait for publication of the book next spring; "The book will shock the world, I can tell you that," he says.

Just about then, things begin to happen in the room. Jewelry twists. A gold and stone amulet hanging around the neck of one "psychic" begins to bend. People pass up several broken wristwatches; Uri touches them and they begin to tick. A man in the crowd concentrates on a figure of the Star of David and Uri reproduces it flawlessly on a pad. At that moment, a Star of David pendant hanging from a woman psychic's neck curls up like a potato chip.

It's time to leave them with their eyes popping out. "Wasn't it great?!!" he enthuses as we head off toward Philadelphia. "What a terrific group!"

The next evening, we have some free time. Uri wants to see a Bruce Lee movie.

An event is about to occur that is hardly one Uri would have wished for. Like all good conjurors, he tries to be "one step ahead" in his actions and his planning. Obviously, he has taken the opportunity to prepare a fork and conceal it beneath a napkin close at hand. It is to be brought out and substituted at the right moment, but Singleton has happened to notice it, and calls attention to it. Does Uri blanch and stammer? Not at all! He is, after all, a pro.

At dinner, in the hotel dining room, I notice a strange-looking object protruding from beneath a napkin on Uri's side of the table. I move the napkin; the object is a fork, which has taken a bend like a folded ribbon. Uri acts startled—"These strange things happen around me all the time," he says. "It's amazing—one time I was having dinner in the home of Ray Stanford, a parapsychologist in Texas, and a meteorite that had been in a Bell jar suddenly teleported through the door and crashed to the floor!" Out of the corner of my eye, I spot a strange-looking fork at the next table. Is it bending? I check it again a few minutes later. It seems to have bent.

We walk to the theater, arriving about five minutes before the show is to start. As we stand, talking, in the lounge, there is a strange, mechanical sound from across the room. I look over and see that the soda dispenser has gone mad; it is spewing forth piles of shaved ice.

"It happens all the time!" Geller says. "Once in Munich, I was three miles away from the Olympic stadium, and I concentrated on turning the lights off and they went off in the whole stadium. Three times at SRI, where they tested me, the candy machines shot chocolates all over the place."

Back in the hotel, I draw three different symbols on three pieces of paper. I fold them up and shuffle them so I don't know which is which, then I choose one and, without looking to see which it is, I put it into an envelope. I then put that envelope into another envelope. Uri asks me to concentrate; I do so, and within about five minutes he says he is getting an image of a circle with an X in it. I open the envelopes and that is the drawing inside.

The next day, it is time to leave. Uri has some TV shows in Washington, and I have to get back to New York. As we are paying the check for a farewell cup of coffee at the station, Uri notices that one strand of the cashier's necklace is bent at a 90-degree angle. The cashier swears it had been straight; we try to straighten it out and can't.

As I rode home on the train, I thought back over the events of the three days. A whole lot of strange things had happened to me and to people around me.

Or had they really?

Trying to figure out whether Israeli psychic Uri Geller is genuine or a fraud is like trying to walk down a twisting hall of mirrors wearing a blindfold through which you can take only an occasional, squinting peek. You're forever catching glimpses of reality; but then each successive glimpse seems to prove the one before it was really only a mirage after all.

The young Israeli psychic who has been enthralling American audiences has a whole bag of tricks, that's for sure.

Take his ability to bend metal objects merely by concentrating on them, willing them to bend.

On the one hand, things really do get bent when he's around: keys curl; spoons and forks twist and break; bracelets and rings crumple.

But on the other hand, all the professional magazines say his bending routines are just tricks, probably incorporating a lot of sleight-of-hand, suggestion, some special strength and possibly some new gimmicks. One magician, The Amazing Randi, claims he has studied Geller and can duplicate all the tricks, using only normal magician techniques and no psychic abilities whatsoever.

You ask Randi if it would be possible for Geller to fool you so many times, and he asks you to think back over all the details of the times Geller bent things. Did you ever actually see something in the process of bending? No. Were you always right there watching every time something bent? No. Come to think of it, it seemed like he was always taking somebody off into a corner or another room, and then two of them would emerge, all enthusiastic about how a key, or a ring, had bent magically.

Now we're getting somewhere. This is a most astute observation, though infrequently made. If Geller notices that you are just a bit too observant—as in this case—all the wonders seem to take place at the other side of the room. But most accounts do not specify this, because it does not seem to be part of the action. This is one of those sins of omission commonly committed.

You think you have him at last, and so you take a photographer with you to see what Geller can do on camera, and this time you make sure that you stay right in the room. But you have to leave the room momentarily, to go and buy some spoons and forks for Geller to try to bend, and when you come back Geller and the photographer are all excited about how the photographer's key bent while you were gone.

So you've finally caught him, you think — the need for silverware was a ruse, just to get you out of the room so he could trick the photographer with no experienced observer watching him.

But then the photographer comes up with a series of photographs which show, with indisputable clarity, Geller holding a key, and the key in successive stages of bending. And the photographer swears he never took his eyes off the key, and Geller never moved it or touched it with his other hand the whole time, and the key just flopped over like a noodle going limp.

And there you are.

I refer you to the Yale Joel article that follows (Chapter 9) for a good point concerning photographers working on Uri. He is in a particularly good position to be able to fool them, since they are looking through the viewfinder most of the time. (The same thing occurs in Andrew Tobias's article from *New York* magazine, "OK, So He Averted World War III, But Can He Bend a Nail?") So Geller is delighted when the writer leaves him alone with the photographer. Miracles are bound to pour forth. Back to Singleton:

Or take Geller's ability to do telepathy and clairvoyance — he's forever reading people's thoughts, or reproducing a drawing someone has done and placed in one or more sealed envelopes.

On the other hand, you've got to believe your eyes. You test him, as I did. You take three identical sheets of paper, make a different drawing on each. You fold the sheets and shuffle them, so you have no idea which is which. Then you place one of the sheets into an envelope and put that envelope into another envelope. And after a 30-minute effort, Geller comes up with a drawing of a circle with an X in it, and that turns out to be what's in your envelopes.

I'm a bit puzzled here. Is this the same event described a moment ago? Then, it only took 5 minutes.

So you think he's genuine for sure. But then Milbourne Christopher, chairman of the Occult Investigation Committee of the Society of American

Magicians, tells you there are many standard ways to perform that particular trick.

And you read Christopher's books on the subject, and you're forced to admit that, yes, maybe if Geller had held the two envelopes up in front of a light, he would have been able to see through them—they were only flimsy hotel stationery. And besides, you did have your eyes closed for a couple of minutes, when he was telling you to concentrate on your drawings and you presumed he wouldn't cheat.

So you figure Geller's probably only a fraud.

But then you talk to Kreskin, the magician who specializes in several forms of thought-reading, and he tells you that while 90% of his act is simply a combination of deception and suggestion and special magical effects, the remaining 10% does involve some very real thought transference.

I differ with Kreskin on some fine points. While admiring him as a performer, and certainly not classing him with the Gellers and such, I fail to see where the "thought transference" angle comes in. However, I must admit that, if a man punches me in the mouth, I have divined his thought without verbal or other sensory cueing: he dislikes me. Maybe *that's* what Kreskin is getting at.

And then, just to complicate matters, Kreskin asks you to look for a minute, he wants to show you something. And he puts a folded dollar bill—your dollar bill—on a bedspread, and he tells it to unfold, and it unfolds. And then he tells it to walk, and it begins to skid slowly across the bed, starting and stopping on his command. And you know you're looking at something at least as impossible as a bending spoon. And Kreskin assures you that what you have just seen has nothing whatsoever to do with psychic abilities, but is just "an effect."

And you suddenly realize that maybe you're right back where you started in the hall of mirrors, not knowing which way is up.

Both Christopher and Randi are perturbed, to put it mildly, about the recent rash of interest in Geller. Both of the professional magicians call Geller nothing more than a clever trickster, possibly the most clever trickster to come down the well-worn occultist path for several decades.

"And I want to emphasize the difference between the two terms," said Christopher. "Geller is a trickster, not a magician. Magician is a legitimate term for a member of an honorable profession. This guy is going after really big money—bigger money than you can get just by being a good magician."

Randi agrees: "It's really convenient to have an act like Geller's. He claims he has these psychic powers that come from someplace outside himself, and he has no control over them. So when he manages to do a stunt, he succeeds, and when he fails to do a stunt, he says that's proof he's not a magician. So when he wins he wins, and when he loses he wins. If I ever went on stage and nothing happened for 30 minutes, the way it sometimes goes with Geller, they'd boo me right out of the house.

"No, Geller is no magician, in the ordinary sense of the word," Randi continued, "but he does have something. He's discovered a completely new approach to magic—something brand new—and it's so naïve, so direct, so simple, that even the magicians can't figure it out right away. I couldn't figure it out myself for quite a while. But I now can duplicate any trick Geller has done."

Randi calls Geller "Just about the most dangerous man to come into the limelight for the past 50 years, because he's into psychic feelings, and when he gets into that, the next thing you know, people will be bringing him their problems, their secrets, and then their money."

Randi, Christopher and Kreskin all agree on one further fact: The more intelligent one is, the easier it is for one to be fooled by a professional magician—and that fact applies to the scientists who have been mystified by Geller at the Stanford Research Institute in California. "The intelligent mind makes a lot more presumptions and assumptions than the less intelligent mind, and the magician learns to manipulate these assumptions to his advantage," says Kreskin. "I'm not the least bit impressed by all that SRI stuff," says Randi.

After talking to all the magicians, to Ed Edelson, science editor at the "News," and to assorted others, I began to feel that perhaps I had been had. So, with the assistance of Randi and Christopher, I set up one final test for Geller, and Uri agreed to try a couple more things for me.

I went to a locksmith and got a duplicate of the strongest, thickest key on my key ring. I tried with all my might and I couldn't bend it, even by pressing it against the corner of a steel desk. Then I made a simple drawing (of an eye), wrapped it in aluminum foil and put it into two envelopes.

I went to see Geller the next afternoon.

He tried for more than half an hour, with me keeping the envelope in my sight every second, to get the drawing. And he failed.

Then he made an effort to bend the key, again with me keeping it in view every second. Again, nothing happened. Uri said that he was terribly disappointed, that this simply had been an all-around bad day for him.

We continued talking for a while, and at one point a spoon which Geller was handling seemed to break in half—when I wasn't looking, unfortunately. Then, a bit later, he tried again to bend my key, and it did, in fact, bend ever so slightly. But my attention had been diverted from it for several minutes at that point, and I can't swear to you that he didn't palm it and pass it to Yasha Katz, his manager, who entered and left the room several times.

I don't think that's what happened. But I can't swear it didn't either.

So that's about it. I left Geller, wiggling the ever-so-slightly-bent key in my pocket, trying to figure out what I really believed about him.

And I guess you'll just have to do the same.

Thank you, Donald Singleton, for a very good account. And I must agree with you: I don't think that Yasha helped Geller in any way. He's a deceivee, not a deceiver. Uri never has to worry about Yasha upsetting any applecart. But then there's Shipi—

3

About the "SRI Report"

It is more from carelessness about truth, than from
intentional lying, that there is so much falsehood in
the world.

—Samuel Johnson

In Menlo Park, California, is located one of the most prestigious
"think-tank" complexes in the world. More than 2,500 top-ranking
scientists operate from this center, which, although primarily a military-
oriented setup, has in recent years devoted more of its time to private
industry. The reported revenue earned by the Stanford Research Institute is about $70 million a year, and though it is located in close prox-
imity to Stanford University, student protests directed against its mili-
tary nature forced the university to publicly disassociate itself from the
SRI operation.

In December 1972, the first whispering of strange goings-on inside
the institute began to percolate up to the press. It was said that the organization was investigating the psychic claims of one Uri Geller. Indeed
they were. Two laser specialists, Harold E. Puthoff and Russell Targ,
whose contributions to science are considerable (Puthoff holds a patent
on a tunable laser that he invented and Targ has invented a microwave-
frequency plasma oscillator), had been involved in the investigation
after Andrija Puharich, the man who "discovered" Geller, introducd
them to the young Israeli. Both Puthoff and Targ had already been pok-
ing about in the wonderland of parapsychology before this, and Puthoff
was already thoroughly convinced of the value of one of the newest
pseudoscientific religions, Scientology. They were thus quite well prepared to believe that a man could do any number of impossible things at
the moment Geller entered the picture.

The famous "SRI Report," more correctly titled "Information
Transmission Under Conditions of Sensory Shielding"—which dealt
with the six weeks of Geller tests and some tests run with other lesser-
known "psychics" during a six-week period—began circulating around
the various scientific periodicals like an academic *Gone With the Wind*.
Publication of the paper would have meant recognition of Puthoff's and
Targ's efforts on behalf of parapsychology, and the two were understandably anxious to see it in print.

Possibly the most influential of all scientific journals is the British publication *Nature,** whose editors received a copy of the "SRI Report" but sent it back for revision and possible reconsideration. In October 1974, the report finally saw print in *Nature,* along with a guarded page-and-a-half editorial introduction insisted upon by the referees of the magazine, who had disagreed for some time over the possible use of the report in the journal. Their editorial made it quite clear that the "SRI Report" was published as an example of the kind of research currently being done in the field of parapsychology and in no way endorsed the report or the research methods used to perform the tests outlined therein.

In this introduction by the referees, it is pointed out that "there was agreement that the paper was weak in design and presentation, to the extent that details given as to the precise way in which the experiment was carried out were disconcertingly vague." There are good reasons *why* the details were vague. Had Puthoff and Targ described the bedlam that existed at the so-called "scientific" tests, no layman—let alone a scientist—would have accepted the conclusions. Even Edgar Mitchell, an avowed believer in Geller, said that the two researchers "gave in to every whim" of Geller and that he was allowed to jump up and run about at will, refusing or postponing attempts at any test, returning to other incompleted ones and, in general, thoroughly misdirecting their attention.

The introduction also expresses other dissatisfactions, which result in giving little status at all to the report. Yet Puthoff, ecstatic that *Nature* published his and Targ's paper, has reprinted the article as it appeared there in an attractive blue folder. *But*—and it is important to note this—he has done what is so often done in a field that has come under great pressure from the larger body of scientific authority. *Puthoff reprinted the* Nature *article without the page-and-a-half introduction!*

For those of my readers who may have seen the "SRI Report" but not the original *Nature* (October 18, 1974) version, I include here the introductory editorial that Harold Puthoff does not consider important enough to print. I think you will find it more important than he does.

The *Nature* article was entitled "Investigating the Paranormal."

We publish this week a paper by Drs. R. Targ and H. Puthoff which is bound to create something of a stir in the scientific community. The claim is made that information can be transferred by some channel whose characteristics appear to fall "outside the range of known perceptual modalities." Or, more bluntly, some people can read thoughts or see things remotely.

Such a claim is, of course, bound to be greeted with a preconditioned reaction amongst many scientists. To some it simply confirms what they have always known or believed. To others it is beyond the laws of

---

* I must add that a few scientist friends disagree with this assessment.

science and therefore necessarily unacceptable. But to a few—though perhaps to more than is realised—the questions are still unanswered, and any evidence of high quality is worth a critical examination.

The issue, then, is whether the evidence is of sufficient quality to be taken seriously. In trying to answer this, we have been fortunate in having the help of three independent referees who have done their utmost to see the paper as a potentially important scientific communication and not as a challenge to or confirmations of prejudices. We thank them for the considerable effort they have put in to helping us, and we also thank Dr. Christopher Evans of the National Physical Laboratory whose continued advice on the subject is reflected in the content of this leading article.

A general indication of the referees' comments may be helpful to readers in reaching their own assessment of the paper. Of the three, one believed we should not publish, one did not feel strongly either way and the third was guardedly in favour of publication. We first summarise the arguments against the paper.

(1) There was agreement that the paper was weak in design and presentation, to the extent that details given as to the precise way in which the experiment was carried out were disconcertingly vague. The referees felt that insufficient account had been taken of the established methodology of experimental psychology and that in the form originally submitted the paper would be unlikely to be accepted for publication in a psychological journal on these grounds alone. Two referees also felt that the authors had not taken into account the lessons learnt in the past by parapsychologists researching this tricky and complicated area.

(2) The three referees were particularly critical of the method of target selection used, pointing out that the choice of a target by "opening a dictionary at random" is a naïve, vague and unnecessarily controversial approach to randomisation. Parapsychologists have long rejected such methods of target selection and, as one referee put it, weaknesses of this kind reveal "a lack of skill in their experiments, which might have caused them to make some other mistake which is less evident from their writing."

(3) All the referees felt that the details given of various safeguards and precautions introduced against the possibility of conscious or unconscious fraud on the part of one or other of the subjects were "uncomfortably vague" (to use one phrase). This in itself might be sufficient to raise doubt that the experiments have demonstrated the existence of a new channel of communication which does not involve the use of the senses.

(4) Two of the referees felt that it was a pity that the paper, instead of concentrating in detail and with meticulous care on one particular approach to extra-sensory phenomena, produced a mixture of different experiments, using different subjects in unconnected circumstances and with only a tenuous overall theme. At the best these were more "a series of pilot studies . . . than a report of a completed experiment."

On their own these highly critical comments could be grounds for rejection of the paper, but it was felt that other points needed to be taken into account before a final decision could be made.

(1) Despite its shortcomings, the paper is presented as a scientific

document by two qualified scientists, writing from a major research establishment apparently with the unqualified backing of the research institute itself.

(2) The authors have clearly attempted to investigate under laboratory conditions phenomena which, while highly implausible to many scientists, would nevertheless seem to be worthy of investigation even if, in the final analysis, negative findings are revealed. If scientists dispute and debate the reality of extra-sensory perception, then the subject is clearly a matter for scientific study and reportage.

(3) Very considerable advance publicity—it is fair to say not generated by the authors or their institute—has preceded the presentation of this report. As a result many scientists and very large numbers of non-scientists believe, as the result of anecdote and hearsay, that the Stanford Research Institute (SRI) was engaged in a major research programme into parapsychological matters and had even been the scene of a remarkable breakthrough in this field. The publication of this paper, with its muted claims, suggestions of a limited research programme, and modest data, is, we believe, likely to put the whole matter in more reasonable perspective.

(4) The claims that have been made by, or on behalf of, one of the subjects, Mr. Uri Geller, have been hailed publicly as indicating total acceptance by the SRI of allegedly sensational powers and may also perhaps now be seen in true perspective. It must be a matter of interest to scientists to note that, contrary to very widespread rumour, the paper does not present any evidence whatsoever for Geller's alleged abilities to bend metal rods by stroking them, influence magnets at a distance, make watches stop or start by some psychokinetic force and so on. The publication of the paper would be justified on the grounds of allowing scientists the opportunity to discriminate between the cautious, limited and still highly debatable experimental data, and extravagant rumour, fed in recent days by inaccurate attempts in some newspapers at precognition of the contents of the paper.

(5) Two of the referees also felt that the paper should be published because it would allow parapsychologists, and all other scientists interested in researching this arguable field, to gauge the quality of the Stanford research and assess how much it is contributing to parapsychology.

(6) "Nature," although seen by some as one of the world's most respected journals, cannot afford to live on respectability. We believe that our readers expect us to be a home for the occasional "high-risk" type of paper. This is hardly to assert that we regularly fly in the face of referees' recommendations (we always consider the possibility of publishing, as in this case, a summary of their objections). It is to say that the unusual must now and then be allowed a toe-hold in the literature, sometimes to flourish, more often to be forgotten within a year or two.

The critical comments above were sent to the authors who have modified their manuscript in response to them. We have also corresponded informally with the authors on one or two issues such as whether the targets could have been forced by standard magical tricks, and are convinced that this is not the case. As a result of these exchanges and the above considerations we have decided to publish in the belief that, however flawed the experimental procedure and however difficult the process of distilling the essence of a complex series of events into a scientific manuscript, it was on balance preferable to publish and maybe stimulate and advance the controversy rather than keep it out of circulation for a further period.

Publishing in a scientific journal is not a process of receiving a seal of approval from the establishment; rather it is the serving of notice on the community that there is something worthy of their attention and scrutiny. And this scrutiny is bound to take the form of a desire amongst some to repeat the experiments with even more caution. To this end the "New Scientist" does a service by publishing this week the results of Dr. Joe Hanlon's own investigations into a wide range of phenomena surrounding Mr. Geller. If the subject is to be investigated further—and no scientist is likely to accept more than that the SRI experiments provide a "prima facie" case for more investigations—the experimental technique will have to take account of Dr. Hanlon's strictures, those of our own referees and those, doubtless, of others who will be looking for alternative explanations.

Perhaps the most important issue raised by the circumstances surrounding the publication of this paper is whether science has yet developed the competence to confront claims of the paranormal. Supposedly paranormal events frequently cannot be investigated in the calm, controlled and meticulous way that scientists are expected to work, and so there is always a danger that the investigator, swept up in the confusion that surrounds many experiments, abandons his initial intentions in order to go along with his subject's desires. It may be that all experiments of this sort should be exactly prescribed beforehand by one group, done by another unassociated group and evaluated in terms of performance by the first group. Only by increasing austerity of approach by scientists will there be any major progress in this field.

At this point, the full text of the "SRI Report" ought to follow. There is good reason that it does not. The report (*sans* introduction) would seem to be a generally available document. And when I wrote to ask permission of *Nature* magazine to use their introductory editorial, permission was granted immediately. I also wrote to Stanford Research Institute (addressing my inquiry to Harold Puthoff and telling him of my desire to include the "SRI Report" in my book). Though I had received no answers at all to some previous letters, I hoped this permissions request letter would be an exception. I have not received the courtesy of a reply to my request. SRI is, I must conclude, not happy that I wish to comment upon its work. Perhaps I can hardly blame them. It is difficult to face the fact that you've been had.

Here, then, is a summary—*in my own words*—of the tests done with Geller at the Stanford Research Institute, Menlo Park, California, during the last part of 1972 and in August of 1973. I have tried to be direct and very impartial.

The "SRI Report" Summarized

The report covers a series of experiments conducted "under laboratory conditions," the results of which suggested the existence of a sense or method by which certain individuals can obtain information without the use of the "normal" senses. One person so tested was Uri Geller, who performed tests to determine whether he could (*a*) reproduce pictures drawn by the experimenters, who were located at positions remote from Geller, who was in an "electrically shielded" room; (*b*) reproduce drawings stored in the memory of a computer; and (*c*) reproduce drawings enclosed in sealed envelopes and of which specifics were unknown to the experimenters.

At all times, say the authors, measures were taken "to prevent sensory leakage and to prevent deception, whether intentional or unintentional."

Over a period of seven days, thirteen drawings were used in tests. For each test, either Geller or the "senders" entered a shielded room, so that Geller was electrically and acoustically separated from the other half of the experiment. Then a "target" would be chosen, in order to avoid the possibility of cueing in advance of the beginning of the test. And to get around the chance that a target might be *forced* upon the experimenters, Geller was not told who would do the choosing or how it would be chosen. Three methods were used to choose the target: first, a random method of opening a dictionary and selecting the first word seen that could be pictorially represented (though not specified in the report, drawings were made and *posted on the wall!*); second, sealed-up pictures were prepared in advance and given to the experimenters during the running of the test, and the identity of these was unknown to the experimenters; third, an arbitrary selection "from a target pool"—on which the report gives very little information—was used.

Working on each of the drawings for periods of from a few minutes to half an hour, Geller either tried or "passed" (he had the option of passing on any test he was not sure of) and his drawing was taken from him before he was allowed to see what the target had been.

The first ten tries were conducted using a double-walled steel room with a tightly sealed inner and outer door. It provided sound shielding and visual isolation as well. There was an audio link (about which nothing is said except that it operated only one way: from Geller inside, to the outside) used to monitor the experiment. The experimenters never discussed out loud the nature of the drawing after it was drawn and brought near the shielded room. No sensory leakage was found in their examination of the room, though nothing is said about what methods were used to determine this insulation.

The tests numbered 11 to 13 were done in the SRI engineering building in order that they could use the display screen of the computer there. Here, Geller was inside a double-walled copper-mesh cage, known as a Faraday Cage. The original was designed by Michael Faraday to conduct experiments in a location free of radio waves and/or magnetic fields. Targets for these tests were chosen by outside personnel, and neither the experimenters nor Geller were aware of the targets that had been drawn from the pool and stored in the computer memory.

The judges were asked to evaluate the results by "blind" comparison of results with the targets. They agreed on the results. Odds of this happening by chance are one in 30 million.

A second set of tests involving Geller were done to test his clairvoyance. In these, no one would know what the test object was, so telepathy was ruled out and the knowledge would have to come by some other sensory apparatus, if at all.

One hundred drawings were prepared and sealed up in envelopes by SRI personnel, then divided into groups of 20 for three days of experiments. On all of these tests, Geller "passed"; that is, he refused to try. Each day, however, he made 12 drawings that he said were associated with the entire pool of 100 drawings. On each of the three days, 2 of his drawings could reasonably be associated with 2 of the targets in that day's 20 test drawings. But the drawings did not correspond in numbers greater than could be attributed by chance.

Another test involved a single die placed in a 3"-by-4"-by-5" steel box and shaken by the experimenters. The face uppermost was unknown even to the experimenters, and Geller accepted the test eight times out of the ten times tried, "passing" on two. He was correct all eight times he tried. The probability of this occurring by chance alone is one in 1,000,000.

The "SRI Report" concludes that "in certain circumstances, significant information transmission can take place under shielded conditions." Factors affecting the results, they decided, are "whether the subject knows the set of targets in the target pool, the actual number of targets in the target pool at any given time, and whether the target is known by any of the experimenters."

Metal-bending, though observed at the lab, was not reported in this paper "due to lack of adequate controls."

I am dealing here only with the Geller substance of the SRI paper, and must ignore the rest, which describes further tests with other "sensitives." But I may mention that the complete narrative of the SRI film showing Geller at work—which was shown at Columbia University on March 9, 1973, to convince disbelievers before the SRI paper was published—appears in the report as well.

There was no way that I could get to see the SRI film. Only the elite of the world of science and journalism were invited, and being of a lower order of life, I received no request for my presence. Besides, the film might well have refused to run under negative vibrations, being the psychic revelation that it was. Leon Jaroff, of *Time*, was invited, but the editorial pressures made it necessary for him to send his assistant, Sydnor Vanderschmidt, in his stead. (Circulating among the celebrities after the showing of the film, she reported that she overheard one of the top U.S. physicists remark with a smile, "Targ does not strike me as being very smart.") So a complaint, made by Targ and Puthoff that Jaroff failed to attend the film showing is hardly valid.

By a rather surreptitious means, I managed to obtain a videotape copy of the last half of the famous film. And what I have seen has caused me several bruises from falling off my chair in laughter. How the great minds at SRI failed to tumble to the simple tricks Geller performed for them, I cannot understand. Even my youngest magic student solved the compass trick right away:

Geller is shown waving his hands about over a simple compass. We are solemnly assured that his hands have been carefully examined with a probe to be sure he has no magnets concealed. Nonetheless, the compass needle deflects! But it moves, not in rhythm with his hand movements, but in time with his *head,* and only when his head approaches the device! Open wide, Uri. What's this magnet doing in your mouth?

Then Uri treats us to some spoon-bending. That's right, folks, these serious men of science sat about watching Geller stroke a spoon, trying to make it bend. And it didn't bulge a degree out of normal. Not while they were watching it, that is! You see, the spoon-bending trick is shown in the film in five segments. In each, we see the Israeli wonder stroking for all he's worth, turning the spoon every which way and concentrating mightily like a man in pain. And every time a segment ends (to wind the camera or to put new film in) the spoon returns to the screen with a new bend in it! Marvelous!

I bothered to study this phenomenon further by photographing the spoon in profile from the television screen at the beginning and end of each segment. Guess what? There is *no change whatsoever in the bend while the camera is running,* but considerable change when no film is being shot—that is to say, *while no one is looking.*

Now, I am not a great scientific mind, so I cannot pass judgment on the methods used by the accomplished scientists who performed these earth-shaking experiments with Geller. But if a simple method like the one I have just outlined was not thought of by the greatest minds in parapsychology, someone is missing the boat somewhere.

The film ends with a display of wondrously contorted rings and silverware all bent by Geller, but the narrative tells us that they are not quite sure of how all of these got bent, I think I know.

Tell me, gentlemen of SRI, if the film you so highly tout proves absolutely nothing about Geller's psychokinetic "bending" powers, why include the sequence? Could it be that you just need to bolster your case, so you throw in the glamor stuff, too? Whatever happened to science along the way? Or is that too unsophisticated a question, and attitude, for you?

I repeat: What I saw of the film leaves no mystery about Geller. It does leave *other* mysteries, though.

4

What Does It All Mean?

A lie travels round the world
While Truth is putting on her boots.
—Charles Haddon Spurgeon

Well, the descriptions given in the SRI paper are certainly not complete, by any means. Russell Targ reported to Dr. Joseph Hanlon, who wrote an analysis of the "SRI Report" for *New Scientist,* that he felt "confident that Geller will cheat if given the chance." So the question is, did he, could he, and would he cheat if the opportunity arose? Certainly he would if he wanted to impress the scientists—and he wanted to do so very much. Could he? Yes, because the experiments were full of loopholes. Let us look into some of these.

First, did the "steel room" really provide electrical shielding? We may never know. All of my requests to see the room and test it have been met with stony silence. Had I the opportunity to test it, I would (*a*) examine the audio line, which could be used to transmit a radio signal inside, unless provided with isolation transformers or other filter systems, or which could be tapped into directly if the vigilance of the experimenters was low enough; (*b*) I would find out if the supply of 110 V.A.C. to the inside of the room was isolated from the other mains—otherwise, a simple communications link could be established by that means (such systems are available at very low cost in any electronics store, and can easily be miniaturized); and (*c*) I would find out if a low-frequency induction system could be set up (such systems are often used to conduct the regular A.C. through the walls) to transmit information.

But hold on a moment! We would need a confederate to transmit the information to Uri! We've already been told that all means were adopted to be sure that no cueing was possible, so we can assume that any person who would be capable of giving information to Uri was excluded from the test area. Not so. Shipi was there, according to Hanlon, "constantly underfoot" during the tests! So we have *both links we need* for a perfectly possible method of cheating on these tests!

Further inquiries within Stanford Research Institute reveal that the famous steel room (referred to as the "Faraday Cage," though the *screened room* more aptly meets that definition) is not anywhere near soundproof. A tap on the outside of the room can easily be heard inside; this signaling is quite possible even while the door is shut. And there remains unexplained an interesting occurrence during the telepathy tests that were conducted with Geller: at the end of one test, the experimenters found it impossible to open the door! They called to Geller and got no answer, though it was obvious he was on the other side of the door and holding it shut with his body, and he would not admit them for some three or four minutes. When they finally got in, they discovered the lock had been tampered with from the inside!

And this is a set of tests done under "controlled" conditions? Funny, I don't seem to be able to find any mention of *these* events in the "SRI Report."

But we've not described just how successful Geller was. And this may surprise you, but I'll be much more generous than the experiment's judges were in deciding which were "hits" and which were "misses."

The results are shown in Figures 1 and 2.

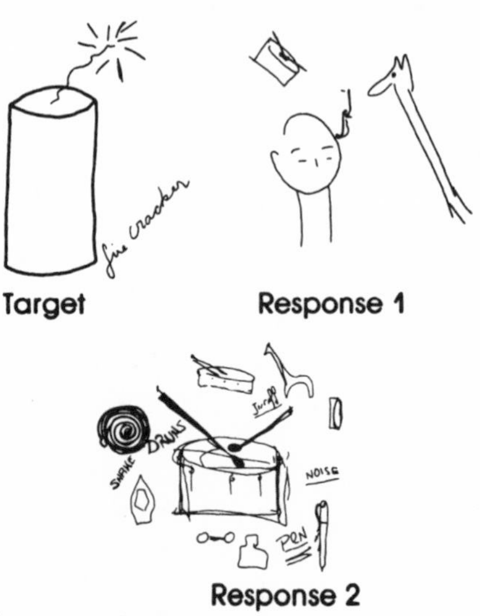

Target   Response 1

Target

Response 2   Response

FIGURE 1 (FUSE) 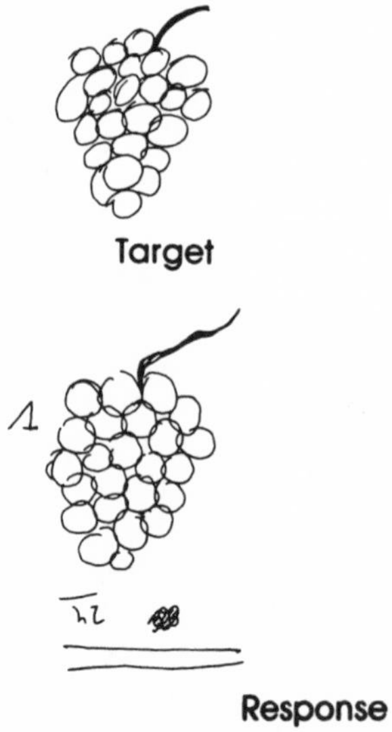   FIGURE 2 (BUNCH)

FIGURE 1. This is *almost* a hit. It has the word "noise" and a human head with a lightning bolt in one ear. If you made an excuse to leave the room — and could have gotten just one *quick glance* at Shipi Shtrang, and he was trying to signal "firecracker" to you, wouldn't he put his fingers in his ears? And wouldn't that mean "noise"* — like a drum? I see the word noise written in the response! *SRI verdict*: a miss. *My verdict*: a miss (but just).

FIGURE 2. Leapin' lizards. Sandy! This is a 100% hit, no question. The system was really working well here. See text p. 48. Even the number of grapes is right. *SRI verdict*: a hit. *My verdict*: a hit.

---

* Hanlon interprets the word beneath "noise" as "pow" — it is not. It's "pen."

DEVIL

Target

Response 1

Response 2

Response 3

FIGURE 3. Of thirty responses to a simple target, only two seem to correspond to the transmission: the tridents. And, of all the response drawings, only two are hastily scrawled—one of them even over a previous drawing—the tridents! Could these have been hastily added as Geller emerged and saw the target? I think so—*SRI verdict*: a miss. *My verdict*: a hit.

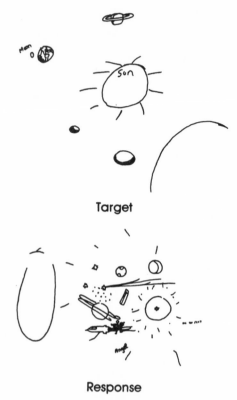

Target

Response

FIGURE 4. Here again, the system worked well. The response corresponds exactly to a verbal impression of the target, though not to a visual (or a telepathic) one. *SRI verdict*: a hit. *My verdict*: a hit.

FIGURES 5, 6, and 7 were a rabbit, a tree, and an envelope in the original series, but were passed over by Uri despite their simplicity. Let's score them as misses!

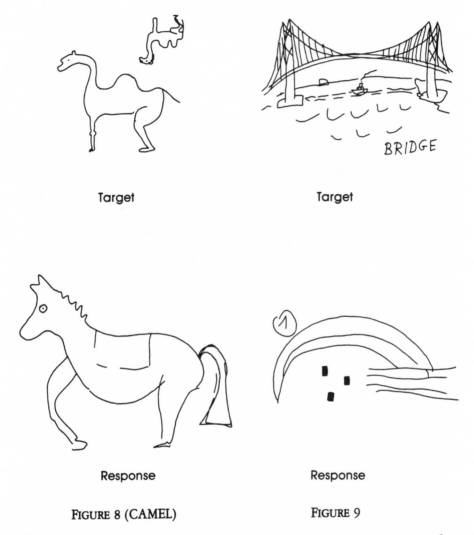

Target

Target

BRIDGE

Response

Response

FIGURE 8 (CAMEL)

FIGURE 9

FIGURE 8. A quick glance at this target might have given Shipi an impression of a horse. Interestingly enough, if telepathy *were* used, this would be one of the most impressive of the results! *SRI verdict*: a hit. *My verdict*: a hit.

FIGURE 9. To an American, a bridge must be a suspension bridge. To Uri, it might mean a rural span. In any case, the response does not match the picture, but could correspond to a verbal cue. *SRI verdict*: "Fair." *My verdict*: "Fair + ."

 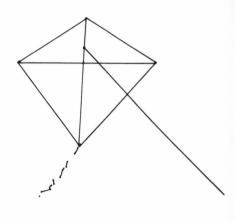

Target

Target

Response

Response

FIGURE 10 (SEAGULL)

FIGURE 11 (KITE)

FIGURE 10. How Uri's name got under the *target picture* I'll never know. But a bird is a bird, and all systems were working, though you can't prove that Uri's drawing is a sea-going bird. But I'll be generous. *SRI verdict*: a hit. *My verdict*: a hit.

FIGURE 11. (This and the next two tests were done in the cage.) No question of it. This shape, which could have been transmitted by simple hand gestures or by a verbal cue, can hardly be drawn any other way. A success! — But—not as a *kite*! As a square with diagonals, yes. Such a response could result from a hand signal that would give only the geometrics. *SRI verdict*: a hit. *My verdict*: a hit.

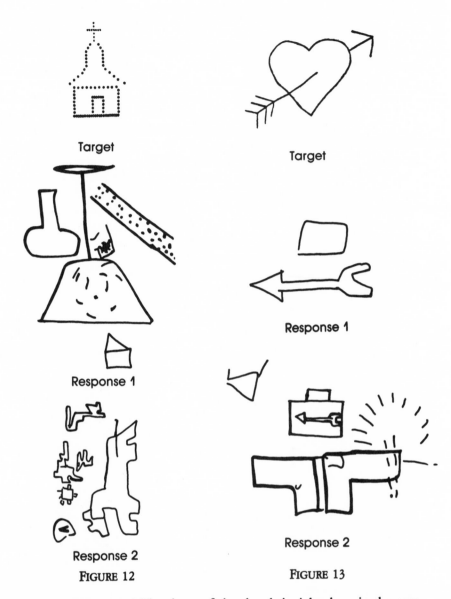

Target

Target

Response 1

Response 1

Response 2

FIGURE 12

Response 2

FIGURE 13

FIGURE 12. Come, now! The shape of the church is right there in the over-turned champagne glass! Or as near as we can get to a shape transmitted by hand gestures. Try it: Ask another person to pick up a drawing while you "draw" it in the air. It should approach Uri's result. Even a bunch of dots got through, as well. Isn't telepathy wonderful! *SRI verdict*: a miss. *My verdict*: a hit.

FIGURE 13. I would accept anything with an arrow in it. They might even have been watching Shipi by now (a bit late!) and opportunities would be getting slimmer. But he's a good man to have around. *SRI verdict*: "Fair." *My verdict*: a hit.

You see, I've given Geller three more hits than SRI gave him, leaving only *one* miss in the whole works—and three passes, besides the one hundred envelopes he passed up as well.

Why? Because if you study the third response to Figure 3 you'll find two tridents drawn among all the other nonsense, and there is a trident in the target. But examine those tridents carefully, and compare them with the other drawings in the three sets of responses. Note that *all* drawings are very carefully made; all lines meet; and all closed curves are closed carefully and neatly. What are the only two drawings in the entire set of *thirty* drawings in the answer that are carelessly—*as if done at the last second, surreptitiously*? Yes, the two tridents! Is it *possible* that Geller made these drawings *after* the target was shown to him. Yes, it's very possible. Lora Myers, writing for *Oui* magazine in September, 1975, reported that she performed a "telepathy" test with Geller in which she had drawn a television set. Geller made a number of drawings in response to this. Lora says, "Then I show him my television set. Exuberantly, Uri flips over the paper on which he had drawn the rose. On the back of his response to my first drawing, the pear, are a few faint lines that look like parts of a square. In a flash, Uri again *seizes* the pen from my hand and draws in a television set over the lines, adding two little knobs, and his name at the bottom.

'I mean look, you saw it,' he crows, setting down the pen. 'The pen is down here . . . I got your television set!'"

The SRI report tells us specifically that the responses were collected before the target was shown to the subject. Given the many statements from persons present at that series of tests to the effect that Geller's every whim was satisfied and that conditions were altered any way he wanted them, I find it not difficult to postulate that on this occasion the performer could have emerged from the sealed room clutching the three pages of responses he'd made—pen or pencil still in hand—and looking up at the target posted in full view, could have hastily added the two tridents to the third page. Note that the two tridents are not only the sole sloppy drawings in the set of thirty, but one of them overlaps the globe drawing, carelessly. It is the only response to do so, as if it were made without Geller looking at the place he was drawing.

My conclusion has to be that Geller emerged from the room, saw the complex target drawing, seized upon the one "theme" that he could quickly sketch in (the trident), and did so, then looking at the result, he tried again for a better version. Ten points for effort, guts, and ingenuity. But no points for drawing.

The other bonus points I've awarded him are in Figures 9, 12 and 13. In Figure 9, I consider that Geller got a bridge—the same *word* that was being transmitted, though not the same drawing of that word. It almost seems as if he got the *sound* of the target rather than the visual impression, doesn't it? Well, consider that possibility. We already have a very possible system (Shipi/electronics) for transmission of data. Why not?

In the case of Figure 1 (a firecracker) he tried with *thirteen* separate responses. (The actual *word* chosen was "fuse" — not "firecracker.") But the human head with squinting eyes and a "pain" bolt entering the ear, the drums and the word "noise" show me that he got very close to the target: a *lit* firecracker. I'll make a bet here. I'll bet that Geller made some excuse to leave the room, promising to hold his hand over his closed eyes, and shot a quick look at Shipi. This poor guy was under pressure to give Uri a signal — very quickly — that would convey the idea of a lit firecracker. Somehow, whatever other methods they had set up were not working at that moment. So, to transmit the idea to Geller, Shipi stuck both index fingers in his ears, shut his eyes, and grimaced in pain. And the signal that gets across is "noise." *Or* a human head with pain in the ear.

Farfetched? Maybe. But, under pressure to produce, it's the kind of thing I would expect *my* confederate to do, and I would probably make the same sort of response. And as we discover more about Uri's record in these matters it seems a more likely explanation than telepathy.

Now my reader will be astonished, perhaps, to find me making the assumption that highly trained men like Harold Puthoff and Russell Targ could possibly allow loose enough conditions to exist during the tests so that Geller could demand to be let out of the sealed room and allowed other great relaxations of security — such as having Shipi Shtrang, certainly the most probable confederate a performer might be suspected of using, to be present and "underfoot" during the experiments. How can I presume so much? Because I have seen what grown men will do to satisfy a deep need to believe. And, because Captain Edgar Mitchell, former astronaut, surely one of the leading Geller supporters, has said, "I was there virtually all the time. I am a co-investigator on all that work . . . Frankly, [there's] a problem that Russ and Hal had — they were so eager to keep him around that they worked themselves into a box by meeting his every whim, and if he threatened to walk off they would relent and do what he wanted. Of course they lost control of the situation, and it just got worse and worse and worse . . ."

So my presumptions are based upon testimony from a man who was deeply involved in the Geller tests. And something else bears mention as well. Mitchell also related — to Joseph Hanlon — that there were a great number of experiments done with Geller at the SRI sessions that they could not report, because Geller simply broke loose from even the flimsy controls they *did* insist on. Thus we see that Geller had a good deal of knowledge about the testing procedures and was not exposed to them "cold turkey" at all. By the time the lab settled down to record results, he was familiar with their methods and prepared to work a way around them to get results.

When I first saw the SRI drawings, one thing above all bothered me no end. The bunch of grapes was *too* good. (Here, too, the chosen word was different. It was "bunch.") No performer in his right mind would reproduce a target that well—but Uri's ego was too much for him. But am I ahead of myself? Perhaps. Let's look over the experimental setup at SRI again.

Unfortunately, it seems I'll never have the opportunity of really doing that. The folks at SRI just refuse to have anything at all to do with me. To get in there would solve a lot of puzzles, but I won't be able to, so I'll have to be content to theorize and relate all the little clues that have passed my way. Joseph Hanlon, in conversation with one of the persons who was present at the SRI tests of Geller, was told that several people there talked openly about a small but important defect of the highly touted "double-steel walled room" used in the experiments. It seems that this room was not designed or built with Geller tests in mind, but had served SRI as an electrophysical recording chamber. It shielded out most electromagnetic radiation and was used for the ESP tests since it was already there.

The room had double refrigerator-type doors all right, but with a rather serious leak. In order to get cables in there for the electroencephalograph (EEG) tests, a square hole was cut in the steel wall *and the space around it was stuffed up with gauze*! There were reports of gauze being found about the floor after the "grapes" drawing was received! My theory? That Shipi made a small drawing of the target—an exact drawing—and pushed it through the hole to Geller. Unwisely, Geller chose not to make a lot of other "tries" (after all, he later made *thirty* responses to another one of these targets!), but made a very suspicious direct "hit" on this one.

Hanlon's informant also told him, "It's the feeling of a lot of people here that they are throwing away a lot of data." I believe they were quite correct.

In Figure 4 (solar system), Geller was right on—not pictorially, but in the spirit of the words. But verbal cueing is indicated here strongly.

The next three, a rabbit, a tree, and an envelope, were "passed" over by Uri though they seem to be very simple, basic objects for a renowned psychic to "pick up." Number 5 was a sealed drawing unknown to *any* of the experimenters, locked in the steel room with no one viewing it. Numbers 6 and 7 were tried while EEG equipment was attached to Geller with outsiders attending him closely. Remember, though, that *these three were performed in such a way that either there was no person who could be a confederate who knew the answer, or Uri was under close surveillance and could not resort to his confederate without detection.* And in the case of the one hundred envelopes, as with the one hundred that were to be presented upon another occasion by SRI *psychologists*

UNDER TEST—REAL TEST—CONDITIONS (see page 52), Geller was unable to perform. *Here, too, no person could signal the answer to him!* ONLY IN THE TESTS WHERE THERE WAS NO POSSIBILITY OF TRANSMISSION OF DATA FROM A CONFEDERATE DID GELLER REFUSE TO TRY THE TEST OR JUST FAIL IT!

But on to the remainder of the thirteen tests. In Figure 8 (camel) I will guess that Shipi saw the drawing fleetingly and mistook it for a horse. I think *I* would, if shown it briefly. SRI has no claim on the art world. The next, Figure 9, was the word "bridge," drawn as an American would think of a bridge; but if received as that word, it would have been *thought of* by Uri as any kind of bridge—perhaps a simple stone puddle-jumper. The seagull (Figure 10) is another in which direct auditory information would transmit a large white bird in any convenient configuration.

The last three drawings were done with Geller in the Faraday Cage. I think the response in Figure 11 (kite) is excellent! It lacks only a string and a tail. And Figure 12 has an overturned champagne glass that, upon examination, resembles the church outline very closely—he even got a bunch of dots as well. That's a remarkable "hit," in my estimation. And Figure 13 (arrow-through heart) has an arrow in the response. I'll buy that! But these three are hardly what Uri would get from a *verbal* cue. We would need something much stronger than that if we were to explain the kite and the church, as well as the arrow. You have probably made the assumption that Geller could not see out of the Faraday Cage in which he found himself for those last three experiments. BUT HE COULD SEE, EASILY! HE COULD EVEN REACH HIS ARM OUT OF THE CAGE! What is to prevent Shipi from signaling these three to Geller? Nothing. And we are not told how long Geller took to perform these tests; so we do not know *that* important factor either. It would have been simple for Shipi to signal with hand gestures.

Do the SRI tests still look as good as they did when first reported? I think not. But we still have the all-important test with the metal box to consider. I think that any of us who would design such a test would insist that at least there should be a catch on the metal box. Was there? No. There was no catch or lock. The simple metal file box was just that. Of course, since the SRI men were sure that with Geller there was no chicanery involved, they did not need to equip it with a catch.

I digress here to chide Dr. Hanlon, who describes in his *New Scientist* account a "radio die" that was briefly on the market for magicians to purchase. He says that it might have been the one used in the experiment, rung in by Uri at an opportune moment. Hardly. The prop die in this case looks like a gigantic parody of a regular die. It is not transparent, as further information shows the SRI die was, and it is huge. Not even Puthoff and Targ would have been deceived by *that* one. I hope to presume that Hanlon had not seen the actual die that is sold for this trick, or he'd not have reported its possible use here.

As for the SRI die experiment, I will beg off an explanation until Chapter 11, where we will discuss a most interesting parallel between Geller and his tricks and another long-gone conjuror from the past.

The conclusion to all this is rather obvious. The SRI did not report exactly what happened. It could not have, because there were seemingly unimportant occurrences that escaped their attention, and lapses in their accuracy. They assumed perfect shielding of Geller, so they did not report whether he was searched for the presence of electronic equipment. (Some readers of the *New Scientist* wrongly assumed that Hanlon meant to imply that Geller had an implanted "tooth receiver" for which none other than Andrija Puharich holds the patent, but I know that such was not Hanlon's intention, though Puharich could *easily* have been the man who constructed the electronic device that Geller perhaps used.) Besides, Geller does not *allow* a search—such procedures are "negative vibrations." (See Rule 4 in Chapter 1.)

Hanlon has an interesting conclusion to make in *New Scientist*. Commenting on a prominent scientist's remark that it was necessary to deal with "psychics" in a special manner and that "you must feed them information bit by bit in a controlled way," Hanlon says: "If this is in fact so, and if this is to be acceptable to science, then it means we must be prepared to accept the paranormal on faith—and tolerate wholesale fraud along with it. I, at least, am not prepared to do so." Amen.

Before we leave the SRI matter, one more peek behind the curtain. The "SRI Report" specifies that in the case of the thirteen drawings there were no tests performed with these that were not reported. But it *fails to say the same* about the one-hundred envelopes that Geller failed to try. Why? Because the following account is not to Geller's credit, and therefore not important enough to be mentioned!

There *were* further tests with these envelopes. After the end of the formal test, on the last day, the experimenters loosened the conditions, and suddenly miracles started to occur. Six drawings were tried, and Geller got one of them perfectly—by clairvoyance *of course*. One of the experimenters (we're not told which) commented that he was sure Geller had cheated. When the facts are studied, that conclusion is quite possibly true.

The facts are these: The six drawings were left lying about the room unguarded, and no one bothered to determine if all six were at times left on the table. Geller was allowed to do his wonted wandering about, even leaving the room, which he did at least three times. Upon his return, he was able to "get" one of the drawings.

In *New Scientist*, Hanlon concludes: "If he [Geller] could do this test under loose conditions but not under tight conditions, is this not worth a mention in the paper?" Charles Rebert, a psychologist working at SRI at the time, had no doubts about this phase of the tests. He told Joseph Hanlon, "I was *there,* and I'm convinced that he cheated."

I leave my reader to his or her conclusions.

I consulted with Dr. Hanlon at length on the Geller matter when he visited the United States, and later I traveled to England at my own expense twice to show him videotapes of Geller in action on several American television shows. Much of the information contained in his account came from my tapes of Geller in action, and from my discussions with him in England.

There are places where I disagree with Hanlon in his conclusions, and some of these have been noted. Further, I must say that I have to agree in some small way with some of the persons who objected to his *New Scientist* article, in that he does seem to have departed in some measure from a strictly scientific approach in his investigation. But any person who had been through the strange ritual that both Hanlon and I went through in trying to fathom the mysteries of parapsychological double-think and devious methodology would certainly, too, have tended to lose his objectivity. The reasoning—or lack thereof—is enough to strain anyone's patience. Rules that do not apply to any other discipline are expounded as being absolutely necessary to investigation of the "psychics." And no reasonable person can accept such loopholes in procedure while attempting to work within a scientific framework.

The *New Scientist* article gave rise to a huge volume of reader correspondence that the magazine ran for a full two months after. Reading these letters now, I am struck by the fact that they all carry on at length about the *philosophical* involvement of the investigators and take Hanlon to task for not having a wider view of the matter. The letters cover in great detail the *possibility* of psi phenomena but fail to deal with the fact that the "SRI Report" was a totally inadequate document prepared by improperly qualified persons under anything but scientific conditions. It proved nothing except that nothing has yet been proved.

Meanwhile, the Stanford Research Institute had by this time come under a great deal of fire, and in a way I must accept some of the blame. I had been cheerfully repeating Geller's claim that SRI had tested him under flawless laboratory conditions and declared him to be genuine. This was far from the truth, and both Geller and I knew it. My reason for repeating the falsehood was this: I knew that surely not *all* the specialists working at the institute had been taken in by Geller, although the director and the two laser physicists obviously had been. I reasoned that, if all the SRI scientists were branded as Geller devotees, some of them would rebel eventually and that psychologists—who should have conducted the tests in the first place, if any were to be done at all—might demand that they be allowed to test the Chosen One. And that's exactly what happened.

I quote from the organ of the American Psychological Association, *Monitor* (vol. 5, no. 2), of February 1974. Titled "Uri Geller: Is He a Medicine Show Hype or a Challenge to Science?" The article, by Jules Asher, says:

> The psychologists at SRI had, according to Geller, originally opposed the Institute's studies of his powers. After the "Time" article, internal politics gave SRI psychologists an opportunity to run their own tests of his alleged paranormal perceptual ability.
>
> They devised an elaborate, double blind experiment employing 100 envelopes with drawings in them. It was to have run over a 5-day period. According to Dr. Charles Rebert of the Life Sciences Division, Geller tried for three days to reproduce the psychologists' drawings but was unable to function clairvoyantly.
>
> "He passed on every envelope," said Rebert.
>
> On the third day the psychologists reluctantly yielded to the physicists' request that the experimental procedures be loosened up. Geller then achieved one "hit," but by that time there were suspicions of foul play and the experiment was abandoned, said Rebert.
>
> "I'm convinced that he [Geller] swapped envelopes on us," remarked Rebert. "He flunked our test."
>
> Targ admits that Geller cannot always function paranormally and he places some of the blame for failures on "non-believers."
>
> "Even the secret introduction of a skeptic who 'knows there's no such thing as parapsychology' can quench his [Geller's] ability," said Targ.

The last statement makes me wonder a bit. (It's Rule 4, remember?) How is it that with Charles Reynolds and myself in the room with him at the *Time* magazine office in New York, Geller was able to perform what he swore were genuine wonders with a fork, a key, and some "telepathic" drawings, whereas he could *not have possibly done so* because of our quite negative attitudes toward him? He performed as well as he has ever performed, yet we were giving out all the negative "vibes" we could muster!

And is it not curious that this Geller test series was never reprinted or mentioned by any of his SRI disciples? And that the press—so very interested in the Geller matter, we're told—never ran a story on his spectacular failure and suspected cheating? Remember what I said earlier about a nonstory? Here's a perfect example. Editors all over the world turned down *that* story!

Nature held the "SRI Report" for more than eight months before they printed it. This is an abnormally long time with 35 issues of the magazine published in the interval. Even editor David Davies, of *Nature*, referred to the report as "a ragbag of a paper," and he realized, along with the referees, that to reject a paper submitted by reputable scientists with the apparent backing of a recognized organization like the Stanford Research Institute would be quite difficult without his having a very positive reason. The world of science works that way: Refusal would have impugned the integrity or competence of the scientists involved, and this is just not done. Perhaps it is a weakness of the system. Scientists, moreover, feel that they must "publish or perish." But editor Davies was astute enough to realize that the *Nature* editorial (written by Dr. Christopher Evans, one of the referees of the journal) should direct his readers to the *New Scientist* article, which put the whole thing in the proper perspective.

Fortunately, *New Scientist* editor Bernard Dixon and *Nature* editor Davies are long-time good friends, so such cooperation was possible. The Geller fans had brought pressure to bear on *Nature* by making it widely known that the SRI paper had been submitted to them; the actual copy had also been widely "leaked" to the scientific world. So *Nature* had little choice. But both editors had the good sense to see that a balanced story would emerge if the SRI paper and the Hanlon story broke together. They arranged it that way. Said Davies, who is a Ph.D. in physics, "You set a scientist to catch a scientist, and you set a magician to catch a magician—or at least you would if Uri Geller would allow it. Perhaps a journalist is the right person in this case. Only a science writer could describe the chaos that exists in some of these labs."

Of course the publication in *Nature* of the "SRI Report" has been touted as a great victory for Geller supporters. The overall picture escapes them. They ignore the *New Scientist* coverage carefully and will refuse to believe that Hanlon is sane in bringing serious doubt into their hero's profile.

Some people never learn.

Will we *ever* know just what happened at the Stanford Research Institute in the last months of 1972 and in August 1973, when Uri Geller and Shipi Shtrang performed there? I very much doubt it. Recognized men of science, as well as myself, have been asking questions of Targ and Puthoff about the hole in the wall of the steel room, about the dictionary used in the "telepathy" tests, about the time taken for each test, about why Shipi was allowed in the test area, and about many other details that these two men have simply refused to answer. A distressed member of the SRI staff has reported that Russell Targ tears up letters requesting such information. And we all continue to wonder about the prestigious Stanford Research Institute and the strange policy it follows in investigating Things That Go Bump in the Night.

The Geller tests at SRI were utterly useless, except as examples of inept and biased research. They proved nothing at all about the purported powers of the Israeli conjuror, but they proved much about the men behind the research.

Does it not begin to appear as if Uri Geller has feats of clay?

I include here not the entire *New Scientist* article, but only that portion which deals with Joseph Hanlon's own *personal* experiences with Geller. He was a good observer and managed most of the time—though not all—to keep his eyes on the performer. But even he was misdirected long enough for miracles to take place. Here you will see how easily someone like Professor Ellison can be talked into giving more information than one realizes and how helpful subjects tend to be in making the experiment a success—though they are often not aware of this at the time.

Transatlantic Telepathy

Investigating the Geller phenomenon second-hand is all well and good, but the strongest impressions necessarily come from personal contact with Uri. I have seen Uri work twice, once as part of a transatlantic telepathy experiment conducted by the Sunday Mirror (10 December, 1973) and the other in the Montcalm Hotel, London (19 June, 1974).

In the Mirror test, Geller was in New York, connected to the Mirror office in London by transatlantic telephone. In the Mirror office were Clifford Davis, the Mirror TV editor who arranged the test; Professor Arthur Ellison of City University and chairman of the executive committee of the Society for Psychical Research; Dr. Christopher Evans of the New Scientist panel; Ronnie Bedford, Mirror science editor; Patricia O'Flanagan and myself from New Scientist; the Thames television crew; and about a dozen spectators. Yasha Katz of Geller's staff, and Sidney Young, from the Mirror, were with Geller in New York. The attempt lasted nearly two hours, and covered a variety of tests. Katz listened on the New York end of the telephone and later told New Scientist (during one of his meetings to discuss our experiments) that Geller's biggest success was seeing a photograph of a car.

In fact, the event was not so clear cut. At my request, Patricia O'Flanagan had provided a set of sealed envelopes containing simple photographs which no one but she had seen. When Uri was already on the telephone, she gave me the sealed envelopes and I selected one, which turned out to contain a photo of a police car and a policeman. Professor Ellison was on the London end of the 'phone and concentrated on the photo, attempting to transmit it to Geller. We could all see and hear Ellison and hear Geller.

The photo transmission experiment took 33 minutes—the first half being primarily long silences followed by encouragement from Ellison. At seven minutes Geller said "I am getting all the time three pictures." Ellison replied "Can you tell us what the three are, just in case one of them matches?" Geller declined and more long silences followed. Finally, at 20 minutes Uri said he could not do it. But Ellison said: "Would you like to tell us anything about the patterns you were getting in your mind when we were all concentrating on the picture?"

Geller replied that he had drawn three different sets of things. First, "three people appeared in my mind with something white underneath." Second, "something long." Ellison immediately replied "That sounds likely, it could be described as something long." Then Geller said it was like an animal—a dog or a horse standing sideways. With no further encouragement at this point, he moved on to the third drawing—which he described as something triangular with a semi-circle coming out of the left side—"a mountain, sort of, with something coming out." Finally, he said he had words in his mind: "pattern, horse, animal, dog, dog, dog."

Although this drew no encouragement from Ellison, he continued to press the dog—asking if there was a photo of a dog somewhere in the room. There wasn't. Only the "something long" had drawn a positive response from Ellison.

Next Geller said that of the three impressions the "biggest one" was the second—an "object that was wide, long, and bright in colour." "Very good," replied Ellison. Geller then went through another series of words—tables, flower, telephone—which drew no support from Ellison.

Then, 28 minutes into the test, Geller began drawing and Sidney Young came on the 'phone to describe what he was drawing. It could be "a car or a pig," Young said, which drew a favourable response from Ellison. Then Young said it looked "like a child's wooden toy—the sort of thing you get from Czechoslovakia where it is just a semblance of a car or a pig—not wheels, not legs, sort of rounded."

Ellison responded "Very good, we can call that a partial success." Then Young described Geller drawing "a fat sausage with, at the rear, a part that comes down and looks like, say, an elephant's foot, then goes along toward the front and becomes a sort of a breast." Ellison laughed and gave a negative response. Geller then announced that he was finished, and asked Ellison what the photo was.

Ellison said it was a police car, and Geller then claimed to have written down the word "car" even though he had not mentioned it before with the list of words in his mind. Later, he claimed to have written down the word "car" twice.

To me, at least, this was hardly a success. Guided by Ellison, he drew a shape that could have been an animal, a car, a table, a hill, or almost anything. Later in the nearly two-hour telephone call, however, Geller made remarks like "I am happy I got the drawing."

When I asked him afterwards, Ellison answered immediately that Geller had, indeed, gotten the car. He called the test "remarkable" and noted that Geller "didn't say a cup or a tree or a human being." Actually, of course, Geller did mention people and his drawing could have been a cup—it was Young who said it might be a pig or a car. But most important, Ellison seems to have been totally oblivious to the amount of help he gave Geller during the entire time. He permitted Geller to offer him three basic shapes from which he chose one, then guided Geller to something that was only vaguely right, and finally accepted Geller's statement that it was, indeed, correct. This is a good example of how Geller is able to draw people into helping him and wanting to believe that he has succeeded, even up to the point of reporting an event that did not happen.

Nothing appeared in the Sunday Mirror about the trial, which surprised me as Geller was hot news at the time. Only later did I find that Geller had insisted and Davis accepted that nothing would be published if the test failed.

Uri Bends My Key—and Rips His Trousers

My second chance to watch Uri work was 19 June when editor Dr. Bernard Dixon and I met with Uri in the lobby of the Montcalm Hotel, London, for more than an hour.

We sat in a secluded corner of the lobby and chatted for a long time. Then Uri offered to try some of his skills for us. He tried to reproduce pictures which Dixon and I drew but eventually "passed" (he said he saw nothing clear on his "mental screen") each time. Next he suggested he try bending metal. I gave Uri my housekey, which he worked with unsuccessfully.

Dixon commented afterwards that he was struck by the extent to which Geller stressed his failures—constantly saying he did not think he could do it and telling us stories about his failures on television and elsewhere. Indeed, he talked far more about failures than successes. The effect, of course, is to make everyone around Geller exceedingly anxious that he should succeed.

Geller suggested we move to the next room—an empty dining room with a few soft chairs near the door. He continued to attempt to bend my key. Noting that it was often easier to bend an object when it was near other metal, he rubbed the key against an upended metal floor ashtray and other metal objects. Even with just the three of us, a high degree of chaos prevailed—at one point I was sent looking for metal and at another looking for a pad. Hotel staff who passed—who by now seemed used to the events—added comments. But still nothing unusual happened.

Finally Uri suggested we move into the corner and sit down on a sofa behind a low coffee table. Bernard Dixon was sent to fetch Geller's jacket. Geller sat down first and I walked around the table and was just sitting down; Bernard was walking across with Geller's jacket. Thus neither of us was watching Geller closely. Suddenly Geller lurched forward, spreading his legs so rapidly that he split his trousers. His hands were down in front of him.

After joking about his ripped trousers, he held the key from the point end, enclosing most of it in his hand, and continued his efforts to make it bend. Geller's hand was slightly arched, however, and I could see clearly that the key was already slightly bent. Suddenly he said it was bending, and slowly moved his hand down the key to expose the bend. The bend was not large and he put the key on the coffee table to show the bend—carefully holding it in a V position so that both ends were off the table and the bend touching. He repeated many times that it was still bending and to prove this he put it back down on the table, now in an L position, with an entire flat side touching so that the other end was higher off the table than it had been the first time. As far as I could see, however, the key was no more bent than when I saw it in his hand.

I cannot actually say that I saw Uri bend my key by non-paranormal means. But I can offer an explanation that I find more plausible than previously unidentified mental forces. First, it should be noted that keys are surprisingly easy to bend, particularly for a person like Geller with strong hands. Few of us ever try it, however, and we assume it is difficult.

But anyone, including me, can bend a key on the edge of a chair. Sitting in a chair with your legs slightly spread, reach down to the bottom of the chair seat and you will feel part of the chair frame. Holding the head of the key in both hands, put the point on the top of the frame and press down. You will be surprised how easily the key bends. With practice, you can do this with a quick, casual movement in which you pull the chair forward towards a table.

To me, the most plausible hypothesis is that, knowing neither Bernard nor I were concentrating at that moment, Uri put the key on the metal rail at the front of the sofa (his hands were in the right place) and then suddenly slid forward. Because the coffee table was too close to the sofa, he had to spread his legs quickly, splitting his trousers.

Faces and Flowers

After the key bend, Uri again tried telepathy. After a couple of unsuccessful attempts—as before he always passed, never showing a final drawing despite attempts on his part—he finally did one drawing. I drew a simple flower, Uri made two attempts, which he rejected, and then said that I had drawn a face. It is, as he noted, not too far off because it does have a basic circle with lines coming out from it. The final drawing is his explanation—that he drew a circle with bumps and then guessed at the eyes and then the rest of the face.

Uri's relative lack of success, his own explanation of how he did the drawing, and some observations by Bernard Dixon allowed us to piece together afterwards a non-paranormal hypothesis for this effort as well. First, it should be noted that in the early attempts which Uri passed, we had time to think and were drawing relatively unusual figures such as a complex fork and an integral sign. But by the time Geller made an attempt, we had little time left with him and I had to think of and draw objects quickly—thus the simple flower.

More important, however, was Bernard's observation that after each drawing, we would carefully hide the drawing, but then Geller would ask us to draw the picture again in our mind. "I found I was making slight head movements, tracing the shape of the drawing. I tried not to, but found it difficult if I was really concentrating hard and tracing the shape as Uri suggested. Watching Joe Hanlon I noted the same effect."

Looking at my drawing and Geller's efforts and explanations, it seemed that Bernard's hypothesis holds up well. The head motions for a flower would be a large circle, several short back and forth motions (petals) and one long curving up and down motion (the stem). This is precisely what Uri drew in his first two attempts exhibiting the fact that it is difficult to tell from head motions precisely where on the circle the other lines should go. Dropping the long up and down motion, and putting the short motions all on the top, seems to suggest a face with hair. And Uri himself noted that he was sure about the circle and bumps and guessed at the face. Because of the haste with which I drew the picture, he could be sure that it was one of the common ones.

Not an Experiment

My investigation of Geller has been surprising to me in two important ways: first that every Geller event that I could investigate in detail had a normal explanation that was more probable than the paranormal one and second, the really strong desire of people to suspend disbelief and accept Geller. On the latter point, I must admit that I, too, was strongly taken with Geller, and that I could not help liking him and being swept up by his enthusiasm — despite the fact that I was looking for tricks.

Many people believe implicitly in Geller — often based on a very few demonstrations of his powers, swept on by their own desire to believe and by the force of Geller's personality. Indeed, some supposedly objective scientists now talk of the "Geller effect" as a fact.

But as Uri himself told me, "a stage demonstration is not an experiment" because "what I do on the stage is under my conditions." Only controlled scientific tests will tell whether Geller actually has paranormal powers.

But we can use our experience with Geller the performer to help develop and evaluate tests with Geller the experimental subject. And if there is any lesson to be learned, it is that Occam's Razor must be our guide — we must reject all normal explanations before we consider the paranormal ones.

In some cases, normal explanations would not mean that Geller is cheating. It is possible, at least, for someone to reproduce drawings watching a nodding head without realising quite how it is happening. But we must also accept the fact — made all the more difficult by Geller's likeability — that a normal explanation for key bending must imply fraud. And on the evidence of Uri's performances, this possibility must be seriously considered.

I once did an experiment similar to the transatlantic test outlined above, in which I was to receive an entire six-word phrase chosen at random by a newspaper columnist. Wesley Hicks, of the *Toronto Evening Telegram* in Toronto, Canada, had me at his office while a local radio personality concentrated, a couple of miles away, on the phrase. One interested party, a confederate of mine, was in the studio with him, and after seeing the phrase, went to a telephone, called a public pay phone on the corner and relayed the message to another confederate. This second person stayed put until I said to Hicks that I wanted to check if the chap at the radio station was ready. I picked up his phone, called the number of the public phone, waited as if the line was not connected yet, heard the stooge give me the phrase I needed, then hung up the phone, saying that the line was "busy." A moment later, I suggested that Hicks himself call this time, to obviate any possibility of trickery on my part (it was a bit late at that point!), and he verified that the experiment was under way.

A bit of concentration and many groanings later, I had reproduced the entire phrase. Question: Did the people of the *Sunday Mirror* take any precautions to see that such a scheme was not pulled on them? They could have, but they didn't. I had been in touch with them before this and they knew where I could be reached, but they chose not to take advantage of my expertise.

And note that this experiment was a flop (though Uri might have planned to use my method to do it), but it never hit the papers at any time—because *Geller had an agreement with them that, if it failed, they would not publish the results!* Do you see now how biased the press is when it comes to a "nonstory"? Geller's failure in print would have destroyed a good source of stories for the *Sunday Mirror* and they decided to cover up the truth and wait for another "miracle" to take place.

Similarly, when a popular television show in Israel, called "Boomerang," blew a taping with Geller, *the show was simply cancelled and the tape scrapped,* because Geller looked bad. It might have been an interesting sight to see the psychic wonder unable to perform because his gimmicks had been discovered by detractors in that audience. Happily, the Johnny Carson show in the United States displayed none of this timidity, and proceeded to broadcast Geller's failure and discomfort in living color.

Time magazine correspondents in Israel reported that a psychologist there named Merari agreed to examine Geller's claims, *with the arrangement that if results were not positive no report would be issued.* To this day—several years after the event—Merari has not been heard from.

Did Geller have the same arrangement with the boys at SRI before he agreed to be tested there? I'll bet he did!

How many other times has Geller had this cozy arrangement with the media and scientists? We may never know. But we can suspect.

Further: The photo that was used in the *Mirror* transatlantic test, you should know, was not just a simple one with a simple theme. It had a great number of items in it: two policemen, six traffic cones, one car, a numbered license plate, three printed words, and a number of trees. If Geller had gotten even one of these objects, he might have been declared a success. The choice of targets was *very* poor, and I'm surprised at Hanlon's choice. The dedicated believers jump at the slightest hint of success and blow it all out of proportion, as you can see. Katz declared it a great success and Ellison declared it a "partial" success.

As for the second encounter with Uri, Hanlon seems not to know about something we're about to become very familiar with in the next chapter. He is not aware of "pencil-reading." Nowhere in his analysis does it occur to him, and his solution of the trick (that it was one of the few shapes he would draw in the circumstances) is very weak. But looking at the series of drawings, we will see that Hanlon's results are compatible with Uri's having done the pencil-reading trick. Hanlon's observation about head movements is, however, quite astute—for which he gets a full ten points.

All things considered, thank you, Dr. Hanlon!

We will hear fully about the Geller matter in the United Kingdom in Chapter 16.

5

Andrew Weil's Search
for the True Geller

A psychiatrist was consulted by a patient with a very peculiar delusion. He was convinced that he was dead, and nothing could be done to dissuade him of this. The psychiatrist tried to reason with him. "Tell me," he said, "do dead men bleed?" "No, of course not!" cried the patient. "That is a stupid question!" The psychiatrist pricked the man's finger with a needle, and a drop of blood appeared. "And what do you conclude from that?" asked the psychiatrist. The patient paused but a few seconds to examine the wound. "Obviously I was wrong," he murmured quietly. "Dead men *do* bleed . . ."

Andrew Weil is an accomplished thirty-two-year-old doctor of medicine who is primarily interested in the study of exotic states of consciousness and has written a book on the subject, *The Natural Mind.* I do not know that I agree with Dr. Weil's conclusions arrived at in the book, but I believe him to be an honest investigator. We both have an interest in the peoples of South America, and it has turned out we are both also interested in Uri Geller. Weil wrote a two-part article on Geller for *Psychology Today,* published in June and July 1974. Weil had already written the first part before he came to visit me, though he had spoken to me on the phone and did not sound at all convinced about my statements on Geller. After the publication of the first part, I received a lot of "nut" mail and weird phone calls from persons wanting to bring me to the True Light of Belief, and I was happy to know that I was to have Weil visit me and thus have a chance to make my case in person.

Andy Weil is one of the most honest men I ever met. It will be evident why I say this as you read his account. The title of Weil's two-part article was the same as this chapter's.

PART 1

Uri Geller is a 26-year-old Israeli who came to the United States not long ago to demonstrate his powers of telepathy and psychokinesis. He claims he can bend or break objects simply by concentrating on them, and that he can make things dematerialize. Since the time I first encountered Uri, over a year ago, I've tried carefully to understand his talents. Dealing with this extraordinary man has been an adventure—a sort of roller-coaster ride, through troughs of skepticism and heights of pure belief. Let me describe what happened.

Last April, I happened to be in Berkeley when Uri Geller made one of his early public appearances. The event took place in a school auditorium, filled to capacity with people who had paid a moderate admission fee to see the Israeli wonder.

The program began with an introductory speech by Andrija Puharich, the physician and parapsychological researcher who brought Geller to this country. Puharich explained that Uri was very tired because he had just tried to demonstrate his powers before committees of Nobel Prize winners from Berkeley and Stanford. He assured us that Uri had passed several rigidly controlled tests at the Stanford Research Institute, a private think-tank which studied the "Geller effect" last fall. All we had to do now was "be with" Uri—give him our mental energies—and we'd see amazing psychic feats.

Are You with Me?

Then Uri came on stage. He was charming, good-looking and boyishly enthusiastic. He said that his day had been exhausting, especially since he hadn't been able to do much of anything for the scientists. The mental set of an audience is crucial to his performance, he explained. If people are with him, all sorts of things happen; if they aren't with him, nothing happens. As an example, he described his inability to perform successfully in the hostile editorial offices of "Time" magazine a short time before. But with the staff of an underground newspaper in the Bay Area he was able to make pieces of silverware break and cause objects to vanish without a trace.

Uri told us he had first noticed his telepathic abilities as a child, when he was able to guess his mother's hands at card games. When he was about seven, he noticed that the hands of his wrist watch would jump forward or backward several hours. Eventually, he learned that these movements occurred when he willed them. Uri kept these powers to himself, and as he grew older he attached less importance to them. But in his early 20s he became interested in them again, started practicing, and finally decided he should use them to make his living. In mid-1970 he began appearing before small audiences. By the end of 1971 he had become famous in Israel. It was then that he met Puharich.

Uri began his demonstrations by picking several female volunteers from the audience. He kept telling us not to be disappointed if nothing happened. "Just 'want' something to happen and maybe it will."

He asked the first woman to write the name of a color on a blackboard. He kept his eyes averted as she wrote "blue" and then erased it.

He asked the audience to "think" the name of that color on the count of three. "And please, no one whisper it," he cautioned. He counted to three. I thought "blue." We repeated this three times. Uri shook his head. "I'm having some trouble," he said. "Once more. One, two, three . . ." There was a long pause. "OK," he said, "I'm going to take a chance. The color I get is blue."

The audience applauded wildly. He held up his hands. "Wait. I must ask: who over here was sending yellow?" A young man in front gasped and raised his hands. "Please don't do that," Uri told him. "It really confuses me." The man apologized, saying he couldn't help himself.

The Stopped Watches

Uri was also successful at the next test: a foreign capital written on the board, erased, and then sent to him mentally by the whole audience. The capital was Prague; he guessed it with no difficulty. He also reproduced several figures drawn on the board.

"I'll tell you how I do this," he said, "I have in my mind a kind of screen, like a television screen, and when I receive something, whatever it is draws itself on that screen."*

Uri then tried to demonstrate psychokinesis, or making things move by means of psychic powers. "If anyone has a watch that is not running," he said, "as long as no parts are missing from inside, bring it up front, and I'll try to make it go." Apparently, his talent at this operation was already well known, because many people had brought their stopped watches with them. Uri fixed a watch by having a woman hold it in her hands and putting his hand over hers. Without touching the woman's hand, he passed his palm back and forth as if trying to direct some sort of energy. He asked his volunteer to let him know if she felt any sudden heat or tingling. She did. He opened her hands and took out the watch, which was running again. He repeated this demonstration with several other watches and got almost all of them to run; one was an antique pocket watch that had been stopped for years.

Andy Weil has observed here that Geller's purported ability to fix "stopped" watches was "already well known." Yes, it is widely known, but not in quite those terms. Geller has many times positively stated that he fixes "*broken*" watches—not just ones that are "stopped." But we will discuss this phenomenon fully in Chapter 12. I just wish to note that Weil has observed more carefully at this point than most persons, who easily substitute "broken" for "stopped" and fail to see the difference.

Elated by success, he said he would try to bend some metal objects. Volunteers rushed forward with an assortment of rings, keys, and pins. Uri explained that objects to which people were emotionally attached

* We will discover how Geller *really* does this in Chapter 14.

were most suitable. He couldn't guarantee success, though, because he was exhausted from his day of failures with the Nobel laureates. He tried bending rings by putting them in the hands of volunteers and again passing his hands over theirs. It didn't work. After several attempts he gave up. "No, it just doesn't want to work tonight." The audience was only slightly disappointed. They had already seen his powers.

One of Geller's cleverest ploys is to fail a certain amount of the time, often much more than he succeeds. The impression given is that Psychic Rule 1 is being obeyed. Miracles just don't always happen when we want them to the most. And, his audience also figures that if the whole thing were just a trick, it would work every time. Since it doesn't, the demonstration must be the real thing. Illogical, but it has appeal!

Uri concluded his presentation by offering to take a group of volunteers on a blindfolded drive through Berkeley. That is, he would be securely blindfolded and would drive a car, using the vision of the other passengers telepathically to navigate. There was no shortage of volunteers, and I heard the next day that the ride had been a success.

We will leave this blindfolded matter to be taken care of later, but I venture to guess that if Weil had seen Geller's demonstration that day his confidence in the superstar would have been badly shaken. This is one thing that Geller just doesn't do well.

A Bias Toward Belief

Uri Geller was now a real person to me, and very likable. Whether he really had the power of mind over matter, I couldn't say. I hadn't seen him fix watches with my own eyes, since I was sitting too far away; but I believed the testimony of those who had. The experiments in telepathy, on the other hand, failed to move me. I had seen stage magicians give similar performances using trickery. The blindfolded driving didn't impress me either, since a person can learn to peek through even the best-fastened blindfold. What I really wanted to see was a key bend or a ring break. For me, that would decide the case.

My prejudice leans heavily toward the belief that such things are possible. I have no doubt, for instance, that telepathy exists; in fact, I think it's so common that we do it all the time without knowing it. I've never seen psychokinesis, but I'm prepared to accept that, too. No mental gymnastics are required to rationalize its existence. The proposition that matter and energy are synonymous on some level is consistent with the most modern conceptions of physics. The propositions that human consciousness is a form of real energy seems to me self-evident. So why shouldn't consciousness affect the physical properties of things?

I didn't see Uri Geller again until the first week in June. By that time he was becoming well known. He had made convincing television appearances with Merv Griffin and Jack Paar. On the latter show he had bent a heavy metal spike. His host was astonished. Meanwhile, favorable articles about him were being published all over the place. "Time" was the only magazine that accused him of being a fraud.

The *Time* magazine episode is one of few where I was present from first to last and had an opportunity to observe Geller up close without being suspected by him. This scene will be discussed later in detail, and will be most revealing of the process of outright lying and of a system of double-think used in judging the Geller matter.

I was living in New York then, and one night Andrija Puharich invited me to a small gathering on the upper West Side where Uri was meeting with some people who wanted to make a feature film about him.

Ten people were there when I arrived, among them Puharich and Geller. Uri had just flown in from California and was looking well, although he said he was tired. The company included a lighting director from a major television network, together with his wife; a young lawyer and his wife; a young woman psychic who was also a protégée of Puharich; and Jascha Katz, one of the two Israelis who managed Uri's professional appearances.

Many of the people present had seen Uri do extraordinary things; some of them had witnessed phenomena they considered miraculous. The lawyer showed me a ring Uri had bent for him and said the experience had changed his life.

And right there is my main point in opposing Geller and his crew. More than one person has had a life changed as a result of seeing these conjuring tricks and believing them to be the real thing. Barbara Walters, surely an intelligent and erudite woman, told me after I had successfully convinced her that Geller was a trickster that she had based the whole past year of her life on the reality of Uri's powers. And *that* much of a change in philosophy is no trifling matter for any human being.

Can you believe that a conjuror bending a ring by sleight-of-hand could change a person's entire life?

"I Am Just a Channel"

After chatting for a while, we drifted into a small living room and sat down, hoping Uri would feel up to trying out his powers. Uri asked us not to urge him. "If something is going to happen, it will," he said. He began to tell us stories of his recent feats. He had "blown the mind" of an astrophysicist by making his fork bend while they were eating dinner together. The day before, on the plane from California, he had "unconsciously" jammed the motion picture projector, causing film to spill out on the floor. "Things like that are always happening around me," he said,

"Sometimes Andrija and I are eating in a restaurant and—'pop!'—a fork on the table is breaking just like that."

It so happens that during a flight to California last year, the projector on *my* flight also broke down, piling up film. But I resisted taking credit for the event, thus missing a great opportunity for becoming a cult figure.

Someone asked Uri what he thought this power was. "I don't think it is my mind," he answered. "The parapsychologists are always talking about the mind, but I think this power comes from somewhere outside of me, and I am just a channel for it." What did he mean by "outside?" "I believe there are other dimensions and other universes, and that this energy which comes through me is coming from another universe—that it is intelligently directed and sent through me for a purpose." Puharich made assenting noises and said that what he and Uri were learning about the nature of this intelligence was astonishing. He didn't want to say more; the subject was too "far out" and would be discussed in a book he was writing.

But Uri added that he thought the people of the United States were unusually receptive to his powers at this time.

In the United States (and elsewhere), yes. But in Israel, no, as we will see in Chapter 14.

"Here is where people really believe in me and where things are going to happen." He described himself as "bigger than Watergate" and predicted that everyone in America would soon hear of him. Already, Uri said, a number of high-placed American officials believed in him. The Defense Department has been especially interested in his ability to erase magnetic tapes at a distance. He describes how he made an airport television monitor go blank in the presence of a U.S. Senator. Uri talked like this for some time.

There is absolutely no basis that I have been able to discover for this claim concerning the Department of Defense. Dr. Ray Hyman, of the University of Oregon in Eugene, is employed by the Defense Department to check up on matters like this, and Hyman knows nothing about it, nor have inquiries to Washington yielded any confirmation of just another of Geller's wild claims. (See Appendix.)

There were some pieces of silverware and a few keys on the table. Uri picked up a key and played with it. Everyone moved forward. "I don't know if anything will go tonight," he said. "I'm really very tired and not feeling up to it." He rubbed the key with his finger and thumb. "No," he said, and dropped it.

Thinking About Ice Cream

"Look, let's try some telepathy," he suggested. He pointed to me. "Why don't you draw any figure on a piece of paper. I won't look." He turned his head away. I drew the sign for infinity. "Now right below that draw another figure." I added a pyramid. "OK, now try to send it to me; just visualize it in your mind." Uri took up a pencil and pad. He assumed a look of concentration, first staring at me, then closing his eyes. He quickly sketched on the pad.

"The first thing I got was a circle that changed to an '8.'" He had drawn an upright "8." Underneath it he had drawn a triangle. I showed him the horizontal "8" and the pyramid. "Dammit," he said, "I saw a pyramid for an instant but then it became a triangle." But I was impressed.

At this point in his investigation, Weil was unaware of one of the basic tools of the "mentalist." And here—I must confess—I will give away one of the magician's cherished secrets: "Pencil-reading" involves watching the end of the subject's pencil or pen while a drawing is being made. A little experimentation on the part of my reader will convince anyone that such an art is not at all difficult to master. As long as the pencil is long enough, Geller is able to cover his eyes, just peeking out from between his fingers enough to see the end of the writing instrument. A guess (a triangle instead of a pyramid, for example) will be just far enough off to impress the believer with how uncertain these marvelous psychic forces are.

A good example of this happened later in Weil's article, with Martin Abend of New York's "Channel 5 News." Analyze this event in the light of the foregoing and it becomes quite clear that Geller did *that* trick by the same means.

"Can you send something to me?" I asked.

"Oh, yes—go ahead, close your eyes."

We both concentrated, and I came up with an ice cream cone, possibly because I think about ice cream often. Uri had been trying to send me a sketch of a boat.

He tried a few more drawings with other people in the room and generally scored well. Then he began to miss. "There's something not right about the energy in this room," he complained. "It's just not working well; maybe it's because I'm tired."

"Can you try the key?" someone asked.

"I'll try," he replied, "but I don't think I can do it." He picked up a thick key and began stroking the shaft. Nothing happened. He placed it in his palm and tapped it with a finger. Still nothing. "Maybe if it were lying on something metal," he suggested. Someone brought him a frying pan. He turned it upside-down and placed the key on it. He jiggled the key and tapped it, but still there was no change. "No, it's not working;

let's wait." Uri seemed a little edgy now. Every once in a while he conversed in Hebrew with Jascha Katz, his manager.

"Do you only have power over metal objects?" I asked.

"Only with metals," he answered.

"Does it make any difference what kind of metal?"

"No, all metals are the same."

"I Am Not a Messiah"

"Do you do any kind of meditation, or go into trances?"

"No, I'm very ordinary."

"Do you use any drugs?"

"No, not even alcohol."

"How do people react when they see you do something that's not supposed to happen?"

"Oh, man, it blows their minds. Most people are really excited and really are turned on. Some people just don't believe it even when they see it with their own eyes. Some guy on the West Coast wrote that I had a laser beam concealed in my belt. Can you imagine that?" He laughed and shook his head. "A few people believe it and think it's evil."

"What do you mean?" I asked.

"Well, like that business with the projector on the plane yesterday. The stewardess was really flustered because she said that never happens. I told her it often happens when I'm on planes. I didn't really mean to cause it; it just happened."

Can you imagine a stewardess getting worked up over an event that "never happens"? Of course it may never have happened to that woman during one of her flights, but it's occurred hundreds of times, and Geller wasn't present. Or does he take credit for all the other occurrences, too?

And though I have no idea who the "guy on the West Coast" could be, such unfounded comments involving advanced technology, such as a laser, are very harmful. They make the critics sound like dummies. And when they make such stupid guesses, they *are* dummies.

"So then some of the passengers recognized me from television, and I bent a few forks for them. And then this big guy from Hawaii came over and identified himself as the security officer. It was very far out. He didn't know what to make of it. So finally he relaxed, but then he asked me how did I know that what I was doing wasn't from the Devil. He said the old Hawaiians believed powers like that were from the Devil."

"How does that make you feel?"

"Well, it makes me feel strange. I have these powers, and they just come through me. I want to show them to people. I want people to know that it's real, that there are no lasers in my belt and no chemicals. I just say to the key, 'Bend!' and I feel that it's going to bend, and it does."

"I imagine that could be heavy for some people."

"Sure, it's heavy for them. But, look, I am not a Moses or a Jesus or a Messiah or anything. I believe in God and I think that everything comes from God, but I don't think this has anything to do with God."

I agree with that last statement. But when Geller cautions his followers not to think of him as a Second Coming of Christ, in spite of the fact that he was born in Israel on December 20, I see full well what his game is. That's exactly what you say to people when you *want* them to think of you as the Second Coming of Christ.

You don't believe it? Okay, try *not* thinking—right now—of a purple ostrich. Convinced?

"Do you have any effects on living things?"

"Yes. One time in a press interview in San Francisco, they gave me a rose bud, and I put it in my hand and the bud opened."

"How about on humans? Did you ever try to heal anyone?"

"Just one time. When I was at Stanford there was this girl who had polio, and I put my hand on her leg, and it started to move for the first time in years."

"Really?"

"Yes. But that scared me. I wouldn't like to do that again."

Not true. Geller, asked by Merv Griffin if he has ever tried "psychic healing," replied that he had not (but he *had*) and that he would "go into it when [he felt] ready." Millions of persons heard him say it on television.

And where is this little girl so miraculously healed? No one knows.

Uri Bends a Key

At this point, the lawyer asked Uri if he would please try to bend a valuable old pin that belonged to his wife and was of great emotional importance to both of them. Uri said he would try later. "What if it really twists or breaks?" he asked.

"Believe me, Uri, it would mean more to us that way," the lawyer told him.

"Well, maybe I'll try this key again," Uri said to himself. He picked up the key—it was a good solid house key—and held the head of it between the thumb and forefinger of his left hand. With his right index finger he stroked the shaft of the key. I was about six inches from him, and the light was good. For a long time nothing seemed to happen. Then Uri shouted: "Oh, look! There it goes!" Several of us pressed closer. At first I saw nothing different about the key. But Uri insisted: "It's bending! Yes, it's bending!" And then I could see that the tip of the key was slightly curved. It had been straight.

Uri continued to rub the key. Now the bend was easily visible, and the key could be rocked back and forth when placed on a level surface.

Uri put it down on the frying pan. "It will continue to bend slowly by itself," he told us. And, after several minutes, the bend did seem to be more pronounced. "Usually, they keep bending by themselves for 24 hours, so by tomorrow morning it will be even more bent. It's as if they have a kind of life for a short time."

For an interesting detail on this "continuing-to-bend" nonsense, refer to the detailed discussion of the *Time* magazine episode (Chapter 7). For a good conclusion of the key-bending as just witnessed by Weil, see Part 2 of this same article. You have some surprises coming.

Now Uri felt "hot." He correctly received two drawings sealed inside opaque envelopes—one of a cross, the other of a Star of David.

The lawyer wanted Uri to deform his wedding band, but the idea didn't carry. The lighting director offered Uri a heavy gold ring, set with stones. Uri examined it carefully. He asked the man to support the ring on its edge with his forefinger. Uri then held his hand over the man's hand and finger, without touching the ring. After trying out several positions on his hand, he settled into one he seemed to like. Again, I was only a few inches from the demonstration.

Suddenly, the ring sagged into an oval shape. Uri exclaimed, "There! Look at that! Did you feel anything?"

"I felt a strong tingling over the whole back of my hand, definitely some kind of energy," was the reply. Uri held the ring for all to see. It was no longer circular, and would not fit back on its owner's finger.

A Fork Like Melting Wax

Flushed with success, Uri took on another house key, and within less than a minute had it bent to about 25 degrees. He assured us that by the next morning the angle would be considerably greater.

Later, someone asked Uri to try to bend a fork. He said he didn't like to work with silverware because it was too easy to bend. As he spoke, he picked up the fork by the middle in a casual way, just to play with it. Suddenly, the fork looked like melting wax and drooped over Uri's hand. "My God! Look at that!" Uri said. "I wasn't even trying to do it." The fork was bent at a grotesque angle. I picked it up. It wasn't even warm.

By now the company was about to break up. I wanted badly to see Uri work on something of mine that I knew wasn't gimmicked. The only metal thing I had on me was a heavy brass belt buckle. I offered it to him. "I never work with belt buckles," Uri said flatly.

There was little doubt in my mind that I had seen genuine psychokinesis—something I had always believed in but never witnessed. I left the apartment feeling absolutely elated.

Remember the fork? Way back at the beginning of this article, the silverware was sitting on the table, and when Geller was asked just now if he would try bending it, he declined. Then we are treated to a spontaneous miracle.

One of the basic tenets of the conjuring profession is that we never tell the audience *what* is going to happen, or *when*. They are thus confronted, at an unexpected point in time, with an unusual event that they are unable to correctly witness and analyze. Somehow, I suspect Geller is more than casually aware of this principle.

There was ample opportunity to get a fork off that table and to prepare it for stardom. And, I wonder, was the ubiquitous Shipi Shtrang there at Geller's side during *this* demonstration? Andy Weil doesn't recall, but I'd put money on it. Andy also does not recall if Geller made one of his oft-reported trips to the bathroom. He visits the bathroom so often that there is a suspicion he suffers from bladder trouble. It is *my* considered belief that his bladder is perfect, but I'm getting personal, I fear.

By August of last year, Uri Geller was even more famous. He appeared on the "Tonight Show" but wasn't able to accomplish much. He tried to detect, telepathically, which one of 10 metal film canisters contained water, and he tried to bend nails, but he couldn't do either. Johnny Carson became impatient and urged him to try other things. Uri balked, saying he couldn't be rushed. It was painful to watch. A few nights later, on the "Merv Griffin Show," he bent a large nail very successfully. Griffin introduced him by saying that his failure on the "Tonight Show" proved that Uri was real, since a stage magician would succeed every time.

We already called that shot. It's called Rule 1. Griffin, who I swear believes in the Tooth Fairy and the Easter Bunny as well, accepted Geller's failure on the Carson show by saying, "That's all the proof *I* need!" But the reason for the failure on NBC is not hard to find. Carson's staff was in touch with me the moment that Geller announced he wanted to appear on the show. Either he was not aware of Johnny's magic background (who can forget "The Great Carson"?) or he figured that Johnny would "go along" with the gag.

Later on, we will discuss the reason that Geller failed on the Carson show. His own reason was that he was "nervous," and that is partly true. He was nervous because he suddenly found that the tests were so well controlled that he would have to depend upon real psychic powers to accomplish anything. *That* would make *anyone* nervous.

Scientists Are Chumps

The possibility that Uri Geller might be nothing but a trickster didn't enter my mind for quite a while. When it did, it came by way of a remarkable man named James (the Amazing) Randi, a stage magician and escape artist who lives in New Jersey and is well known in New York from a radio show he used to do for children. I had heard that the Amazing Randi was out to expose Geller as nothing but a stage magician and that he could duplicate most of Geller's demonstrations.

Excuse me, Andy, but the radio show was for adults, not kids. I was fired from radio station WOR when I stepped on a couple of sacred cows. Much like I'm doing right now, as a matter of fact.

"That guy is dangerous," Randi told me over the phone. "He's a good magician, nothing more, and he's going to go on a Messiah trip or get into psychic healing. That's what bothers me." I told Randi what I had seen Uri do. "Of course, it looks real; that's the point of magic," he said.

"But how could Uri have bent the keys?" I asked. "He didn't," Randi replied. "They were bent already; he just reveals the bend by sleight-of-hand movements that make you think it's bending."

That didn't sound very convincing. I had seen the key when it was straight and I had seen it in the process of bending.

"What about the scientific tests?" I asked. Randi guffawed. "Scientists are the people 'least' qualified to detect chicanery," he said. "They're the easiest to fool of all. If you want to catch a burglar, you go to a burglar, not to a scientist. If you want to catch a magician, go to a magician.

"Do you know why Geller couldn't do anything on the 'Tonight Show?'" Randi went on. "Because Carson used to be a stage magician, and I got to Carson, and we figured out exactly how to safeguard the props that were going to be used. All Geller needs is 30 seconds alone with those props and he can tamper with them. But we fixed him good."

A few days later, I met with Uri privately at his East 57th Street apartment. I asked him what he thought about people who said he was a mere stage magician.

"I am not a magician," he said vehemently. "Look, the people who are supposed to see these things will see them, and those who don't, don't. I don't care if people say I do magic tricks. I know that it's real. And it's all good publicity."

On a Friday afternoon in mid-September I went again to Uri's apartment. This time I came equipped with several keys, a threaded steel bolt and a stopped watch. The watch hadn't run for a long time; if jarred it would go for a few seconds and then stop.

Five reporters were there when I arrived, four of them from the "Rolling Stone" and one from Boston's "Real Paper." The table was littered with bent spoons, a bent key, a gold ring on a piece of paper, a watch; drawings of geometrical figures, and several tape recorders.

Uri seemed tired but enthusiastic. He told me to ask him anything. I said I'd prefer to sit and listen first. The talk focused on astral projection and flying saucers (Puharich has described seeing Uri enter a flying saucer in Israel) but also included many questions I'd heard before. When did Uri first notice his powers? Did he meditate? Could he heal people?

One of the "Rolling Stone" reporters asked if Uri could teach his powers to other people. "How can I?" he answered. "Where would I begin?" I asked him if there were any verification of the bendings reported by home viewers of his television appearances. "Oh, yes," he replied. "Just last week I heard that in the Texas attorney general's office in Austin, a secretary was listening to a tape of a radio show I did there, and a fork started to bend in the presence of four witnesses."

A woman from the "Rolling Stone" told me that he had fixed the watch on the table just by holding his hand over it. The "Real Paper" man reached for the watch. Suddenly he became excited. "Has anyone reset this?" he asked. Everyone looked at the watch and gasped. Apparently, it was now four hours ahead of where it had been. Uri picked it up and exclaimed: "My God! Look at that!" He put it down. Moments later it had advanced again. "It's always like that," Uri explained. "You never see the hands moving; you just find them in a new position."

I can hardly believe that Uri said that. It's quite true, of course, because that's the only way it can be done. I've taught the trick to many other magicians, and they agree that it's a pussycat of a trick. It's easy to do, and has a great effect on the audience. We've coined a name for it. We call it "Urianalysis."

. . . I said I had a broken watch with me, but as I drew it out of my pocket I had a funny feeling that it would already be running. And so it was, quite steadily. Uri took credit for this, even though he hadn't known the watch was in my pocket. I wondered to myself if he had mobilized my latent psychokinetic ability. We correctly set both watches and left them side by side to see what would happen.*

Manic Atmosphere

The "Rolling Stone" people told me that the ring on the piece of paper had levitated earlier, or at least had dropped from mid-air onto the table. They had also seen a key bend. I took out my collection of three keys and my long bolt and put them on the table. The bolt rolled a little — I think because I bumped the table. "Who moved that?" Uri asked, very excited, grabbing me by the shoulder. "Did you touch that?" I said I didn't know, and it became another miracle.

I asked Uri if he would try to bend one of my keys. He took up a short brass one. "OK, I'll try, but don't be disappointed if it doesn't work. I'm very tired and I don't know whether I can do it now." He stroked the key while I hunched over him. Nothing happened. "No. I'm too tired. Maybe later. I had to do two early morning performances in Cleveland on television, and I'm exhausted."

The phone rang. It was someone in Denver who wanted Uri to do a

---

* See Chapter 12 for the Watch Trick.

show for 10,000 people. Jascha Katz took the call. The atmosphere was almost manic now, and the "Rolling Stone" reporters began to get headaches. "There's a lot of energy in this room," one of them said.

We're about to hear about the previously touted stunt with Abend. Using your new expertise, analyze *this,* class.

Then the director of the Channel Five (WNEW) news arrived, together with Martin Abend, a political commentator for the same channel. The news director had spent the early part of the afternoon with Uri and was now a solid convert. Uri had detected metal in film cans, caused a key to bend, and succeeded at ESP. Channel Five was going to do a feature on Uri that night and wanted Martin Abend to comment afterward.

Abend seemed unsure about all this. "It's not my line," he kept saying. But the director kept telling him that he would have an amazing experience if he would just suspend his doubts and watch.

"But if it is real, I can't say that over the air," Abend protested. "Do you know what kind of a storm we'd stir up?" He frowned. The "Rolling Stone" people urged him to be openminded and told him proudly that they had always been believers. "Just try to help him — you'll see."

Pretty soon the reporters left, leaving me with Uri, Martin Abend, and the news director. The director was keyed-up, anxious for Uri to convince Abend. Abend drew a geometrical figure and Uri looked away; but Uri was not able to reproduce the figure. Then he tried to bend a key and failed. Finally Uri sent the news director away, saying, "You're making me nervous."

Abend drew two intersecting circles. Uri received two circles tangent to each other, then two circles, one inside the other. Abend was impressed. "That's really something," he said. "I can do much better when I'm not tired," Uri told him. "No, that's 'good,'" Abend replied. There was another unsuccessful attempt at key-bending.

Did you solve it? If not, you've flunked the course. It was "pencil-reading." Geller made two guesses, based upon the technique we've learned about, and failed to guess the right configuration. But Abend declared it was "good," so everyone was happy. Now mind you, it *would* have been good, *if* there were no such thing as pencil-reading. But there is, Virginia. By this technique, two circles are just two circles. Uri was trying all the possibilities.

I've got to go," Abend said, "I have to get back to the station." The television people took their leave, telling us the show would be on at 10 o'clock that night.

Tête-à-Tête

Uri and I were now alone, sitting together on a couch. I told him I hated to ask him to perform again, but I had never seen him bend anything that belonged to me.

"Let's try the key again," he suggested. We did, but with no luck. "What else do you have?" he asked. I brought out two other keys on a small chain attached to a little knife. "I used to have a knife like that," he said and put it into my hand. He covered it with my other hand, then put his hands on mine. He concentrated intently. Then he looked at the other keys and asked which one I was most attached to. I wasn't sure. He piled all the keys into my hand and put the knife on top. Then he repeated the operation. I felt a pulsation and told him so, but there was no change.

"Dammit!" he said, "Why can't I do anything?"

"Don't be disappointed," I told him. "I'm very patient, and if nothing works now, we can try some other time."

Uri seemed agitated. "Don't you have anything else metal?" he asked. "Maybe in your boots." He pointed to my boots that I had left across the room.

"No, all I've got is a belt buckle, and you told me once you never worked with belt buckles."

"Let's try it," he said. I took off my belt and put the large brass buckle in my palm on top of the three keys and the knife and chain. I covered the pile with my other hand. Uri put his hand on top. More intense concentration. Suddenly, I felt a distinct throb inside my hands, like a small frog kicking. I told him so. "You did?" he asked excitedly and opened my hands. I could see no change in the buckle. He pulled out a long steel key and cried out: "It's bent, yes, it's bent! Do you see?" I did not see at first. But then I noticed a slight bend. It was very exciting. Uri put the key on the table to check it. Yes, it was definitely bent.

The Making of a Convert

Uri was almost jumping up and down for joy, and I shared his emotion. "Let's see if we can bend it more," he said. He touched the key to the other keys and stroked it again. After a few minutes the bend was about 25 degrees. Uri patted me on the back, making me feel that I had participated in the miracle. "It's good you felt it jump, man," he told me. "Not many people can feel that." I was elated.

Well, now, let's examine that last statement of Uri's. After a bit of experimentation, I was able to discover that if you hold a key in your palm with the length of the key across the width of the hand, then close your hand firmly with the fingers straight—that is, the first two joints of the fingers not curled under—after a moment you will feel a distinct and rather startling throb. It's your own pulse, but it sure feels weird. It was so effective when I did the key trick for a secretary at WNEW Channel 5 in New York that she screamed and threw the key into the air when it "jumped" vigorously in her closed hand. I was as much startled as she was! The phenomenon varies greatly for different persons, but try different orientations of the key, and different pressures. It will work.

> He ran into the other room to tell Jascha Katz of the success, then hugged me warmly. I gathered up my things, thanking him profusely and telling him I had seen exactly what I wanted. He walked me to the elevator. As we were saying goodbye, I heard a "plink!" and the long steel bolt bounced off his left arm onto the floor. "Is this something of yours?" he asked, picking it up.
> "Yes," I said, "I brought it along but must have left it inside."
> His eyes widened. "My God! Just like their ring. You have just seen a materialization!"
> I wasn't sure about that materializing bolt, since he could have pocketed it and made it appear by sleight-of-hand; but the other powers I had seen that day seemed extraordinary and impossible to deny.
> I was a convert.

Thus endeth Part 1 of Andy Weil in Wonderland. Stay tuned for Part 2, wherein Weil gets a surprise or two.

During the conversation quoted in Part 1, between Weil and myself on the telephone, I invited him to come out to visit me at my home, where I would give him the Geller Treatment—but without any of the divine or supernatural pretensions. You must realize that I went into this project without the protection of the "humble act" that Geller professes. I had admitted, in advance, that I was an out-and-out fake, merely an actor pretending to accomplish miracles by using trickery. I could therefore not prevail upon Andrew Weil to allow me failures for over an hour or so and then suddenly come up with a winner; I could not ask him to excuse me from the room for long periods of time; nor could I feign surprise if an already bent or broken fork suddenly were discovered on my table, as happened with Don Singleton in his meeting with Geller. I was very vulnerable.

When I answered the door to Weil, I was immediately impressed by him. Not only did he sport a huge lumberjack-type beard, which I consider a mark of good breeding, but he was the huge, affable, open type of person that Geller must have rejoiced over. I don't think Andy could tell a lie or steal an apple if he had to. I liked him immediately, and he liked me. But he would brook no nonsense about his subject, and with a few exceptions he believed in Geller very firmly.

I almost felt sorry for what I had to do. I knew that in the next hour or so Andy was going to be badly shaken up, and I wanted very much to preserve his faith in his own powers of observation while convincing him that he had been only one of hundreds of competent people who had been "taken in" by Geller's skill and reputation. That they are fooled is only testimony to their humanity; it does not reflect on their mentality. I wanted Andy spared any undeserved embarrassment.

Here is the second episode in the education of Andrew Weil. It was preceded by an editorial backview of the previous Part, the month before, and as Part 2 it was subtitled "The Letdown."

PART 2

If a man deceive me once, shame on him.
If twice, shame on me. — PROVERB

Later that night I watched the Channel Five news. There was Uri again, in a long segment, bending a key, receiving drawings, locating pieces of metal hidden in cans. The reporters presented him as unquestionably real—there was "no possibility" of deception.

Then came a round-table discussion between the reporters and a professional magician who wanted to discredit Uri. The magician came off badly. He didn't believe in psychic phenomena and said Geller had to be a phony. Martin Abend, the political commentator, defended Geller by recounting his own experience earlier that evening.

"I drew two intersecting circles," Abend told the magician, "and tried to send them to Geller. Now I think that's an unusual sort of figure. Geller first drew two circles tangent to one another. Then he drew two intersecting circles. It was an amazing thing."

I noted with interest that Abend had not reported this incident correctly. In fact, Uri had come closest with the tangent circles. Uri's second attempt to reproduce the hidden figure had been one circle "inside" another. Initially a skeptic, Abend had remembered what happened in a way that made Uri look even better than he was.

Ten points for Weil here. He has correctly noted that in recalling the event, Abend made an error in Geller's favor. The errors are seldom made the opposite way. I know from experience that persons who are under pressure to convince their listeners are apt to do just this process in order to (subconsciously) further convince themselves as well.

Several years back, I was confronted by a man with the description of a magician performing an apparent miracle that I *knew* had not happened. He grew more and more eloquent, and hyperbole filled the air as he recounted how this wonderful gentleman had been wrapped in a straitjacket and then handcuffed, stuffed into a steel box, and thrown into a swimming pool after the box was soldered shut! When I pointed out to him that his description had to be at fault, since such a box would not sink as he had averred it had, he got very testy and began getting disagreeable. And as I explained that a man cannot be handcuffed and straitjacketed at the same time, since the hands are encased in the sleeves of the jacket and wrapped about the body, he became so belligerent that I feared for my safety. He began ranting about how we magicians wouldn't believe it if we saw it with our own eyes. I was able to deflate his enthusiasm when I told him that he was describing the stunt *I* had done in New York for television about a year before. I felt I was in a position to know more about it than he was. He has never spoken to me since that time.

The Amazing Randi

Nevertheless, I called several friends to tell them about my evening with Uri and about my new faith in him. By then, I was sorry I had made an appointment for the next day to see James (the Amazing) Randi, a professional magician who wanted to expose Geller as a trickster and who had once raised a few weak doubts in my own mind. After all, what could Randi possibly show me?

The Amazing Randi lives in New Jersey, in a house guarded by two beautiful macaws. On the door is a Peruvian mask, which sends forth martial music when you ring the bell. The door opens from the side opposite the doorknob. Inside are mummy cases, clocks that run backwards and other strange and incongruous objects that advertise the inhabitant as a creator of illusions.

Randi turned out to be a delightful host, talkative and funny, with a twinkle in his eye and a roguish look that always let you know he might be up to some trick. I told Randi what I had seen Uri do. He listened attentively but made no comments. When I finished, he invited me over to a table covered with envelopes, paper, nails, nuts, bolts, and aluminum film canisters.

"What shall we try first?" he said. "Some telepathy?" He invited me to take a piece of paper and three envelopes. "Go to the other end of the room or out of the room," he instructed. "Draw any figure you like on the paper, fold it up, seal it in an envelope, seal that envelope in another envelope, and that in the third."

I followed his instructions and brought the sealed envelope back. Deep inside was a drawing of two intersecting circles.

"We'll put that aside now," Randi said, setting it down on the table. He handed me a carton of sturdy four-inch nails. "Pick any six that you think are perfectly straight." I did. I also looked to make sure they were all real nails. "Now put a rubber band around that bunch and set them aside." I did so.

"Meanwhile, let's try one of Mr. Geller's favorite tricks." He picked 10 film canisters and told me to stuff one of them full of nuts and bolts— "so tightly that it won't rattle if moved." He went out of the room while I did what he told me. "Now mix them all up," he shouted from the kitchen. When I had done so, Randi came back and sat down at the table.

He studied the canisters and moved his hand over them without touching them. "I'm going to eliminate the empty ones," he told me. "When I point to one and say it's empty, you remove it. And set it down quietly, so I can't tell anything from the sound." He made passes over the canisters, just as I had seen Uri Geller do on television. "That one's empty," he said confidently, pointing to a canister in the middle. I removed it and set it aside. "Don't tell me if I'm wrong," he said. "That one's empty." He pointed to another. Randi had a great sense of drama; I felt involved in his performance. He eliminated another canister, and another. Finally, there were just two left. He passed his hand over each one as if feeling for emanations from the metal inside. "That's empty," he said at last, indicating the one on the left. I removed it. It was empty. The remaining can was full of nuts and bolts. He had neither touched the canisters nor jarred the table. I was amazed.

You will read later that Geller stomped about on the floor during the break in the Carson show, since that is one method of determining which can is "different" from the others. Since Andy and I had discussed that method, I allowed him to believe that it was the *only* method, and he was watching me very carefully with this maneuver in mind. Thus, when no jarring of the cans or table was evident, he was doubly amazed. And I had set him up purposely in this way. At that moment, he was completely in the dark as to how I'd done the trick.

"Now," Randi told me, "that was a trick. And I'm going to show you how to do it. But I want you to promise you won't reveal the method, because we magicians aren't supposed to reveal secrets. This is a special case."

I gave my promise and Randi taught me how he did it. It was simple — so simple a child could master it. In fact, Randi said he had taught the trick to several children. It is based on a subtle but easily perceptible difference between the full can and the empty ones, a difference that can be seen by anybody who knows what to look for.

"What if the canister is filled with water?" I asked.

"It's the same idea — you just look for different things. Do you remember when Mr. Geller tried to do that on the Tonight Show?" Randi asked. I thought I did. "Let's look at it," he said.

Studying the Tapes

Randi had a video-tape machine in his house, together with recordings of most of Geller's television appearances. "I learned how he does most of his tricks by studying these tapes," he explained.

We relived the famous "Tonight Show," where Uri had failed, according to Randi, because Randi and Carson (a former magician himself) had safeguarded the props. There was Johnny Carson telling Uri to go ahead and do something. Uri stalled. There were the film canisters, one full of water. "Carson and I handled those cans in a way that eliminated the difference," Randi said. Uri was moving his hand over the canisters. "No, I'm not getting it," he said, and gave up. So ended one of Uri's most famous disasters.

But, as we have already discovered, it was not the "disaster" that Andy says it was. It served to convince the believers of the wisdom of their belief in Geller. Remember: If it were a trick, it would work every time. That's Rule 1.

"Now look at this," Randi said. He turned on a video-tape of the "Merv Griffin Show," where Uri had appeared a few nights later. I heard Griffin tell his audience that Uri's failures with Johnny Carson had convinced him Uri was real, since a trickster would never have failed. The high point of the show was the bending of a nail.

"All right, back to the table," Randi said. He picked up the bunch of six nails. "Let's find one that's absolutely straight." He rolled each one back and forth on the table, keeping up a constant patter while eliminating any nails that had "little woggily-woggilies," as Randi called them—slight irregularities which kept them from rolling smoothly. He ended up with one nail he liked, holding it between thumb and forefinger, midway along the shaft. "Now, keep your eye on it," he said, "I'm going to try to bend it." He moved it back and forth slowly and gently between his thumb and forefinger. I hardly knew what to expect.

Suddenly the nail began to bend before my eyes. "Look at that," Randi chuckled. Sure enough, it was bent about 30 degrees, and by a stage magician.

I shook my head in astonishment. "Not bad, huh?" Randi asked. I allowed that it wasn't bad at all. "That's incredible!" I said. I took the nail. It wasn't warm or unusual in any other way. Just bent.

I reiterate: Weil is no dummy. He wasn't chewing the mushroom or imbibing the grape when he saw this happen. He was merely watching a magician doing his thing. And please recall that he *expected* trickery.

Then, before my eyes, Randi showed me in slow motion how he had substituted a bent nail for one of the straight ones, how he had concealed the bend from me until the proper moment and how he had then revealed it while rubbing the nail between his fingers. But I had "seen" it bend. Suddenly, I experienced a sense of how strongly the mind can impose its own interpretation on perceptions: how it can see what it expects to see, but not see the unexpected.

"Now, let's watch that tape of the 'Merv Griffin Show' again and see how Uri does it," Randi suggested. Sure enough, there was Uri Geller manipulating three nails just as Randi had. And under Randi's tutelage, I could see that one nail was never really shown in its entirety to the closeup camera, even though Uri was claiming to hold up each nail, one at a time, to prove its straightness.

I must admit that without the facility of a video recorder, I'd have been hard-pressed to prove Geller's methods as convincingly as I did. And, by means of tape, the proof is right there to be witnessed again and again. The "moves" cannot be denied.

But do you recall the sealed envelopes? After all this carrying-on, with trips to and from the video machine, and coffee with cookies, what has happened to the envelopes?

Andy will fail to recall one event here. I "accidentally" spilled a cup of coffee on the table and there was a moderate flap over the cleanup. (You'll note he doesn't even report the coffee! It seemed not to be a part of the proceedings.) I daresay the envelope went out of his sight for a few seconds. It's possible, but I couldn't swear to it.

Secrets of the Envelope

"Ready for the telepathy?" Randi asked. "Let's try that sealed envelope." He went back to the table, sat down, took pad and pen, and held the envelope to his forehead. "You concentrate on the figure," he told me.

He started making marks on the paper, attempting to reproduce the secrets of the envelope. First he drew an equals sign; he seemed to be way off. "Now don't tell me how I'm doing," he said, "Just let me work on it." Slowly he extended the lines, then made them cross into a flat "X." He muttered to himself while working. Then the lines began to curve. "Oh, I see it now," he said happily. And there on the pad appeared the two intersecting circles, exactly as I had drawn them. Obviously, Randi had known what was in the envelope. I opened the envelopes, one by one, took out the folded paper, and showed it to Randi. "Well, well," he said, pleased with himself. "Look at that."

Whoa! "Obviously, Randi had known what was in the envelope." Not necessarily, at all. This is an unwarranted assumption. And I'm somewhat disappointed that Andy chose the same drawing that Abend had used. But we wonderworkers are faced with that problem, aren't we, Uri?

And please remember that the drawing was sealed inside three envelopes!

Randi showed me how he did that one, too. There is only one way to know what is inside an envelope without using paranormal powers: you have to get your hands on the envelope for a while and use your eyes.

"People come back from seeing Uri Geller," Randi told me, "and they say, 'He never touched the envelope.' But if you question them carefully, what they really mean is: he never touched it in ways that 'they' think would have let him know what was inside. That's the basis of stage magic. You take advantage of little opportunities to do the dirty work, when you're certain people aren't going to notice you. Geller is a master opportunist."

"Have you ever seen him doing the dirty work?" I asked.

A Glance at the Blackboard

"I sure have. I was at Town Hall the other night. The thing that really irks me is how much people let him get away with—things they wouldn't let a magician get away with. He asked a woman to write a foreign capital on the blackboard, and she wrote 'Denver?' The whole audience was annoyed at her for not following instructions. At one point, you could just see every head in the audience turn to glare at her, and right then old Uri just shot a glance at the blackboard. It's that simple. And when he broke a zodiac ring at the end, he said, 'Let's try two rings at once.' What he did was click off his microphone for an instant, wedge one ring into the other, and give a hard squeeze so that the zodiac ring broke where the setting was joined."

Since the account above appeared, I've had a few doubts about this as a solution for the "foreign-capital" stunt. Though I was accompanied that evening by several magicians,* including Stanley Palm, Milbourne Christopher, Charles Reynolds, and the late Felix Greenfield (who was very instrumental in laying Geller's ghost on behalf of the magicians, until his untimely death), and we all gasped when we saw the blatant methods used by the Israeli, it is possible — indeed, probable — that he usually depends upon a confederate in the front row to give him hand signals on this one. Or, as we will see later, he might well be using a sub-miniature radio device for the same purpose. But I've gotten to know Uri pretty well. I know he would rather use the Chutzpah Method. For those of you who are not familiar with the word, it is a word in Uri's mother tongue that is defined as "the quality possessed by the young Jewish lad who is convicted of murdering both parents, and appeals to the court for leniency on grounds that he is an orphan." It denotes extreme nerve or cheek.

"And you saw that?"

"I saw it. Everybody looks for complicated explanations, and the explanations are always simple. That's why you don't see them. And the people who are easiest to take in with that sort of thing are intelligent people, especially scientists. The people who are hard to fool are children, because they look at what they're not supposed to look at. Scientists are pushovers."

"Has the Stanford Research Institute ever had a professional magician act as a consultant in their studies of Geller?" I asked.

"Never! Isn't that unbelievable? They get insulted if you suggest it, or they say that a magician would put out 'bad vibes' that would interfere with Uri's abilities."

That situation has changed. Now, SRI, in its great wisdom, has called in a magician briefly as consultant. Not *before* Geller's tests there, mind you, but *after*. With them, the alarm system is installed after the robbery.

It is interesting to note that when Geller did a subsequent series of tests there (see p. 52), he failed. Any connection?

"All right," I said. "I'm impressed with everything you've shown me and told me. But last night Uri Geller bent one of my keys for me. Can you do the same?"

"Got a key?" Randi asked. I brought out the brass key that Uri had failed to bend. "Give it to me." Randi took the key and played with it for a while. "Yes, I think that will work," he said. He sat down across from me and held the key under my nose, rubbing it between his thumb and forefinger.

"Look at that," he said, "I think it's going." The key was bending. In a trice it was bent to about 30 degrees, looking for all the world like a Geller production.

"No!" I protested. My faith in Uri Geller lay in pieces on the floor.

"All I needed was a moment in which your attention was distracted to bend the key by jamming it against my chair; I made the bend appear just as I did with the nail." Again I had seen not just a bend, but actual bending.

This "jamming-the-key" business is of course a gross simplification. It's a little like describing a color-television receiver as a box with a lot of electronic stuff in it, without getting at some of the processes by which those parts are designed and arranged. But it is, nonetheless, true.

"Have you ever tried to bend a key with your hands?" Randi asked. "I've assumed I couldn't."

Randi showed me how he could bend a key with his hands, and I was able to do the same, although with difficulty. I saw clearly that with practice one could get very good at bending metal objects quickly and surreptitiously, without recourse to lasers concealed in the belt or any other complicated devices.

Randi also made a fork bend for me, although he couldn't simulate the fork I had seen melt over Uri's hand. He astounded me with other tricks; and even when I knew what to look for I couldn't see him doing the dirty work.

Andy, fork-"melting" is now part of my repertoire. Come see. The price is right.

"Do you think," I asked Randi, "knowing what I do now, that I could see Geller doing it?"

"I doubt it," Randi replied. "He's very good. He can take advantage of any situation. And people want to believe in him."

I remembered how Martin Abend had misremembered Uri's telepathic performance, and how I had embellished some of what I'd seen when telling others about it.

"What about the time I saw Uri make a ring sag into an oval shape without touching it?" I asked.

"Look, I can't explain all of what he does, especially if I haven't seen it. I repeat, he's good. And he probably has many different techniques available. But if an accomplished professional has a chance to watch him closely, it can all be figured out. That's why Uri won't come near me or any other magician."

"How did you get a chance to watch him up close?"

"First by masquerading as a reporter when he was interviewed at 'Time.' And then by studying the videotapes."

"Do you want to expose him?"

"I'd love to, but I don't think that will be easy. The fact that I can duplicate his feats by magic tricks proves nothing. The only way would be to catch him substituting a bent nail, or jamming a key against a chair leg; that will be difficult."

I thanked the Amazing Randi for his time and went on my way, suitably amazed. I had never before had the experience of going from such total belief to such total disbelief in so short a time. Nor had I ever doubted my perceptions so thoroughly. Uri's unwillingness to perform in the presence of magicians seemed especially damning.

Not to the believers, Andy. Remember the special rules "psychics" work by. Anyone around with "negative" thoughts makes the demonstration fail. And we all know how "negative" magicians are. They are realistic, and there is no more negative attitude in the view of the "psychic."

Since then I have thought a lot about Uri Geller and have talked with others about him. One person I spoke to was Ray Hyman, a professor of psychology at the University of Oregon in Eugene, who teaches a course called "The Pseudopsychologies." It deals with astrology and various psychic and occult phenomena. Hyman describes himself as an "open-minded skeptic who has never seen a genuine psychic phenomenon." He doesn't know what kind of evidence it would take to change his mind. Hyman was once a magician, and he spent a day at the Stanford Research Institute watching Uri Geller last December. He decided that Uri was "a very good magician but that he could replicate most of what Uri did by simple tricks.

"What I find most interesting about Uri Geller are the reactions to him," Hyman told me. "For instance, the physicists at Stanford were irate at the suggestion that Geller might be tricking them. They were physicists— real scientists—and I was only a psychologist. I was astounded that they had never bothered to check up on Uri's background in Israel."

Selective Perception

People who believe in things like telepathy and psychokinesis are sometimes accused of thinking wishfully. I have always thought that people who "denied" the existence of such things were also thinking wishfully, for they, too, ignore certain types of evidence while paying attention to others. Leon Jaroff, the editor who did "Time" magazine's first negative story about Uri Geller, once said: "There has never been a single adequately documented 'psychic phenomenon.' Many people believe in things like this because they need to." That view discounts completely the evidence of direct experience. It, too, is based on a need to see things a certain way.

Sorry, Andy. I'll stick with Leon on this point. Your definition of "direct experience" is something I would like to know more about, too. Was not the experience of having a key curl up in your hand a "direct experience"? When the fork "melted" over Uri's hand, had you not just been through a "direct experience"? Yet you admitted to me, as you left my house, that you had discovered you were not capable of judging these things. You realized that you were able to misreport and exaggerate events in which you felt directly involved. How, then, can you give such value to "direct experience" when *you alone* judge for authenticity?

Selective perception of evidence is the basic method by which we construct our models of reality. Many systems of thought urge us to distinguish between reality and our models of it. For example, one of the important themes in Don Juan's philosophy, as transmitted by Carlos Castaneda, is that what we call "objective" reality is nothing more than a consistent model—one of many possible models—constructed out of learned and habitual ways of selecting evidence and interpreting perceptions.

As a student of psychology and of drugs, I have always been interested in the concept of "set," the body of expectation that determines experience. When I conducted research on marijuana I found that people who were unfamiliar with the drug, in the absence of any encouragement to get high, felt nothing at all even after receiving large doses. On the other hand, subjects who are ready to get high can get high on a placebo. In other words, our unconscious needs and expectations can lead us to experience things that other people rarely notice, while at the same time they lead us "not" to notice some things that other people see perfectly well.

It might be possible to take more conscious control over the process by which reality is shaped and made to seem objective. "Wishful thinking," though it has a negative connotation, is an appropriate term to describe this process. We all engage in it, often unconsciously, to bring things into reality according to our needs, and to make them leave reality according to our needs.

That is why certain questions like, "Is Uri Geller a fraud?" or "Do psychic phenomena exist?" are unanswerable. The answer is always yes and no, depending on who is looking and from what point of view. Each of us has the power to make such phenomena real or unreal. The first step toward making them real is to believe that evidence exists. As for Uri Geller, I wish him good fortune and the wisdom to use his abilities well. From knowing him, I have learned an enormous amount about the way I see things and the need for great care in evaluating evidence—especially the kind of evidence which seems to prove things I want to believe.

At this point, when Weil drags in this silly "multiple reality" philosophy, I lose him entirely. Andy, that's a terrible cop-out. And I think the readers of this book feel that, too. I *know* what Uri Geller is, and my readers are rapidly discovering what I already know.

6

The Man Who "Discovered" Uri Geller

A scorpion, who could not swim, approached the
bank of a stream and begged a frog there to carry
him upon his back to the other side. The frog complained that the scorpion would sting him. But the
scorpion replied that this was impossible, as he himself would drown with the frog. So the pair set out
across the stream. Halfway over, the frog felt a pierc-
ing pain in his back. The scorpion had stung him. "Is
that logical?" he cried. "No, it's not," said the scorpion as they submerged together, "but I can't help it.
It's my nature."

—Orson Welles: Mr. Arkadian

Dr. Andrija Puharich, M.D., the man who "discovered" Uri Geller
and brought him across the Atlantic to America, has a colorful and somewhat enigmatic background. Early in his career, after graduating in medicine, Puharich became fascinated with the possibilities of telepathy and
established a council in 1948 to attempt enhancement of any telepathic
powers in individuals by means of electronic devices. He was convinced,
after research along this line, that telepathy exists, and was instrumental
in bringing to this country the Dutch performer Peter Hurkos, whose
checkered career soon left Puharich without a wonderman to exploit.

In 1960, he traveled to Mexico to participate in the secret rituals of
the Chatina Indians. A part of those rituals involves the use of certain
hallucinogenic plants, and as a result of these studies Puharich wrote two
books, *The Sacred Mushroom* and *Beyond Telepathy*. He discovered
more "sacred mushrooms" in Hawaii when he was made a "kahuna" priest
there.

Though Puharich owns a number of patents on subdermal receivers
originally designed to aid the deaf by transmitting information to them
via radio frequencies through the receivers hidden in or on the body, he
has failed to convince the U.S. Patent Office that his other machines,
designed to enhance ESP powers in humans, actually have any merit, and
he cannot obtain patents on them. Patents are only issued for things
that really work.

Brazil, and a performer named Arigo, beckoned in 1963, and Puharich headed up a team sent there to investigate this man, who claimed he was able to heal by magical powers and to perform operations by "psychic" means. (It is interesting to note that the same man who wrote a book on Arigo [*Arigo — Surgeon of the Rusty Knife*]—John Fuller—also wrote not only several UFO books, but Uri Geller's "autobiography," cleverly titled, *My Story*.) Arigo carelessly allowed himself to be killed in an auto accident, and his wonders ceased, we presume.

Now Puharich was ripe to "discover" another miracle-monger, and just as Geller was in heavy decline in Israel, Puharich arrived to snap him up and exhibit him to the world. This was in 1971.

Just how did a man of the learning and intelligence of Andrija Puharich ever get sucked up into the Geller following? It seems a mystery, until we look into it more fully. His experimentation with hallucinogenic substances might very well be a good part of the answer. Throughout his writings on Geller, he wonders if what he has seen is really true, or if he might be hallucinating. We wonder, too. When he sees a full-size metal file cabinet vanish before his eyes in his home, and repeatedly watches UFOs cavort across the sky that no one else can see, we wonder. And when he sees the Egyptian hawk-god, Horus, bringing him messages of comfort in-between instructions and assurances from a mysterious IS (Intelligence in the Sky) we wonder further. Yet here is an outwardly sensible, sober member of the scientific hierarchy telling us these wonders, and other fantastic throwaways like Geller's ability to dematerialize tape cassettes and to change base metals into solid gold!

Before the Geller matter, I had pretty well lost track of Puharich. I'd seen him on an old Perry Mason television spot, in which he was called in by the sleuth to advise on a matter of parapsychological import, and I was aware that he had been present when the editor of a prominent psychic publication discovered, via infrared photography, that the ghosts being called up by his spiritualist friends were nothing more than these same performers dressed up in luminous costumes to please believers. Though I'd considered him capable of falling for a Brazilian with a handful of chicken livers posing as tumors, I hardly thought someone of Geller's quality would fool Puharich for a moment. But Andrija jumped right into the fire happily. A glance at his book *Uri* will prove that. I recommend it to my readers who collect bizarre reading matter, and suggest that it go on the library shelf next to the "Oz" stories and *Winnie the Pooh*.

In London (June 1975), during the showing of a totally unconvincing and superficial film about the work of Brazil's Arigo—the "surgeon of the rusty knife," produced by Puharich—a member of the audience asked Dr. Ted Bastin, a prominent scientist totally convinced of the wonders of parapsychology, whether he felt that Puharich was still as believable as he had once been. Reference had been made to the book *Uri* at the time. Replied Bastin, "I used to think him a reliable reporter. But after meeting Uri, he changed." Bastin referred to the book as "an absolute disaster." He understated the case. *Uri* had probably done more to destroy what authority Puharich once held in the scientific community than any other single publication—even the most derogatory of them.

Of all the endless pages of supernatural wonders that occur in *Uri* I can only say that if a lot of time and money were available, a large portion of the nonsense could be revealed as such. But enough talent has already been expended to disprove the contentions of these masters of invention and hyperbole. Everything that Puharich sees instantly becomes a miracle, and Uri or his magical friends in the flying saucers are responsible for all such wonders. I will content myself with quoting a few pages from the book in which Puharich details an event at which I was present. In this case, the transpositions of facts and omissions and additions of details are evident to me because I was actually there at the time.

In the Appendix to this book, you will find a statement signed by persons in attendance at the event to be described; the document was submitted to these persons, and they signed it after reading the annotated account. My corrections of Puharich's version are, to the best of their knowledge, true and direct. Let the sample from *Uri*, which follows in Chapter 7, give my readers an idea of the worth of the rest of Puharich's book.

7

The Time Magazine Episode
with Geller

Scientists especially when they leave the particular
field in which they have specialized, are just as ordinary, pig-headed, and unreasonable as anybody
else, and their unusually high intelligence only
makes their prejudices all the more dangerous . . .
—Professor H. J. Eysenck, University of London

On Sunday, February 4, 1973, I received a call from my good friend
Charlie Reynolds, a well-known photographer who has done a good deal
of work for *Time* magazine, is picture editor of *Popular Photography*
magazine, and is also an amateur magician of some considerable clever-
ness. Charlie long ago decided that he would concentrate on learning to
do three of four conjuring tricks exceedingly well, instead of doing fifty
of them badly. I recommend this tack for all amateurs.

Reynolds is well versed in conjuring theory, and when he heard
through a friend at *Time* that they were going to be witnessing a
demonstration by Uri Geller, he called and offered his services as the
photographer. John Durniak, picture editor at the magazine, realizing
Charlie's value as an expert observer who might be of use in that capacity
as well, accepted readily. Charlie also suggested that I be called in to
pose as a reporter, since Geller was said to refuse interviews before magicians. Since I had never met either Puharich or Geller, I knew that I
could safely pose as a *Time* employee. The date was set for that Tuesday.

I'd not heard of Geller at all until I was told about him by Reynolds.
The stories that were then related to me made me feel that I might be
wasting my time with just another flash-in-the-pan trickster who would be
ushered promptly out into the cold. I did not reckon with the gullibility of
those who had already put their approval on his tricks as genuine miracles.

I arrived at *Time* with a miniature tape-recorder under my raincoat.
I felt that it would be better not to even tell Charlie that I was about to
record the proceedings, and I placed my coat nearby with the machine
hidden inside. I was introduced around, but not as Randi; and, though
I already knew Rita Quinn, Durniak, and several others, everyone I had
not met seemed less than curious about my presence.

Equipped with yellow pad and pencil, I assumed a reporterlike
pose and we awaited the miracle-workers. Charlie was not asked to take

pictures until it seemed that *Time* was interested enough to want some. I remember particularly that Leon Jaroff, a senior editor of *Time*, was disgruntled about the whole matter and resented being called in. He felt—and rightly so—that the matter belonged with *Time*'s theater department. But, since he had earlier become involved with the matter of SRI's participation in this circus, he folded his arms and looked glum, casting an occasional fierce look in my direction. I ignored his discomfort and prepared to face the foe.

I had not seen Puharich in many years. He was now a mustachioed, frizzy-haired, aging hippy type, and I managed merely to nod at him as I was introduced under my real name, which begins with a "Z" and was apparently convincing enough. Both Charlie and I passed muster.

Then the boy-wonder entered. He was strikingly handsome, smiling, and quiet. I did not know at that time of his fashion-model background in Israel, but could see that he would be a success with the women whether he was a "psychic" or not. I was impressed.

Puharich immediately announced that he would leave the room, saying that it might be suspected that he and Geller were "in cahoots," to use his terminology. He left, closed the door, and *Time* began speaking with Geller. There were some ten people in that room that day. All of them will verify that what I say here is absolutely true.

I will now begin Andrija Puharich's account of what transpired, and call attention to the myriad misstatements, half-truths, and sheer inventions present in his version. He wrote the following for publication in his book, in order to try to take the edge off Uri's dismal failure that day. His account turns the event into what he refers to as a "lynch." It was more of a suicide.

From Puharich's *Uri*, here is his version:

> The next day I received a phone call from Charles Reynolds, who represented himself as a photographer for "Time" magazine. He said he wanted to meet with Uri. I put him off until I could check his credentials. I found out that he was a magician and a free-lance photographer. He was part of a "Time" cabal to lure Uri into a confrontation with magicians in an attempt to discredit him. I talked the problem over with Uri. I advised him that every indication had showed me that a lynch was in the offing. I even suspected that someone at "Time" was being pressured to do a hatchet job on Uri and myself. We decided to go ahead and demonstrate for "Time," and that no matter what happened, it had to be for the best. I called Charles Reynolds back and made a date to have the "Time" staff meet Uri on Tuesday, February 6, 1973.

Hold on. Let's go back over that, please. Puharich begins by saying that Charlie "represented himself as a photographer for *Time* magazine." Yes, that's true, because Charlie *is* a photographer for *Time*. After all, Puharich represented *himself* as a doctor.

Then Puharich says he "put off" Charlie until he could "check his credentials." Nonsense. With whom did he check? There was nowhere he could have discovered that Charlie was an amateur magician, and he certainly could not have suspected it from a phone call. And Charlie is as much a "free-lance photographer" as any of the *Time* cameramen. The "cabal" was nonexistent: *Time* was merely looking into a story by calling in experts as a matter of proper procedure. And I'm damn sure Geller would never have consented to appear before two magician-observers. He never had before, and hasn't since, if he's known conjurors were present who were competent enough to solve his tricks. Puharich's dark mutterings about "someone at *Time*" being pressured into a "hatchet job" smacks of juvenile paranoia. But back to the good doctor's highly fictionalized account:

> We met in the offices of John Derniak [sic]. Present on behalf of "Time" were editors Fred Golden and Leon Jaroff, magicians Charles Reynolds and James Randi, photographer Peter Basch, some secretaries, and Uri and I. I opened the meeting by stating emphatically that Uri was not a magician and had submitted his claims to science for judgment. One of the magicians immediately made the statement that Uri was known to be a magician, based on material in "our Geller File." Uri explained that he was not a magician; that he had appeared in Israel and Germany in stage shows where magicians had performed; and that his powers of telepathy and psychokinesis were real. One of the "Time" editors informed us that everything was being taped; we consented.

Stop right there. No statement was made by either Charlie or myself—at that point—that Uri was known to be a magician. And neither of them—Puharich or Uri—had *any idea* that there were magicians in the room. The most suspicion Geller raised was when he asked me what my function was before handing me a fork. I lied that I was just "taking down notes" on the meeting. Uri seemed satisfied and roared ahead, digging his own grave.

And neither of the *Time* editors there said anything about the proceedings being taped. No one but myself knew of the tape machine, and neither of the performers had asked. Note that whenever Puharich has to put fictitious words into someone's mouth he fails to specify who it is.

> The atmosphere was that of a kangaroo court. Uri was damned if he refused to demonstrate and damned if he did demonstrate; he chose to run the gauntlet and demonstrate. He asked me to leave the room so that the charge of collusion would be eliminated. I did not observe what Uri did for these people, so my report is secondhand. Uri was annoyed by the hostile atmosphere and made a slow start with a telepathy demonstration,

but he did eventually succeed. The magicians said they could "duplicate" this "trick." Then Uri bent a fork by lightly stroking it. The magicians said they could duplicate this "trick" by using slight of hand and misdirection. Then Charlie Reynolds offered his own apartment key to be bent. Uri bent it by concentration, and it continued to bend after it left his hands. No one said a word about this "trick," and it has never been mentioned to this day by the editors or "Time" or by the magicians. A secretary from "Time" called us later that day to tell us that the key had gone on bending by itself after we left.

The "telepathy demonstration" that Puharich quotes Uri as saying he performed was the saddest, most transparent act I've ever seen. He asked us to draw simple shapes on our pads. I was careful not to allow my pencil to show above the top of the pad, and he got nothing from me, though he made several attempts. One of the secretaries present was not so careful, and Uri, pretending to cover his eyes with his hands but actually boldly peering out from between his fingers, got a fair version of what she had drawn. Jaroff, very sour on the matter, mumbled out loud that Uri was "peeking!" and wanted to get out of the room at all costs.

Geller then decided that he would "project" some thoughts to us. He wrote something down on his pad, then said he would try to project the name of a foreign capital to us. He asked us to exclude the Israeli capital, since that would be too easy! We tittered appropriately at this remark, and Uri went into a concentrating pose. He asked the man beside me what city he'd "received." "London," announced the subject. Lo! Geller had written both "Paris" and "London" on his pad, but "London" was crossed out lightly. Uri cursed his luck, explaining that he should have stayed with his first impulse, allowing us all to believe that he'd originally wanted to transmit "London" but had changed to "Paris." Suddenly one of the crowd announced that he'd gotten "Paris," and Geller gratefully turned to him and asked him to pick a digit between 1 and 10. "Seven," announced the man. Eureka! Uri showed a scrawled "7" on his pad. Charlie and I looked at one another, suppressing smiles.

We were amused, because Uri could not have known that at that moment we both had in our pockets copies of a letter addressed to Martin Gardner of *Scientific American* magazine from Ray Hyman, who had been present during an aborted attempt by Geller and SRI to latch on to some Department of Defense funds. In that letter was a description of exactly the same routine, using the same cities and same numbers. It's an old set-up; in fact I believe I first saw it on the back of a cereal box when I was a kid. Geller looked pretty amateurish to us at that point.

Of course, there is no possibility that we said—as Puharich claimed— that we could "duplicate" this trick. We'd have been ashamed to, anyway. We were not about to show our hand yet.

The key Charlie offered was the key to an office at *Popular Photography*. Uri bent it all right—but *not* "by concentration." He simply put the tip of it against the tabletop and pushed. Charlie and I both *clearly* saw him do it. The fork trick was equally bold, and when Uri asked me at one point, "Did you see *that*?" with wonderment in his voice, I dryly replied, "Yes, I certainly *did*!" When Uri took the key and rushed out of the office and down the hall with it, we were not in the least surprised to see that it had been further bent, but the statement that "a secretary from *Time* called" later in the day to report that "the key had gone on bending by itself" is obviously untrue, since Charlie put the key in his pocket at the conclusion of the trick, and it left the office with him!

Puharich entered the room and came directly over to me at the conclusion of the show. I was turning off the tape recorder in my coat and didn't try to hide it from him. He called me by my professional name and asked rather loudly if I had enjoyed "trying to catch Uri." I replied that I had enjoyed "*catching* Uri," not just "trying." Puharich had been in conversation with a secretary outside the office and learned who I really was. What torture it must have been for him to discover, after he was out of the room, that his Trilby was inside being observed by *competent* people!

But back to his story:

> Uri was in deep gloom as we left the offices of "Time." Now he felt the full weight of the lynch that was being organized against him in the United States. We also found out that the "Time" correspondent in Jerusalem had filed a report on Uri which said that scientists from Hebrew University claimed they had caught him cheating. This, too, proved to be a lie, but it suited the policy of the editors of "Time."

Yes, it suited the policy of the editors of *Time* to tell the news as it really happened. I find it hard to believe that Puharich had never seen an account in the papers that told of the Jerusalem event. I quote now from the *Jerusalem Post* article, "Telepathist Geller Termed a Fraud," of October 5, 1970:

> Uri Geller, a performer who has won a wide following as the possessor of "strong telepathic powers," was last night termed a fraud by four Jerusalem computer unit employees.
>
> The charge was made by one of the men, Mr. Yosef Allon, in an interview over the evening radio newsreel. Confronted with Allon, Mr. Geller told the radio interviewer he would have to "consult first" before deciding whether to sue for libel.
>
> Explaining how his suspicions were aroused, Mr. Allon said he went to a Geller performance and was as impressed as anyone else in the audience until Geller did a card trick that he, Allon, had been doing for years.

A closer study of each of Geller's "telepathic feats" was then made by Allon and three colleagues at the computer unit of the Government office Mechanization Centre, Danny Zehavi, Yitzhak Ziskind and Alexander Eshed.

Last week, they demonstrated the results by performing a series of Geller's acts before an impressed audience of the University psychology department. The four then explained that the feats of "thought transference" were accomplished mainly by sleight of hand.

A member of the audience was Dr. Moshe Caspi, of the University's School of Education, who had also seen Geller perform. He told the radio newsreel last night that the four were not only as good as Geller, but made fewer mistakes.

Among the acts that Allon claims to have successfully imitated is that of driving a car blindfolded, allegedly guided only by the "concentration" of his passengers on the contours of the road. Allon declined to reveal publicly how this is accomplished.

I think that it is obvious by now just how Puharich has misrepresented the actual events at the *Time* office that day. It just did not happen the way he said it did, and we can prove it. Soon after the debacle, the president of Stanford University called Ralph Davidson, the publisher of *Time,* and tried to get the story squashed. Davidson is a member of the SU board of governors. And the SRI public relations man (who has since quit the organization) called Wilhelm of *Time* to see what could be done about the story. Puharich et al. realized that the story would be a factual one.

The Puharich account continues:

> Since the war was clearly on, I had to mobilize my forces. My goal was simple—to keep the human race from talking itself into a "crucifixion" state of mind. I officially informed the editors of "Time" that Uri's powers were real and that science would affirm this in due time. I organized a group of prominent citizens who believed in Uri's powers to act as an Operations Group. The Operations Group was to raise funds for research, keep in touch with media executives at newspapers, magazines, television, etc., and spread the word among leaders in American society that a major issue was in the making. The Operations Group consisted of Judy Skutch, John Tishman, John Douglas, Stewart Mott, Maria Janis, Byron Janis, Ruth Hagy Brod, and others. One of the first tasks of this group was to counter whatever "Time" did. The editors of "Newsweek" were approached, and they assigned Charles Panatti [*sic*] to do a Geller story. After several weeks of work Panatti turned in to the editors of "Newsweek" a favorable story about Uri. [This story has still not been published at the time of this writing.]

Well, the *Newsweek* article has appeared now, and as expected from Panati—who is an ardent adherent of the Things-That-Go-Bump-in-the-Night School—it was a total whitewash of the SRI matter and made Geller's team look like persecuted innocents. As an example of the evasiveness of Panati, let me tell you of an interesting pair of episodes involving that gentleman. Early this year, I appeared on a Washington television show with him to discuss his book *Supersenses*. During that program, I pointed out the fact that his treatment of Geller consisted only of favorable items, with not one detracting comment in the book. His reply was that he was "merely a reporter" and that he just reported what had been said. I said that I doubted he had never seen a negative write-up on Geller, and he had no answer. At that point, the show host asked me to demonstrate the Geller routine. The producer of the show had made a drawing in the privacy of her office, several floors away, sealed it in a series of three envelopes, signed the outer envelope, and sealed it with tape. She had also obtained a box of 10-penny nails for the show, and some were on the table behind us.

I asked the other participants to hold the nails, and, à la Geller, one of them bent over at about 30 degrees. Panati had no explanation. I asked the producer to turn away and not view a television monitor or the set as I made a drawing in full view of the camera. It was, I recall, a person on a blanket lying with a pair of sunglasses nearby and the sun shining down. When I'd finished, she allowed us to open the envelope. The two drawings were identical. Panati said nothing.

Months later, Panati appeared with Geller on a program over Channel 9 in New York City. Unknown to them, I was concealed in the tape room downstairs, since my very presence in the studio would have caused Geller to beat a retreat. I was on the phone to the control room, suggesting questions that might be asked. One question was to Panati. It was: "Isn't it true that Randi appeared with you on a Washington television show and duplicated a couple of Geller's tricks?" To which Panati replied: "Yes, but he lied! He said he had a copy of a magazine in his car, and he didn't!" To this day, I'm thoroughly puzzled by that answer, but it is obvious that he was evading the question that was asked. It seems to be the way of these folks.

Incidentally, the Channel 9 program was called "Straight Talk." I think it was badly named.

Puharich continues:

> I activated the Scientific Theory Group that had been in existence since the Life Energies Conference of 1970. They were apprised of the pressure being built up by the editors of "Time." They knew that the scientific stakes were high—just as high as they were when Copernicus startled the medieval Church of Europe with his findings about the earth and the sun. The influence of this group was enormous in the councils of state; they gave authoritative assurance to the National Science Foundation that Uri's powers were real and that scientists had best keep open minds. Another member, Dr. Gerald Feinberg, invited Targ and Puthoff to dispassionately present their findings on Geller at a Physics Department Colloquium at Columbia University on March 9, 1973.

In the meantime "Time" magazine had requested the results of the SRI research. Leon Jaroff of "Time" told the president of SRI that if SRI did not give them a report on their findings with Geller, "Time" would go ahead with an unfavorable story about both SRI and Geller. The president of SRI said that "Time" would have to wait, like everyone else, for the report on their findings, to be given on March 9, 1973, at Columbia University. Neither man would budge from his position. For me the last few days before the final showdown were packed with action.

I cannot print Leon Jaroff's response to this tirade by Puharich. *Time* was wanting information on a news story; SRI was trying to get the blessing of a hearing at Columbia with a film that proved nothing except that they had a camera and some film.

I will say little more about Puharich except to include the next two paragraphs that follow in order. They speak volumes.

On Sunday, February 25, at 7 P.M., I handed Uri a Mexican five-peso silver coin that weighed thirty grams. This was the same one reported on in Israel. I asked him to bend it in his left hand. As he clenched it in his fist, it vanished. We talked about what IS might do with the coin, and I suggested that it be made into a "thought transmitter" and returned to us. At 8:30 P.M. a 1925 silver dollar fell by my right foot. I examined this coin and it turned out to be a silver dollar given to me by Henry Jackson in 1948 as a token with which to start a Round Table Foundation. It had been in storage in a jewelry case in my bedroom on the second floor. However, the silver dollar had been bent by means unknown since I had last seen it.

At 9 P.M. the phone rang and Uri got up to answer it, crossing in front of me. As he went past me, a coin fell from the direction of the ceiling, hit his shoulder, and fell at my feet. It was the Mexican five-peso silver coin—but now it too was bent.

One begins to wonder if anything mundane *ever* happens to Andrija Puharich.

8

The Wonderful Teleportation to and from Brazil . . . or How Not Knowing Enough About the Subject Can Be Very Embarrassing

It is a double pleasure to deceive the deceiver . . .
— Proverb

In the November 1973 issue of *Today's Health,* under the title "Behind Science's Growing Fascination with Psychic Phenomena," appears the following extract:

Under Dr. Puharich's guidance, Geller says, he has learned to leave his body and journey to distant places. Once, he recalls, he lay on Dr. Puharich's sofa in New York, in the presence of five witnesses, and transported himself to Rio de Janeiro. Walking along Copacabana Beach, he approached a man and asked for money, in Portuguese—a language he previously had never spoken. The man gave him a thousand-cruzeiro note, which materialized in his hand on that couch in Ossining. Dr. Puharich says he has the note. The five persons who saw it materialize, however, do not wish to be identified, according to Geller.

But the trip to Brazil was so frightening, Geller says, that he will never leave his body again. "It was scary," he declares. "I was lying there on the couch and then there I was, suddenly, in another place. I was there just as really as I'm sitting here talking to you. To prove it, I even had sand on my shoes when I came back. But it was all a terrible feeling, because it was a double feeling—there I am and yet I can really feel my body sleeping somewhere else. And I was very scared because the journey back to my body is not sure. I mean, what if I couldn't get back? Oh, if somebody is up there protecting me I'm sure it can't happen, but I don't really know that. That's why I don't ever want to do it again."

Strangely enough, I am unable to find this incident in either Puharich's book *Uri* or in Fuller's book *My Story,* which is supposed to have been written by Geller himself. Such an important event would seem to be one that should be touted in both books. Especially since there is a positive piece of evidence—the thousand-cruzeiro note—that has not been "dematerialized" by the fiends from the flying saucers, as has happened

98

to all the other artifacts so conjured up. But in that very piece of evidence we find the reason neither Puharich nor Geller chose to perpetuate this particularly silly piece of juvenile fiction.

You will note, among other things, that the following description of this event from the pages of *Psychic* magazine differs substantially from the account above. In a court of law the case would be thrown out. But just to be sure, let's peruse the "Letters" column of *New Scientist* of November 14, 1974:

"One experiment I did with Andrija (Puharich) was when he asked me to go to Brazil out of the body. I got to this city and asked a person where I was and he told me it was Rio de Janeiro. Then someone came up to me and pressed a brand new one-thousand cruzeiro note in my hand and it appeared in my hand on the couch by Andrija—to prove I was there."

That is an extract from an interview with Geller in the June 1973 issue of Psychic, a magazine published in San Francisco. Perhaps because I know Rio de Janeiro well, this incident stuck in my mind long after I had stopped marvelling at all the other things Geller is supposed to do.

Accordingly, I wrote to Psychic pointing out that Geller's story was more interesting than it might seem, for two reasons: one, there are no longer any Cr $1000 notes in circulation in Brazil, and two, the people of Rio simply do not hand money to strangers, though they often relieve them of it.

My letter was printed in the December 1973 Psychic, along with Dr. Puharich's reply in which he gave the serial number of the note and said he hoped I could identify the issue, I then proceeded to do this.

In February 1967, Brazil's new cruzeiro, equivalent to 1000 old ones, came into law. Old 1000 notes printed in the U.S. and Britain were overprinted, and in March 1970 newly-designed Brazilian-made notes went into circulation.

The Geller note was not overprinted and was made in the U.S. I managed to establish, with the cooperation of an official in Brazil's Central Bank, that the note in question probably went into circulation in 1963—10 years before the alleged teleportation incident. To double check, I wrote the American Bank Note Co., which confirmed that the note had been shipped from New York on 17 April, 1963.

I should point out that, in the humid climate of Rio, banknotes do not remain "new and unhandled" (as Puharich stated this one was) for more than a few months; certainly not 10 years. Moreover, in a highly inflationary economy, people do not keep money for that long.

In March 1974 I wrote Puharich asking if I could have the note finger-printed. A stiff new note should retain a print, and everybody in Brazil has their fingerprints on file. If somebody handed the note to Geller, his prints might be on the note and I might be able to locate the donor. I also asked if Geller gave any other details of his alleged trip to Rio—scenic evidence which I could help locate and photograph.

No reply. Now, as it happens, Dr. Puharich visited Brazil in 1963, by a strange coincidence. One thousand cruzeiros were only worth about 50 U.S. cents in those days, and he might well have kept a note as a souvenir, or just not bothered to change it back when he left. Geller, or somebody else, might have found the note down a crack in the Puharich sofa (money often finds its way down cracks in sofas) and produced it quite normally in March 1973, after the supposed out-of-body flight took place.

In May 1974 I sent an outline of the facts in this letter to Psychic, and have since sent two follow-up letters. As of this writing, no reply.

Having since read Puharich's book Uri (Anchor Press/Doubleday 1974), I note that this banknote is the only piece of evidence not to have been dematerialised by Geller's friends from outer space! The banknote incident is not mentioned in the book.

This incident does not explain any of the other reported feats of the man who, as a German magazine says, makes "kaputte Uhren zu ticken." But it does suggest to me that further examination of Geller's alleged paranormal abilities can lead to totally normal hypotheses as to how he performs his feats.

Guy Lyon Playfair

Apt. 1106
546 Av. Prof. Alfonso Bovero
Sao Paulo, Brazil

I am also not terribly surprised to find that the five witnesses that Geller claims have not only wished to remain anonymous but, in the second account, have vanished! A teleportation, perhaps?

From this evidence, it seems inescapable that the whole thing was another of Geller's sleight-of-hand attempts, and a particularly bad one at that. But he obviously felt that, if the opportunity presented itself, he could get away with *anything* in front of Puharich.

But note: Here we have direct evidence that Puharich really believes in Geller's powers. Why else would he have cooperated in giving the serial number of the marvelous bill? Surely, if he'd been in on the thing, he would have given a more compatible number. But, then, maybe the other elusive witnesses would have told on him. Geller wouldn't even trust witnesses who had vanished.

Consider this: Subjected to the same close scrutiny and research, how many of the wonder-worker's other stunts would fall apart? Thank you, Mr. Playfair, for an excellent piece of work.

But we're not finished. Let's examine just one more account of the Brazil matter. In it, the mysterious man whom Geller approached and then who, in the second account, approached Geller, *now becomes two persons* who Geller approaches. Puharich puts a message in his head, and supplies the appropriate language for the task, and the five vaporous witnesses are once again not there in the room. It is hard to believe these are descriptions of the same event. The following excerpt is from Jon Lipsky's account, "Uri Geller: The Psychic You Have to Believe," in the

Real Paper, October 17, 1973. Come, come Jon! Do I *have* to believe? I'm finding it difficult!

He was lying down, eyes closed, in Ossining, New York, the home of his scientist friend, Andrija Puharich, trying to project himself to Brazil. Suddenly he saw colors flash past him, like the kaleidoscope in "2001." When the colors cleared he was on a plaza with wavy inlaid lines: Rio or Brazilia. Not just in his mind, his whole physical body. Inside his head, though, he could hear Puharich's voice: "Bring back money!" A couple was walking towards him, just strolling. He asked for money but of course they couldn't understand his language. Puharich supplied some Portuguese or Spanish words. That did the trick. Uri had no shirt pocket, so he clutched the paper money in his fist. Then he was back in Ossining, New York. Puharich, who had seen nothing out of the ordinary in Uri's behavior, asked what happened. Uri opened a fist holding the cruzeiro currency.

He couldn't relate the other teleportation trip. That information was being saved for a book by Puharich. Uri and his entourage are as careful as a rock band about their publicity and make no bones about it. "Bring back money!" was an appropriate phrase. In any case, the experience was too much for Uri, and he won't try it again soon.

If, by chance, you still *do* believe, don't feel bad. You are joined by millions of others who will believe, no matter what evidence is presented. Remember Barnum.

9

Photographs Through a Lens Cap

"I don't believe in astrology."

"Why not?"

"Because I'm a Sagittarius, and we're very hard to convince."

Yale Joel is one of those very quiet, charming souls and hardly looks like the popular version of a former *Life* magazine photographer. He has no hat pushed back over his head, no cigarette butt hanging from the lip, and doesn't talk like James Cagney at all. But he is a veteran of the business, a man who knows what a camera will and won't do.

Then he ran into Uri Geller. He was taken completely unaware by the bouncing psychic, and he, along with son Seth, were taken for quite a jolting ride when they interviewed him. In all innocence, Yale lunched with photographer/magician Charlie Reynolds and myself, and as we had him carefully relive the episode he passed from utter bewilderment to complete understanding of what had happened—with only an occasional nudge from us. Small factors he had forgotten to take into account suddenly popped up, and his picture of the Geller event began to clear. By the time dessert arrived—and *I* had broken a spoon or two for him as well—both Yale and Seth were a lot smarter than when they had sat down.

Here is the account of Yale's Adventures in Wonderland. It was entitled "Uri Through the Lens Cap: The Strange Adventures of a Veteran *Life* Photographer, a 17-mm Lens, and a Roll of Tri-X" and it appeared in *Popular Photography*, June, 1974.

I might accept Uri's power to repair watches, bend table utensils, and sketch hidden chairs. After all, these are not my fields. But photography is another matter. Photography is my profession. And as a "Life" magazine staff photographer for some 25 years, I have obviously taken more pictures than Uri ever psyched out. I also teach a photography workshop in my own studio. And I know what a camera can do. I know you can't take a picture—any kind—with the lens cap sealing the lens. I have tried it several times myself, accidentally. It won't work.

Yet I must report that Uri attempted to make it work.

Here is what happened:

I was on assignment photographing Geller in New York in color and black-and-white, assisted by my son, Seth. After several hours of spoon-bending and other amazing feats, Uri may have become bored with performing the same old routine for my camera. He peered into my shoulder bag. "Do you have a spare camera for me to take pictures through the lens cap?" he asked matter-of-factly. Did I have a spare camera? That bag was literally spilling over with cameras and equipment of my profession. Two Nikon-Fs, with a fast 35-mm f/4 medium wide-angle; a 24-mm f/8 extreme wide-angle; and an 85-mm f/8 medium tele lens. Also a Pentax equipped with a 17-mm Takumar f/4 extreme wide-angle "fisheye" type lens with a 160-degree field of view.

For those of my readers who are not familiar with cameras and their parameters, I must explain that a 17-mm lens is a *very* wide-angle lens that takes in about as much of an angle as the human eye does. For example, a 50-mm lens (on a 35-mm-format camera) is considered a "normal" lens, since what you see through the viewfinder with that lens is about the same "size" image you see normally. But looking through this 17-mm job, one sees almost out of both sides of the camera as well. And it has tremendous depth of focus; that is to say, objects a few inches away and those across the room are equally sharp under ordinary settings.

To continue:

"How about the Pentax?" I suggested. (That lens has a real solid lens cap to protect the somewhat bubbly shape of the front element.)

"Okay, tape the lens cap for a secure seal, and load the camera with film," he answered. As I threaded the Tri-X onto the take-up spool, Uri admitted this would be a tough assignment for him. But he felt Seth and I were sympathetic guys who responded positively to his seemingly amazing powers, and therefore, the chances of a successful lens-cap penetration were greatly enhanced.

Uri told Seth to choose a large picture book off the shelf and find a poster-like full-page picture. Seth settled on a striking close-up of an eagle. Uri's idea was for Seth to sit across the room staring at the eagle with maximum concentration, while Uri would try to transmit the eagle through the sealed lens cap onto the film.

So Seth concentrated on the eagle.

I concentrated my Nikon on Uri.

Uri raised the Pentax with cap swathed in black tape, lens practically touching his forehead. His tightened facial muscles and closed eyes testified to his intense effort. He proceeded to click off 12 or so exposures. (I had set the camera for 1/60 sec at f/4, a perfect exposure for pictures in the given light, but without a lens cap.) Along about the fifth or sixth exposure, Uri intimated with a gurgle that he had established contact with the eagle. "I can feel it getting through," he cried, as he urged the image through the lens cap.

I was busy shooting him with my Nikon, and keeping pace with his exposures. If Uri got a decent image on that film, I could see the Kodak ad . . . "Now you, too, can shoot psychic pictures without a camera or lens—on Kodak film." I also wondered what mysterious ASA speed he was shooting at. Frankly speaking, I didn't take this lens-cap photography seriously. Yet, I found myself caught up in the crazy atmosphere that Uri generates when he performs. It's a kind of frenetic, exciting, child-like "out-of-the-world" nimbleness: bending spoons, fixing watches, busting keys, all presumably accomplished by an enthusiastic, engaging superpsychic.

Meanwhile, Uri set the Pentax on the coffee table, and we flew to the next experiment.

During our luncheon, I could not get Joel to recall that he had ever left Uri alone with the camera, or let him sneak it away. He kept maintaining that it was "in full sight" all the time. Then we asked him to go over the events carefully, and when he began relating the "sealed-drawing" test that we are about to hear of, his face paled as it occurred to him just where Uri could have had the opportunity to fiddle about with the camera. This opportunity is about to occur:

Uri said he would attempt to receive telepathically a drawing which we were to make in an adjoining room. At this point, Seth and I went into the bedroom and closed the door. Seth decided to sketch a chair, and I photographed him at work. We placed the drawing inside two envelopes as Uri had instructed us and returned to the living room three to five minutes later, where Uri was waiting for us. Uri had no trouble in duplicating the chair which Seth had drawn.

This is a point in Yale's article that the believers all jumped on. They *had* to accept the evidence that Uri had cheated in the "psychic-photo" stunt, but they chortled that the Joels had no explanation for the "sealed-picture" test. And Yale *was* pretty shaken up over that one, until we made him recount in detail every small happening of the session. Then it developed that Uri had asked to have the double envelope placed inside a larger manila envelope, but not sealed, since he wanted to use the larger envelope "to send off some photos" later. They recalled that Uri often handled the package, even allowing the open end to go into his lap occasionally, after which he left the room to visit the bathroom for what seemed like a long time. He returned, sat down, and began fiddling with the envelope again—and suddenly announced that he "got" the picture. And he was right: When they again shook the envelopes out of the manila one, Uri quickly tore open the envelopes (to destroy the evidence of manipulation, do you think?) and showed that the two drawings were identical.

Yale left this analysis out of his article, because it was not pertinent to the photographic theme of the story. But in doing so, he left the believers smugly happy that Uri had triumphed, at least in one direction.

Then I reloaded my Nikon with color for more sealed lens cap pictures. Uri once again held the same Pentax, still with the original roll in it, to his forehead while I shot him in color this time. When he had finally completed the roll, I immediately unloaded the Pentax and placed the film in my pocket to keep it apart from the others. There was no way Uri could have gotten to the film after that point.

As we shall see, it was a bit late by this time. But note the reasoning: Since the film is where the phenomenon is supposed to occur, you control the film and all is well. Now Uri can't "get to it."

By this time, I could see that Uri had shot his bolt. In fact, we were all slightly exhausted from the bizarre happenings. Enough was enough. After all, I had Uri's hot roll of Tri-X in my pocket, and I could hardly wait for Seth and I to get home to develop the psychic film in my workshop darkroom. So off we went.

Next scene is well after midnight at my Photography Workshop. Seth's faint incredulous voice echoing from downstairs, "Come on down, I see an exposure on the film!" "Is it sharp?" I yelled, grabbing my magnifying glass. Seth was holding the film as though it were radioactive. He was really shook-up. So was I when I put the five-power glass to the one and only exposed frame. The image was well-enough exposed, a bit thin, clear and sharp, except for the empty blob in the center. Not a bad try for an amateur, I mused. Finally, the enormity of what had possibly occurred with the film hit me!

Do I have a transparent lens cap?

Had Uri Geller really accomplished the impossible?

Who the hell would have thought . . .

This "was" a traumatic moment in the history of photography.

Here am I, a recognized professional photographer, years of experience with lens caps, and Uri one-upsmanships me with my own lens cap, my very own Pentax, even my film. I couldn't believe it. And yet, there was an image on that crazy roll of Kodak film!

Seth hung the film to dry as I prepared the enlarger for an 11 x 14 print of that mysterious image. Meanwhile, filled with awe (it was well past midnight), I telephoned Uri to tell him the amazing news. Yasha Katz, his manager, answered the phone. I blurted out the earth-shaking news to Yasha, and asked for Uri. Yasha told me that Uri was asleep, and he would not awaken him even for this bombshell event because he had a performance that evening at Town Hall, and besides, even a psychokinetic needs his sleep. I was stunned by Yasha's blasé acceptance of Uri's picture of the century, but knowing managers, I told him I would phone Uri at 10 A.M.

Yasha is quite accustomed to "bombshells" with Uri around. He has witnessed a great number of the superman's miracles, including the teleportation of a 150-pound planter from inside the apartment to the hallway. He had been downstairs getting a newspaper, and left Uri "asleep" upstairs on the sofa. Moments later, as he returned, he was confronted with this monster planter in the hall, and he excitedly burst in on Uri, "waking" him, and saw that Uri was astonished at the event, too! Together they lugged the thing back into the apartment, and Yasha's "proof" that Geller had not merely dragged it out there was that though *both* of them had carried it back inside, Uri had a "strained back" from his part in the effort. I wonder just when Uri *did* strain his back?

Back to the darkroom. By this time, the film was dry. I examined it critically under the light of the wide-open Focotar lens of my Focomat enlarger. No dust imbedded in the emulsion. Good. Clean negative. Fine. Carefully, I slipped the frame into the film holder. The image on the easel, slightly flat. Needs a No. 4 Polycontrast filter to bring out full contrast, I judged. Seth developed the test strip while we pondered the mysteries of photography. What's left to explore after this caper? Finally, a print emerged in the developer. Both of us were literally spent. Here it was about 2 A.M. I made an extra print for Uri, and we went to bed. Even photographers need rest.

Promptly at 10 A.M., I was on the phone with Uri. "Uri," I asked, "what were you thinking about when you did it?" His answer—"To tell you the truth, I was concentrating on a star in the sun." I told this pearl to Seth, who promptly remarked, "I guess he was thinking of himself!"

That day, at the Time-Life building, on the 28th floor (where most all the ex-"Life" photographers now rent office space) I showed Uri's picture to the dean of photo-journalism, the venerable Alfred Eisenstaedt. I asked his opinion of how the picture was taken. He took a quick look at it, and opined that the center blob looked like someone had held a lens cap in front of the lens. I then told him how Uri apparently shot it through the taped lens cap, and the picture was therefore the product of a supernatural phenomenon. Eisenstaedt's eyes blinked like a shutter. "Impossible!" he exploded.

I ran into Ralph More in the Photographer's Lounge. Now, Ralph is an expert photographer-technician type. He has taken every conceivable technical kind of picture of the astronauts for "Life." What a fertile, imaginative photographic mind that Ralph has! The only possible picture he may have missed up on is shooting the astronauts through a lens cap. So I showed him the Uri picture. Ralph's reaction? "How did that lousy lens cap get in that picture?"

George Karas runs what's left of the old "Life" lab. By this time, my euphoria about Uri's supernatural photographic talent was fading fast. So I asked George, as I showed him the picture, "Who the hell would take such an awful picture, George?" He glanced at it, and offered, "If whoever took that picture had held the lens cap further away from the lens, it might have been a decent photograph."

Could Uri, or somebody else in the room, have surreptitiously removed the lens cap while I was in the other room photographing Seth? That was the only time when Seth and I were out of sight.

FIGURE 1. The photo that Geller took of himself, supposedly with the lens cap in place. Photo by Geller. Print by Yale Joel.

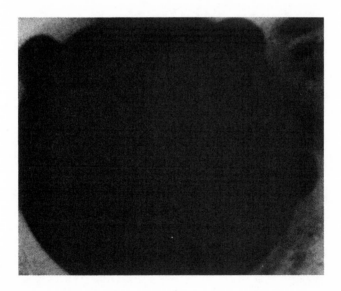

FIGURE 2. Randi duplicates the effect, admitting that the lens cap is held in his hand. Photo by Randi.

Right. And Yale admits that they were out of the room for at least four or five minutes, ample time for Geller to have rewound the film to the fifth or sixth frame, shot the picture after removing the lens cap, and replacing the black tape again, winding forward to the former film position and replacing the camera again in its original position.

It was our feeling that he could have, and perhaps did. Assuming this is the case, Seth and myself and the editors of *Popular Photography* closely duplicated Uri's "through-the-lens-cap" pictures without resorting to supernatural means.

Uri, I'm sorry to say, the consensus of expert photographic opinion, including my own (after due reflection), is that your lens cap is showing. (I mean my lens cap.)

You really didn't reckon with the extreme depth of field of the extreme wide-angle 160-degree 17-mm Takumar f/4 "fisheye" lens.

Besides, what the hell happened to the eagle?

10

The Persons Behind the Geller Myth

Remember, we can't be responsible for the safety of
writers who do hatchet jobs on Uri!
— Connie de Nave, Geller's publicist

I have felt it necessary to mention certain inconsistencies in the
work of Dr. Andrija Puharich, since he was one of the principal persons
behind Geller's arrival in the United States and author of the book *Uri*,
which purported to tell the story of Puharich's dealings with Geller.
Now we turn to some of the others who have put time, money, and talent into making Uri the psychic superstar of the seventies.

Judith Skutch, a prominent and wealthy supporter of "psychic"
causes, gave a huge amount of money to promote Geller here. She was
flabbergasted to see him bend her silverware, and threw a raft of parties
at her posh New York home to present the "psychic" to the curious and
famous. Presently, her interest in Geller seems to have faded. She had
confided earlier to Dr. Stanley Krippner, of Maimonides Hospital, that,
though she became convinced that Geller had real powers, he used trickery when he appeared on television as a performer. It's the old business
(see Rules for Psychics, 2 and 3), as Andrew Tobias said in his excellent
article in *New York* magazine, September 10, 1973, titled, "OK, So He
Averted World War III, But Can He Bend a Nail?": "In other words,
until a feat is explained, it is done by supernatural means; thereafter, it
becomes a regrettable, but excusable, case of showmanship." Ms. Skutch
suspects the television stunts but is persuaded by the personal touch, so
accepts the latter as proof of Geller's genuine powers.

But Dr. Ray Hyman, of the Psychology Department of the University
of Oregon at Eugene, was in the company of Geller with a representative
of the Defense Department when that gentleman asked an important
question. I quote Hyman: "During lunch, he put the question to Uri
directly. 'Did you ever use trickery during your demonstrations to convince others?' Uri became very serious and literally oozed sincerity. He
said with deep conviction that he *never* used trickery. He related that
during his performing days in Israel many people wanted to sell him
secret devices or tricks. But he refused them all. 'Don't you see . . . that
if I ever stooped to trickery, I would not be true to myself? And, if I were
caught just once using trickery, I would be finished.'"

Well, Judith, Uri says he *never* uses tricks; you say he *does*; and
that makes him either a trickster or a liar! *Or both.*

But Ms. Skutch has currently turned to another major discovery in the world of the wonderful. A young chap who makes ball-point pens follow him around the living-room rug, and who had a message tapped out on an electric car-door lock that sent him into the faith-healing business, has captured her fancy, and she is out to reveal his gifts to the afflicted. Incidentally, the tattoo on the car door was signed by none other than God himself. Might as well go to the top right off . . . And it must be so, because the *Village Voice* newspaper believes it. See Van der Horst's article in the *Village Voice* for December 23, 1974.

What of the two Stanford Research Institute scientists—Puthoff and Targ—who have put Geller in the enviable "approved with reservations" category? Their quite inconclusive tests of Geller at SRI have already been dealt with here, but what are the two scientists doing in this particular vineyard, trampling out these particular grapes?

Harold Puthoff is, among other things, a devout believer in the pseudoscience/religion called Scientology. It was formerly known as Dianetics, but when the value of painting it religious became obvious it was redefined as such—and prospered. To go into the postulates of Scientology would insult the reader's intelligence; I will merely refer you to Dr. Christopher Evans's excellent handling of it in his book *Cults of Unreason.*

That Puthoff could also as a physicist endorse the Scientologists' "E-Meter" device (a sort of electronic Ouija board) makes me seriously wonder about his competence. Any high-school senior could work up a test for the meter's validity, yet Puthoff has failed to see through this modern version of what has been used by water-diviners and chiropractors for longer than either of us has been around.

Describing a report made by Targ and Puthoff about a purported miracle of Uri's, Ray Hyman has this to say about the attitude of these two scientists:

> While the band was resting on the center of the table with no one touching either the table or the band, the band was seen to rise up on end, split in half, and form itself into the letter "S." That story quickly faded into the background and I have not heard anything more about it. My guess is that it got built up through second-hand retelling. When I was at SRI, I tried to pin down the details and/or the origin of the story. As with all my other queries during that fateful day, I found it difficult to obtain satisfactory answers from either Targ or Puthoff. My review of my notes makes it even more striking about how evasive and elusive I found their answers to be. The heart of science, as I was taught, is the ability to deal with phenomena about which precise conditions for occurrence can be specified precisely and communicated unambiguously. Neither Targ nor Puthoff was either willing or able to spell out to me any of the conditions under which many of the alleged phenomena took place.

I asked them about his alleged ability to bend rings . . . They told me Uri had bent the one that was in the form of a figure-8. He apparently had been holding it in his hand at the time it bent. So I asked them if he could bend them without touching them. They told me he could do it either way. I asked Puthoff if he or anyone else at SRI had seen Uri do it without touching the ring. They never did answer me. They simply assured me that he could do it either way.

Randi, we tend to think of the Targs and Puthoffs as dupes and fools. But this is a mistake. It is also tempting to think of the [scientist] as having special skills for detecting trickery. This also is a mistake. Targ and Puthoff have been well trained and have succeeded in a difficult area of science. They have fallen for Geller for two reasons: they do not realize that their training and skills cannot be automatically extended to areas outside of laser and quantum physics, and secondly, let's give Uri credit— Uri is obviously good at what he does.

I must agree with that last observation, of course. I demur, however, concerning how I think of these two scientists. I have never thought of them as stupid at all. On the contrary, they have demonstrated that they are reputable men of science who have contributed substantially to the good of mankind—in other fields. I am angered at Geller and his ilk, who have wasted the valuable time and talents of these men—not to mention huge amounts of money—by leading them to believe in supposed miracles. That is the major trespass that I lay at Geller's door.

In passing, I find it of interest to note that Targ's father, now editor-in-chief at Putnam's (they published Mitchell's book *Psychic Exploration*), was once an occult-book dealer in Chicago. Seems like a family trait.

I turn now to the man who is perhaps the best known of all those who support the Geller legend, though he, too, has had serious second thoughts about the *Wunderkind* recently. I refer to Captain Edgar D. Mitchell.

That name, I hesitate to say, might be unknown to many of my readers, and it is a sign of the times that this can be so. Not too long ago, the daring men of space who were taking rockets into the void were heroes without parallel. Schoolchildren spoke their names in awe and followed every stage of their exploits minutely. When a rocket went up, we all held our breath until they were once again safely on Earth. Parades, interviews, and unheard-of media coverage followed every one of their efforts to open space to mankind. Then, after more than a dozen Apollo flights had brought the far frontier of space under rein, these men faded from view. A few television commercials and magazine ads used their likenesses, and suddenly they were swallowed up in anonymity.

One such is Captain Mitchell, who walked upon the moon during the successful Apollo 14 venture. Shortly after the flight, Mitchell resigned from NASA and founded the Institute of Noetic Sciences, to study "theoretical and applied consciousness research." Mitchell now came into prominence again as one of Geller's firmest supporters.

Thoroughly annoyed about Geller's scrap with Puharich (they were fighting, among other things, over an advance on one of the Geller books that Puharich failed to split with the "psychic"), Mitchell has said in an interview that Uri refuses to do anything unless promised "money, girls, or considerable fame." However, I am concerned here with Mitchell's ability to deal with the hard facts behind Geller. Has he made good decisions from the evidence presented? What I've heard of his judgment seems to show that he has an overwhelming desire to believe in paranormal occurrences and faculties, and I feel that the following examples may indicate that his need to prove what he believes to be true overrides his scientific discretion.

I will quote three versions that he himself gave of the famous set of ESP experiments he clandestinely performed on the way to and from the moon. The first account, extracted from the *New York Times* of January 9, 1974, and entitled "Ex-Astronaut on ESP," seems quite straightforward. Read it and see if you are impressed with the case he makes for the reality of ESP:

> PALO ALTO, Calif. — During the Apollo 14 lunar expedition, I performed an extrasensory-perception experiment—the world's first in space. In it five symbols—a star, cross, circle, wavy line and square—were oriented randomly in columns of 25. Four persons in the United States attempted to guess the order of the symbols. They were able to do this with success that could be duplicated by chance in one out of 3,000 experiments. This in parapsychology experiments is considered reasonably successful.

There follows a lengthy account of how Mitchell became interested in the subject, and the moon experiment is not referred to again. Now, based upon what you have just read, you must be left with the impression that there is indeed some significance to the experiment, since guessing the cards in an ESP deck by chance alone would have yielded results of 5 to 1, not a whopping 3,000 to 1! But we are not told how many cards were "transmitted," nor how many correct or incorrect "calls" were made, nor by what means the odds were calculated. Mind you, in an article of this type, we cannot expect an enormous amount of detail, but I am pointing out that the overall impression is quite strong that the moon experiment was a great success—and that Mitchell has ample reason to crow about the test.

Now we will see another account, published a few months after the space event, also in the *New York Times* (June 22, 1971) and fully three years before the previous article. I have several times given this account to reasonably intelligent persons to read, and have shared with them a total confusion. We simply do not know what really was done during the moon-trip experiment, and are left with numbers and procedure in a totally confused mess. I will be charitable and assume that the error may lie partly with the reporter or typesetter. But surely it cannot *all* be thus explained.

Here is the *Times* article; it was headed "Astronaut Tells of ESP Tests." Make of it what you will, though the main point of the account is yet to be made.

DURHAM, N.C., June 21 (AP)—Capt. Edgar D. Mitchell Jr., the Apollo 14 astronaut who performed extrasensory perception tests during his moon mission last February, said today that such tests might prove more important to man than space exploration itself.

"It's a very important phenomenon," Captain Mitchell said at a news conference. "We're much too uninformed, unknowledgeable in this mechanism of telepathy or ESP to project its uses, but I think once we start to understand what the mechanism is, then we can start talking about uses."

The captain said that his own ESP experiments during space travel had produced results "far exceeding anything expected." However, he added that scientifically, the experiments were only "moderately significant."

The astronaut said that when he left for the moon he took along a deck of 25 homemade cards with ESP symbols: a star, a cross, a wave, a square and a circle.

He said he had planned to concentrate on 25 symbols a day at the rate of one every 15 seconds, with one concentration period a day for six days.

Worked on 4 Days

"As it turned out, I was only able to work on four of the days," he said—two on the way to the moon and two on the way back.

Captain Mitchell reported that he had made arrangements with four persons stationed in different cities. He declined to identify his contacts, but one man, Olof Johnson of Chicago, has said that he is a psychic who cooperated with the astronaut.

He said that of 200 guesses sent to him by his contacts, 51 had agreed with the notes he made while attempting to transmit signals from his sleeping quarters aboard the rocketship.

Two of his four contacts performed better than the others, he said, but at least one reported having received messages more often then they were sent because of an unforeseen change of schedule.

The astronaut came to Durham from his Houston home base to analyze the results of his tests with Dr. J. B. Rhine, head of the Foundation for Research on the Nature of Man.

Studies on Transmissions

The foundation conducts inquiries into the possibility of spiritual or other nonphysical life in man, including the reported transmission of messages from mind to mind by extrasensory perception.

Captain Mitchell said that he had told his contacts the schedule of his rest hours during the flight but that he had been unable to pin down just when during the rest period he would try to transmit messages.

He said he had assigned numbers to the card symbols, then had concentrated on the symbols after noting the number he had chosen for each attempted transmission.

The contacts on earth were expected to receive the symbols by extrasensory perception and write them down. Captain Mitchell said that he had planned to compare his numbers series with the series of symbols returned to him in sealed envelopes by the contacts.

He reported that two of the four contacts had submitted more accurate series of symbols than the other two, though he rated the accuracy of all four as "very good."

Well? Do you share my confusion? *More important*, do you still have the impression that the experiments were a success? They are referred to here as "far exceeding anything expected" and, *in the same paragraph*, as only "moderately significant." How can that be? Certainly the two descriptions are not compatible! But we have failed to consider the special language that is employed by parapsychologists. Our ignorance of this exceptional system of logic and language has been our undoing, no doubt.

In the third account — coming up — we will discover the most amazing fact of all.

But before we do that, let me tell you that the Olaf Jonsson (correct spelling) who will be referred to is looked upon in psychic circles as one of the miracle-workers of the trade. I am not surprised that the press managed to discover he was one of the participants in the space experiment. After all, his phone and typewriter were both in working condition, and he is not known to be shy with reporters.

Here follows the third version of the moon test, again in Mitchell's own words. This time, the excerpt is from his book *Psychic Exploration*. In it, he finally tells the horrible truth about the experiment he has been touting as an example of ESP proof. But this should not be in any way a deterrent to the real believer. Mitchell's last lines prove that.

By 1971, when the Apollo 14 mission was scheduled, I had become an avid psychic researcher in my spare time. The opportunity that the lunar expedition offered me to experiment with telepathy in space was too good to disregard, and I think any scientist whose interests and inclinations paralleled mine would have taken it. I never intended to make the experiment public in the manner that it was — as a sensational story in newspapers and other media around the world. I had decided on the experiment only a few weeks before lift-off, and it was to have been a purely personal investigation. I did not request permission from the National Aeronautics and Space Administration (NASA) because it seemed better to do it without sanction rather than risk having permission denied. Furthermore, because of experience with "news leaks" I did not even seek the counsel of established professionals. These precautions were to no avail, however.

My colleagues in the experiment were four people on earth who tried to receive by telepathic communication the targets I attempted to send them on several days of the voyage. Three of them prefer to remain anonymous. The fourth—Olaf Jonsson of Chicago—was suggested by one of my friends at the last minute and his participation was arranged by telephone. We never met before the launch, although I have met him since. Through a news leak—the source of which is still unknown to me—and through excellent detective work by the press, Jonsson was found and revealed the story to the press, with results that brought widespread attention to us and to the whole field of psychic research.

Briefly, my experiment involved four transmission sessions during rest periods programmed into the flight. Two of the sessions were completed on the way to the moon and two were completed on the return trip. I used random numbers from 1 to 5 set up in eight columns of twenty-five numbers each. Just before transmitting, in order to minimize the possibility of precognition, I assigned each number to one of the symbols of the standard Zener cards used for some ESP tests—a cross, a square, a circle, a star, and parallel wavy lines. Circumstances during the flight made subsequent evaluation of the data difficult. We were forty minutes late during lift-off, which caused the first few rest periods to start forty minutes late as well. Thus, the arrangement I had made with the receivers meant that some of the sessions appeared to yield precognitive results, not telepathic ones.

Upon return to earth, the data was analyzed independently by Dr. J. B. Rhine of the Foundation for Research on the Nature of Man, by Dr. Karlis Osis of the American Society for Psychical Research, and by me. The results were statistically significant, not because any of the receivers got a large number of direct hits but because the number of hits was amazingly low. The statistical probability of scoring so few hits was about 3000:1. This negative ESP effect, called "psi-missing," is something that has frequently arisen in other psychic research work, and theorists are attempting to explain its significance. In any case, it offers good evidence for psi, because the laws of chance are bypassed to a significant degree.

I am reminded of the story of the lady who goes to the Little League game to watch her son pitch, and comes away with the glowing comment that her son was a fine pitcher because he hit the bat every time, no matter how hard the batter swung. It's the second-from-last sentence that gets me particularly. Mitchell says, "This negative ESP effect . . . has frequently arisen . . . and theorists are attempting to explain its significance." Yes, the "theorists" may be doing just that, Captain Mitchell, but we common folk have long ago decided what it's all about. *We* call it *losing.*

There are others whom I might put under fire in this chapter. Yasha Katz is one, but I have already stated that I cannot justifiably do this, since he claims no scientific standing, is probably not one of the perpetrators of the hoax, and has never claimed any expertise in the judgment of such matters. I consider him an innocent victim of the set-up.

Professor John J. G. Taylor, of King's College, London University, has written a book entitled *Black Holes,* and I opened it to gain some insight to the man who has been so loudly on the side of the Gellerites in England. I cannot claim to follow the physics involved in his study of the phenomenon known as a Black Hole, but I am able to see that when he fills page after page of a scientific book with quotations from the Bible there is something lacking in his objectivity as a scientist.

Arthur Clarke, whose magnificent science-fiction tales have enthralled me for many years, and who wrote the screenplay for the epic *2001* motion picture, has described the conditions for the tests at Birkbeck in London as "incredibly sloppy"* and said that he was "certainly not impressed by some of the scientists who got involved with Geller." Yet Clarke is—at this writing—"continually changing" his mind. But at least he does not claim any expertise in the subject and is willing to defer to those who *are* competent.†

Professor John Hasted of London University, who was present at the Birkbeck tests, stated after their completion that "in my lab, he wasn't a phony." At a later date, when interviewed by Joseph Hanlon of *New Scientist* magazine, Hasted confided that he had not been at all satisfied with the tests, and that he'd made the "wasn't a phony" statement "to keep Geller happy." They were desperately afraid that he might leave and not let them conduct further tests! Hasted even told Hanlon that he himself was sure he could do the Geiger-counter tests under the conditions Geller had been allowed. Geller wasn't searched for such things as batteries, radioactive substances, etc., "because it would put him off." Hasted added that the Geiger-counter test was a "weak" one and that he discounted it altogether. How perceptive of him.

Dr. Jack Sarfatti (recently changed from the spelling "Sarfatt") became quite excited about the Birkbeck Geiger-counter tests and, when it was suggested to him that they should have searched Geller for a "beta-source" (any radioactive substance that would cause a Geiger counter to register), Sarfatti thought for a moment and declared that he found the suggestion "surprising and ingenious." Words fail me.

---

* *Exactly* the words used by Professor Ray Hyman to describe the conditions at SRI during the Geller tests!

† Clarke is now a total disbeliever in Geller's claims.

Dr. Sarfatti, a prominent physicist, said, in *Science News,* early in 1974: "My personal professional judgment as a Ph.D. physicist is that Geller demonstrated genuine psycho-energetic ability at Birkbeck, which is beyond the doubt of any reasonable man . . ." But in January 1975 he was saying that he thought he was "probably fooled" at Birkbeck and felt that Geller and his whole crew were "frauds." Bouncing back, after exchanging notes with other experimenters, Sarfatti said, "As of now, I simply do not know if he is genuine or not. It's 50/50 as far as I can see, given my present information."

Getting back to Professor John Taylor: He is rather unusual, to say the very least. There are not many leading British mathematicians who can lay claim to having been a consultant to *Forum* magazine, a British sex-advice publication. I would presume that his advice on this subject reflected his academic prowess, which is universally acknowledged as prodigious. At King's College, London, he serves as Professor of Applied Mathematics and has several books to his credit. Nevertheless, one book, *Superminds,* has caused even his staunchest admirers to throw up their learned hands in dismay.

In this book, which deals with Geller and others, notably children, Taylor says: "Some of the [SRI] experiments were scrutinized by a magician on television monitors for possible sleight-of-hand procedures (none were in fact detected); the experiments were performed on what is termed a 'double-blind' basis wherever possible, which means that neither he nor the experimenter could know the answer beforehand."

First of all, Taylor's statement about the magician is not true. Where he got that idea, I cannot tell. There was no magician present. And, second, he fails to note that WHEN THE TESTS WERE DOUBLE-BLIND, THERE WERE NO RESULTS! URI PASSED ON ALL OF THEM. The single exception is in the "die-in-the-box" experiment, and we have discovered that both the reports and the conditions for those tests were enough to completely discount them. (See Chapter 11.)

Describing the metal-bending trick, Professor Taylor naïvely reports: "One curious feature of the bending process is that it appears to go in brief steps: a spoon or fork can bend through many degrees in a fraction of a second. This often happens when the observer's attention has shifted from the object he is trying to bend. Indeed this feature of bending not happening when the object is being watched — 'the shyness effect' — is very common. It seems to be correlated with the presence of skeptics or others who have a poor relationship with the subject."

Translated, this says that people who pay close attention ("who have a poor relationship with the subject") have to be distracted or they will catch him cheating.

During a visit to England in early 1974, I first heard of Taylor, who had just recently become enchanted by Geller. A BBC-TV David Dimbleby program had featured Geller and they had asked Taylor along to judge the performance. Just what kind of expert he was supposed to serve as seems unclear. Whatever his presumed expertise, he failed when confronted with Geller; he fell for "the lot" as the English say.

Taylor was not at all dampened by the evidence that subsequently developed to put this BBC program into the same category as the other Geller shows. Upon further questioning, and looking into their experience with Geller, the director and producer of the program pointed out that after Geller asked for spoons and forks to be brought to the studio he also asked that they be placed on a tray in his dressing room. They were under guard, we're told; but, when the producer walked by the room shortly thereafter, he found that Geller was there *alone* with the cutlery. Uri had sent the guard on an errand!

During the BBC show, Geller held the cutlery in the usual fashion, hiding the prepared one and allowing the others to be freely handled and examined. Sure enough, the one he favored was the one that broke on the program. And Taylor was hooked but good. His statement, used by Geller on the jacket of *My Story,* says: "The Geller Effect—of metal bending—is clearly not brought about by fraud." Dr. Hanlon says, in *New Scientist,* "Taylor was amazing. After the fork-bending, he stated that 'science has no explanation of this,' when he clearly had no idea of what had been going on!"

Colleagues say that there is no hope of talking sense to Taylor. When I called him while visiting there, he spent not more than thirty seconds with me by phone, and answered my offer to visit and enlighten him with, "I have all the evidence I need!" And he hung up on me. But now he has another bit of unsolicited evidence, and though I'm sure it won't shake his confidence in nuttery one bit he might do well to incorporate it into his experience.

During my summer 1975 visit to England, I counted on Taylor not knowing what I looked like and on his well-known penchant for publicity. He is a former student of acting in New York (he is a card-carrying member of Actor's Equity), and his theatrical leaning has obviously predisposed him to the limelight. With all this in mind, and having the commission from *Time* magazine to look into the set-up there as well, I attacked Fortress Britain, disguised as a journalist.

Carefully removing all traces of my present name from briefcase, camera, and wallet, I showed up at King's College to see Taylor. I'd phoned early that morning, at an hour when I had not expected to find him in, nor his secretary either. I was right. Then I'd continued to call at ten-minute intervals, until I got his secretary and mumbled about being "in from New York" and a "deadline." She assured me that Professor Taylor would be happy to see me.

This was calculated so that I could arrive at his office with him primed and ready to accept me. And it worked! He invited me in and I began the interview. He started by showing me several of the sacred relics fashioned by the children whose marvelous powers are described in *Superminds*. One such was a spiral/triangle piece of twisted aluminum rod that was produced by one of the "benders" who has done a lot of metal destruction for Taylor. When I pressed him for details, he looked a bit uneasy and admitted that he'd not actually seen it bend—he had only seen it *after* it got bent. Seems that *the kid is allowed to take it all along to his room and reappear with his little sculpture!* I had a hard time concealing my astonishment—not at the wonders described by Taylor, but at the credulity of the man.

Next, I was given a transparent plastic tube to examine. It had a pair of red rubber stoppers at each end of its twelve-inch length, with a dab of black sealing wax on the side near each end, holding a screw in place that penetrated into the stopper. He assured me that the sealing wax was secretly marked so that he could detect any tampering. Inside

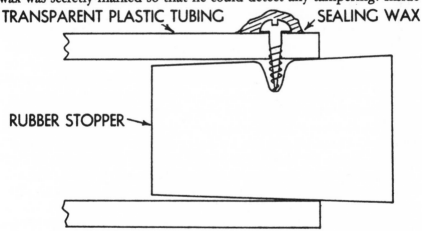

TRANSPARENT PLASTIC TUBING — SEALING WAX

RUBBER STOPPER →

FIGURE 1. Cross-section of Taylor's "sealed" plastic tube. The stopper simply pulled out to the right; the screw did not hold it.

was a six-inch piece of aluminum rod folded into a flattened "S" that he said had been "Gellerized" into that shape by a sixteen-year-old subject of his while the tube was sealed! I examined the relic carefully and noted that the stopper in one end had the "contact" marks I would expect to see (by this I mean the "wet" appearance that results from smooth rubber contacting the inside of glass or smooth plastic), whereas the other end looked quite unsealed.* I experimentally pulled at the rubber cork

---

* This is also evident in a photo in Taylor's *Superminds*!

while sliding the rod back and forth and admiring it, and almost blew the whole scheme; it was fully loose in the tube! Quickly, I jammed it back in place and returned it to Taylor. He had been turned away and hadn't seen the stopper pop out.

For the first time, I realized how *very* gullible he had been. Not only had he *not* seen this bending take place—again, *this* child had been allowed out of the room with the object—he'd only observed that it had already taken place while not being watched. But the tube could have easily been opened, then re-stoppered!* Simple observation proved that, and I had not expected that I would be able to remove the cork so easily. It was quite startling. The screw-and-sealing-wax precaution hadn't mattered a bit. It was a very poor piece of preparation, and the sixteen-year-old who fooled Taylor must be laughing himself to sleep.

The professor turned to his bookcase to produce another wonder for me, and I opened my briefcase, slipping an aluminum "standard test strip"† off the desk as I bent down to set the case there. Taylor didn't notice. He presented me with what appeared to be a carefully sculptured mess of paper clips resembling a four-footed critter. I'd heard of this artifact before and knew it was presumed to be a dog. "It looks just like a dog," I marveled brightly. "That's exactly what it is!" the professor confirmed, obviously pleased at my discernment. "And this is *me*!" he declared, handing over another mess of wire that vaguely resembled a lumpy man. I waxed enthusiastic. "May I photograph these?" I asked, and began fussing with my camera, meter, lenses, and such. At the same time, I bent the aluminum rod over double. Taylor didn't notice. I asked about another book of his—which sent him to the bookcase—and I put another bend in the rod, and another, until I had a "V" with turned-down ends. Taylor didn't notice. I made haste to add these new bits of data (about the other books by Taylor) to the notes, which in actuality I was scratching an identification on the Randi artifact I'd just created. I printed, "Bent by Randi—July 1/75" with a handy lockpick I had in my briefcase.

I now stepped to the window with the "dog" figure—which Taylor said had been created by a ten-year-old by putting paper clips in his pocket and extracting them afterward in the form of psychic sculpture (saints preserve us!)—and began setting up a photo. While Taylor was busy at the other side of the office, I quickly placed the Randi piece beside the "dog" and made an exposure Taylor didn't notice.

---

* In October of 1975, I demonstrated with this very tube before Taylor and a BBC crew that this was indeed possible. I removed the stopper and replaced it, as I had done before. In replacing the stopper, the sealing-wax cracked. After all, it had been put to considerable strain at least three times!

† Measuring 1/4 x 1/16 x 5 inches.

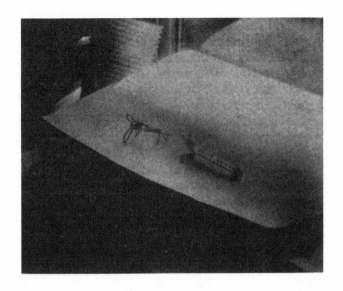

FIGURE 2. Professor Taylor's windowsill, with the "psychic sculptures" by one of the children and by Randi. (Engraving enhanced for legibility.)

FIGURE 3. Close-up of the sculpture Taylor did not expect to find among his collection of bent junk. (Engraving enhanced for legibility.)

By now, I had seen about enough. Taylor begged off showing me the lab where the holy events had transpired, and I busied myself with putting away the camera equipment, asking further questions about the watch tricks that Uri had done. Taylor was amused and told me he put no value in those things at all. It was the old story. What he solves is a trick; what fools him is genuine.

I needed to complete one more step. Picking up my briefcase, I placed it on one of two leather chairs against the wall. At the same time, I pushed the palmed aluminum artifact between the two chairs. Taylor didn't notice. I knew that he would eventually find it and that a glimmer of common sense might tell him he'd been fooled. He hadn't even watched the kids, but allowed them to have any conditions they wanted, even to taking the stuff out of the room; I'd been before him *every moment* in a cramped office, and he had fallen for every device I tried in order to misdirect him. And now a mysterious artifact would materialize between two chairs, marvelously bent. Will wonders never cease?

As I left Taylor's office, he mentioned that he was on his way to Coventry. Whether he was going of his own accord, or being sent, I did not determine.*

At a talk given in July 1975 in London, Taylor declared that he does *not* believe in: spiritualism, levitation, materialization, precognition, plant communication, or Kirlian photography. To those of my readers unfamiliar with these terms, I will say only that they are various nut theories and convictions of the last century or so. (See Glossary.) Taylor declined to follow these convictions because he had "no evidence" for them, though that hadn't stopped him from spending most of his book *Superminds* describing them. But he *does* believe in spoon-bending— *because he can't figure it out!*

During his talk he also said, "There is no chance of fraud—at least in some of the cases," and that during experiments he had made "one videotape—obtained not under ideal conditions." He also has decided that, when it comes to studying the fractures Geller obtained in metal objects, "Certain parts of fracture science are *art*." And later in the speech, he referred to the human body possibly being sensitive enough to detect the "electricity flowing out of lamp sockets when the bulbs are not in place." Comments on these remarks would be superfluous; anyone with any scientific training can assess them as the unscientific nonsense they are.

Re Puharich's book *Uri*, Taylor equated it with "twaddle." My dictionary defines that word as meaning: "Talk not worth hearing." So the professor *does* make some sense, sometimes!

---

* My English friends will need no explanation of this. For others, I must explain that "to be sent to Coventry" means to be ostracized by one's fellows.

In reply to one lady present, who asked a question about his lack of belief in spiritualism, Taylor replied, "If you don't appreciate modern knowledge and where it's at, then you'll continue to enjoy spiritualism." Strange words from him! I am reminded of the Chinese saying I saw in a prized manuscript at the British Museum: "Looking for Truth is like riding an ox in search of an ox."

But there is no denying that John Taylor has great expertise in his chosen field: mathematics. He is particularly incensed by the fact that Puharich's "twaddle" in *Uri* includes a great revelation from the powers who direct Geller's life from flying saucers. It is a mathematical formula that he describes simply as "wrong."

The most revealing thing at the Taylor lecture was that he evoked great dissatisfaction from most of his audience—not for his spoon-bending statements, which they ate up with glee, but for his bias concerning the other nut beliefs for which he said he had no proof. For that audience, he wasn't far-out enough! One spectator left abruptly after accusing Taylor of having a "closed mind"!

We were also entertained that evening by a gentleman pulling on a huge flagon of sherry and warning all to beware of the invaders from "the moon of Ganymede." We took note of his admonition, and Taylor even addressed him by his first name.

I'd paid the equivalent of $1.35 to hear the lecture. I couldn't have stood another 5 cents' worth.

Shortly thereafter, before I was to give a presentation on conjuring for the scientists at King's College in London, I was asked by Farooq Hussain if I wanted to have Dr. Ted Bastin, a prominent Gellerite, present at that meeting. I had to say no to this suggestion, though I wanted very much to meet him eventually. Bastin has been a staunch Geller supporter; it would not have been wise to admit him to that group, since he would then have been in a position to reveal my presence to the people at *Psychic News* before a certain article came out. (See Chapter 17.) However, on the last day of my stay in England, I decided to chance a meeting in hopes of being able to bring Bastin around to a sensible point of view concerning Geller.

I'd seen Bastin at a film showing to announce the publication of John Fuller's book on Arigo, the so-called "psychic surgeon" of Brazil. On that occasion, both Dr. Chris Evans (of the National Physical Laboratory) and I had been totally amazed at Bastin's acceptance of the film as proof of the supposed powers of the Brazilian. We had seen a series of pictures of boils being opened and a cyst being removed from a man's scalp, along with several shots of a blunt knife being run up under a few eyeballs. When I'd pointed out to Bastin at the time that what even he admitted was only a cyst removal was written up in the book as removal of a "scalp tumor." Bastin wasn't fazed in the slightest. He'd shown a remarkable ability to disregard every detraction and just declared that he still believed, regardless.

On July 16, I made an appointment to meet him in a laboratory at King's College and—in the company of Bastin's lovely wife, Dr. Ted Richards, Anne Kernaghan (a technician), Dr. David Dover (a physicist), and Miss Jill Purse—we sat down to discuss the Geller matter. Bastin described an occurrence at a supper during which a spoon had been broken as Geller stroked it while both ends were held by Bastin. In pressing for details, we discovered that this spoon was not quite as Bastin had first described it to us. He had said that he picked up this rather distinctive spoon, and challenged Geller to bend it. It developed that it was not the only such spoon present—there were several other identical spoons about the table. And Geller was not alone. At least one of his ubiquitous cast was also there. When I theorized that Geller had suggested, "Let's try bending this spoon," Bastin could not deny that it was very possible he'd done just that. In short, it was the old Geller Spoon Trick in all its glory. Mrs. Bastin recounted a similar Geller event that had taken place in Genoa.

I asked Anne Kernaghan to try to find us a regular steel teaspoon, which she did, going to her office for one, and I offered it to Bastin to examine carefully. He declared it genuine, though he felt it was a bit less sturdy than most. I handed it to Mrs. Bastin, who grasped each end between thumbs and forefingers. I stroked and rocked it for about ten seconds while she held it about a foot from her eyes. She declared that it was feeling plastic and seemingly melted as she held it. Suddenly, it twisted sideways and broke in two.

In his analysis, Dr. Bastin recalled that I'd washed the spoon by running a few drops of water onto it, since it was sticky with sugar and had coffee stains as well. He theorized that I had surreptitiously bent it to weaken it while doing this and that it would take only "eight or ten" bends to accomplish this. Hardly. When I suggested that the way to determine this properly would be to obtain an identical spoon and try it, he simply refused the suggestion, even over the objections of his wife. I can now tell him that I have done so, and it took 260 bends to break an identical spoon—a feat which the most adept conjuror could not perform, unnoticed, in front of an audience!

Bastin threw away the spoon I'd broken.

Dr. Bastin went on then to describe how Geller had "apported" a set of his screwdrivers out of his kit bag to the nearby stairway, where they were discovered, each broken off at the base of its shaft. When I failed to marvel at this and suggested that Geller or an accomplice had simply swiped the tools, broken them, and placed them on the stair, Bastin refused to consider that as a possible solution. He preferred to believe it was a miracle. Besides, he said, Geller would have needed a special tubular tool to break such screwdrivers. I offered to break one of a new set Bastin had with him, to test me. He agreed, and I simply reached over and inserted the end in a water tap, bent it back and forth about fifteen times, and it broke off. But, Bastin objected when he examined the tool, when Geller did it only the steel shaft showed a bend, not the metal sheath handle! I didn't really know how I could get through to Bastin at that point.

I suggested to Bastin that his position was a little like throwing a dart over your shoulder, noting the exact spot it hit, then challenging someone else to do the same, hitting exactly the same spot! Geller had broken the screwdrivers any old way, and now I was expected to do the precise same fracture! And, since we have no idea what tools might have been used (or what tap!), we are naturally now in the position of being unable to hit the same spot with that dart!

Mrs. Bastin showed me her keyring with a key Geller had bent by about 5 degrees. She held the bunch of keys up, with only the Geller key hanging down. I took it between my thumb and forefinger and asked her if that was the way Geller had held it. Dr. Bastin interrupted, saying that it had been held much differently, but his wife agreed that my handling was identical. I rubbed it for about five seconds and released it. To everyone's surprise, it was now bent *considerably* more—at about a 30-degree angle! Bastin asked me if I had a chemical on my hands. I told him that I did not, that there *was* no such chemical.

I next wrote a few things on a piece of paper, then turned it face down on the table near Mrs. Bastin. I asked her to think of a number, to think of a city, and to make a simple drawing. She did so, and I asked her to turn over the paper. I was exactly right on all three counts, except that the drawing merely had its two parts reversed. I asked Dr. Bastin what had happened to a small object he'd placed on the table, far away from where I sat. He looked about, and found that it had "teleported" right through his body, and was now on the lab bench behind him, having passed through his very solid body in order to reach the table.

As we left the laboratory, Dr. Wilkins's* secretary, Miss Win Adams, was leaving the elevator. I asked her to describe what had happened the day before in her office, and she told Dr. Bastin that she had not only had two keys bend under her control, but that she had asked me to fix her watch, which had been stuck at 7:07 *for four days*. I'd placed it face down in her hand, and when she looked at it, it read 5:30! Not only that, but when she held it to her ear, it was running! She'd set the correct time, and *the watch had been running ever since,* keeping perfect time for over twenty-four hours!

---

* Dr. Wilkins enters our drama in Chapter 17.

Bastin didn't have much to say about that. In fact, he could not explain the broken spoon, the key that bent on his wife's key ring, the watch, or the other tricks that had fooled him. But he chortled that I hadn't broken the screwdriver *exactly* as Geller has broken it!

I was hardly very happy as I left the college. It was depressing to see Bastin so convinced of an illusion. There was no victory in the conference for me at all. I'd merely shown him duplications of major "miracles" also performed by Geller; in his mind, mine had been tricks, Geller's genuine. His idea of reality is a strange one, indeed.

As I've said, there are some things I cannot forgive Geller for. His deception of Dr. Ted Bastin is one of them.

John Hasted, whom I've already mentioned in this chapter, is another Gellerized physicist. He is a fixture at Birkbeck College of London University, and I found him to be a likable bear of a man who I'm sure is incapable of deception—except when practicing it upon himself. He eagerly described to me a session with Geller back in June 1974, which occurred in his office.

One of the photographs in *My Story* shows Professor David Bohm and Professor John Hasted with Geller during this remarkable episode.*

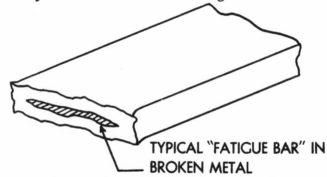

TYPICAL "FATIGUE BAR" IN
BROKEN METAL

FIGURE 4. Appearance of a typical "fatigue" fracture of a metal bar.

Also present were an assistant named Nikola and the photographer who took the picture. His name was Shipi Shtrang, not to my great surprise.

Geller had already been to this location twice before. Thus he was already familiar with the layout and was well prepared. Hasted told me that the group was in the office for barely "two minutes" when Geller asked for a spoon, which was given him from the desk drawer. He held it at the tip, and began to shake it back and forth. Great excitement ensued, as the spoon "became plastic" and wobbled about. Geller handed the

---

* Bohm, when I interviewed him, denied that he ever endorsed Geller and was less than satisfied with the "experiments" that were conducted while he was a witness.

spoon to Hasted, who laid it down carefully, since it was still floppy. It broke a few seconds later.

When I asked what had happened to the pieces, Hasted reported that they had been examined by a fracture specialist to see if such things as typical "fatigue fracture" signs were present. A "bar" (see Figure 4) would indicate such a fracture, obtainable by bending the metal back and forth until the structure breaks down and it falls in two. No such "bar" was seen. The conclusion was that the break was a "psychic" one.

Hasted was ecstatic over this event. He had seen and handled a spoon in process of breaking! He declared Geller to be the real thing.

At the beginning of my visit to Birkbeck (I went there in the guise of a reporter, feeling that as a conjuror I would not be welcome) Hasted invited me to the coffee shop upstairs, where we chatted at length on the experiences he'd had with Geller. He went into great detail about how "happy" they'd had to keep Uri. He said they had to fawn over him and flatter him. Then miracles would occur. I knew that I would have to duplicate the Geller tricks to make him re-think his conclusions; so I asked him to secretly pocket the teaspoon he'd been using. He did so, though he looked as guilty as a bank robber. We went to his office downstairs.

In the office, I questioned him about how Geller had held the spoon. I invited him to hold the one he'd brought by both ends, and I twiddled it about my thumb and forefinger. It began getting "plastic" as we watched and suddenly separated into two pieces.

Hasted colored a bit. He seized his magnifying lens and explained that he was looking for "fatigue bars." He found none. "Did you bend that while I was on the phone?" he asked. I told him quite honestly that I hadn't. (He'd had a call from astronaut Edgar Mitchell in the United States.)

Hasted dropped both pieces into the wastebasket. "Don't want to get them mixed up with the real experiments" he said with a smile. He seemed not at all perturbed that a "reporter" had walked in off the street, sat right beside him, and done a Geller! He hastened to state that he had always worked with keys, not spoons, since keys are much shorter and require more force. They are also less likely to be subjected to trickery, he said.

But he had examined the spoon I "melted," and he'd found no trace of signs that would indicate I had used a trick! Why did he not conclude that he had just seen a psychic event? Because I was just a reporter—not a wonder-worker. He had no predilection to believe that I could psychically bend metal, and so he discarded the evidence. It did not fit his picture of the world. Had he sent that spoon in for an analysis, he would have discovered no difference in the analysis of that one and a Gellerized one—unless the analyst were told which was the "real" one. Then it would depend upon the analyst's prejudice, if any.

The professor then showed me a set of chart recordings that had been obtained with Geller while he was trying to influence both a Geiger counter and a magnetometer.

I must explain. The Geiger counter will produce a "spike" on a line being drawn on a roll of graph paper traveling under a pen. The recorder is the kind of device used on a polygraph, or so-called "lie detector." If there is no atomic particle registering on the Geiger counter, there is just a continuous straight line; when a pulse comes through, the pen is pulled to one side and registers a "spike." The magnetometer, which registers magnetic fields, was also connected to the chart recorder, and produced a parallel straight line, with its own set of "spikes" as it registered magnetic pulses. And lo! Hasted had noticed that while Geller was putting the whammy on both machines, *both* chart lines registered pulses, twice, *at precisely the same instant!*

Now there are just three explanations for this, two of which have occurred to Hasted. Geller would like us to believe the first, which is that he produced a burst of radioactive particles and a magnetic field simultaneously. Hasted does not accept this, because he has postulated the second explanation, which is that Geller can produce voltage across his fingers as he holds the Geiger counter probe, thus making it register a false pulse to the radioactivity chart line and a true electromagnetic pulse to the other line.

Professor, there is a third solution as well. I heard a great deal from you that day on how carefully you had monitored the instrumentation, but I did not hear anything about who was watching the *chart recorder.* Did it occur to you that Shipi—or Uri—could have "pulsed" the recorder just by kicking it? Try it. It works. I've tried it, and it has worked for me. And it produces exactly the kind of dual pulse I saw on your chart record-ings, both "spikes" occurring at precisely the same instant! But you may not like this interpretation, since it proves no supernatural occurrence, just a bump with the foot or elbow. The first two explanations require rejection of all that we know about physics; the third is quite mundane and is a far better solution.

You might recall, professor, that your counterparts in America—Targ and Puthoff—obtained single-sided pulses when Uri tried to hex a sensitive weighing device. And no one thought to try testing the chart recorder then either, though they spent a lot of time jumping up and down on the scale device itself. Again, an alternative explanation of that event will not be popular at SRI.

To return to Professor Hasted's remark on why he preferred to use keys, rather than spoons, with Geller. He had shown me a very short, thick key as an example of how difficult an object could be to bend with-out it being noticed. He'd taken it from his top right desk drawer for me to examine. I'd put it back again.

Well, if Professor Hasted will look at that key—it's in the upper right drawer—he'll find a 40-degree bend in it. And I'm sure he has found his paper knife bent over double as well. Further, if he will check with the colleague I mentioned in my letter to him, he'll find that a block of clear plastic he used to have on his desk is now in the possession of that gentleman. It was teleported, of course.

Why? Do I amuse myself going into these offices doing silly things like Geller does? No, I've done them to prove that it is possible—even without Shipi Shtrang around as a helper—to get away with almost anything. I think my case is proved.

I liked Hasted. I still do, and I hope he takes this account of my skullduggery as a prank. I meant it that way.

Geller didn't.

So we see that the Gellerites are a mixed bag. They all seem, however, to have fallen under Uri's spell. Arthur Clarke, in a personal communication to me, says, "Uri seems to have an extraordinary ability to influence people and make them *want* him to be genuine—I guess the vapid word 'charm' (to which you are obviously immune!) is the only one appropriate."

Yes, Geller has charm, all right. He has the mesmeric panache that all great performers need, and the Gellerites can hardly be blamed for falling under the spell. But they may find that awakening is an unpleasant experience.

One person aroused from a pleasant hallucination is Professor J. W. Juritz, of Cape Town, South Africa. In an article that told of his tests with Geller, Professor Juritz said, "We're baffled, there is no explanation . . ." In the tests, similar to those done for Taylor and for others at Birkbeck in London, Geller had managed to bend keys, start and stop watches, reproduce sealed drawings, and deflect the compass needle by 30 degrees. Juritz was impressed, and said so in print. But two weeks later, he reconsidered.

Allow me to digress momentarily. It is a difficult thing for a man of science, especially when he is a respected physicist like Professor Juritz, if he discovers that the truth has escaped him and he must recant on a previously stated opinion. Not many men of science can do so, and in many cases where the admission is unavoidable they have resorted to all kinds of devious semantics to get around an out-and-out admission of error. But we can rejoice that Professor Juritz and others have had the courage and dignity to express themselves so directly. We know we can trust a man who is not afraid to admit his error, as understandable as this error is.

Said Juritz: "We were a very bad team of observers. Every experiment failed the first time it was attempted, and only succeeded some time later after attention had in the interim been diverted to other activities."

The professor even bothered to experiment with a small magnet concealed upon his person, to see if he could make the compass needle deflect. He could, and did. He also noted that, "None of the alleged bendings etc., was actually seen to happen, but only to have happened. The conclusion is obvious—Uri relies upon the age-old conjuror's trick of diverting attention."

Juritz ended his recantation by saying: "No self-respecting physicist can accept the claims of Geller and continue to teach physics."

Now let us turn to a period in time many of us never knew. We will find an unusual set of parallels between the Geller of today and his antecedents. It will make for interesting comparisons.

11

The Spaniard with the X-ray Eyes

The New Nonsense—really bits and pieces of the
old, brought back and given a "now" look by entre-
preneurs who know their market—arises when men,
having abandoned faith for reason, find the task of
living by reason too difficult for them.
—Charles Fair: The New Nonsense

More than half a century ago, the great magician and escape artist
Harry Houdini published a small booklet that he distributed among his
audiences to further his fight against the frauds of his day. It dealt
mainly with one "Margery" (the operating name of Mrs. Mina Crandon,
the wife of a prominent Boston surgeon), whom Houdini battled for
some time on behalf of *Scientific American* magazine. This journal had
offered a prize of $5,000 to anyone who could demonstrate to their com-
mittee's satisfaction that a supernormal event had been produced in
their presence. Houdini was a member of the committee, for they had
the good sense to employ the services of an expert in order to detect any
chicanery.

But the last few pages of Houdini's booklet dealt with the marvelous abilities of Joaquín María Argamasilla, known as "The Spaniard with
X-ray Eyes." In reviewing the comments of Houdini on this wonder-
worker of fifty years ago, I was struck with the similarities to the demonstration Geller did with a metal file box in which was concealed a single
die, shaken about by the SRI experimenters. First Houdini's account;
then, read my analysis of the reports of Geller's performance. I believe
you will find the comparison interesting.

Argamasilla was a huge man, dwarfing Houdini (who was not a
very large man even in his "elevator" shoes). But the indomitable
escape-artist depended only on intellect and expertise to put a stop to
the career of the X-ray wonder. Soon after the appearance of this booklet,
Argamasilla went out of business permanently.

Notice that prominent scientists of Houdini's day had been fooled
by the demonstrations of this faker. Are we to assume that scientists of
today are any faster at detection when faced with an unusual performance? Richet, one scientist very much convinced by Argamasilla's
show, was France's leading parapsychologist, though that term had not
yet been coined. He was also an eminent and respected physiologist and

acknowledged discoverer of the phenomenon that came to be known as anaphylaxis. (It proved important in immunology and led to research for which he received the Nobel prize, in 1913, for Physiology and Medicine.) In short, Richet was a trained observer and an astute, educated, and intelligent man. But he was no conjuror, and therefore he was taken in by the Spaniard as easily as any person is taken in by a good performer in the conjuring arts.

The spelling and grammar of Houdini's original have been corrected and slightly modernized, with no changes made that alter the meaning or intent at all. Since Houdini turned out this booklet in a hurry, the illustrations and construction are a bit slipshod, but his meaning is clear. Herewith his account of the Argamasilla exposure, entitled (in the booklet) "Joaquin Maria Argamasilla: The Spaniard with X-ray Eyes":

This phenomenal mystifier essays to perform or accomplish the impossible; he makes claim to a power of supernormal vision, X-ray eyes and a penetrating brain; however, his claim to supernatural power is acknowledged as being limited, he seemingly not being familiar with the English language. He is always accompanied by his promoter, who serves in capacity of interpreter.

This promoter presented Argamasilla as a youth of nineteen; his appearance and mannerisms indicate a more mature personality. As credentials, this young man brought letters purported to have been written by the Nobel prize winner, Prof. Richet, and from Prof. Geley, likewise from noted scientists of Spain who attested to the fact that Argamasilla unqualifiedly came through all tests and that he had proved conclusively to their satisfaction "that he could read through metal."

It was claimed that the Spaniard with his X-ray eyes could penetrate metal "provided it was unpainted," giving precedence to gold — and in sequence, silver, copper, zinc, tin and iron. His most popular test was reading through the hunting case of a watch, the hands having been set at random just before the watch was placed in his hands, and that is just what seemingly he did, to the amazement of scientific onlookers — and this youth's handling of the watch was so innocently done as to ward off suspicion.

As in the case, always, with the first presentation of such unnatural things, a weird, uncanny impression is made on the mind of the lay investigator; having been thrown off guard by the art of misdirection he is susceptible to the superstitious element lurking in the minds of the assembled gathering — there is infection to existing superstition, particularly so when logical deduction seems foreign to the production.

Aside from reading through the closed hunting case of a watch, this Spaniard lays claim to visually penetrating metal when in the form of a box. It is true the box must be of convenient form and unpainted. Argamasilla carries two types of boxes, one made of solid silver, represented by

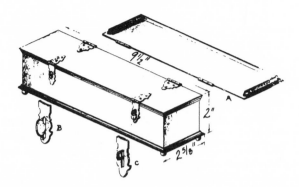

FIGURE 1

illustration Figure 1, the top or lid of which is hinged to the back wall and secured at front by two hinged hasps, but it will be noticed that one of these hasps is engaged by a "turn buckle," "B," while the other one is fitted to a projecting "staple" "C," to accommodate a small padlock. The underside of lid "A" is provided with a flange at the two ends and along the entire length of the front edge, and this flange serves to intensify the mystery, as it apparently renders surreptitious opening, revealing a view of interior, impossible.

The other type of box is represented by Figure 2, three walls of which

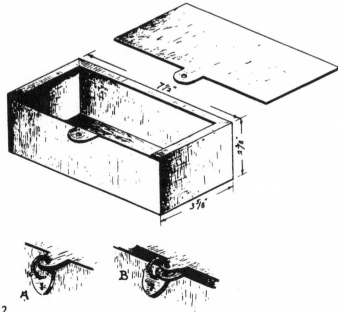

FIGURE 2

are crowned with horizontal flanges in conjunction with lug strips on each end wall under flanges, constituting a runway for a sliding lid.

The front wall is minus such flange, but, centrally situated; it has a flange lug bent at right angles and projecting upward. The sliding lid has a similar lug and both are pierced to accommodate a small padlock.

This box is of sheet iron, or "steel," and since the visual performance is supposed to take place as a result of penetration through the metallic lid, to demonstrate economically, the one box is made to serve the purpose with lids of copper, zinc, tin and iron.

The watch: any hunting case watch borrowed from a spectator serves the purpose. There is no special preparation to make. It is only necessary that the hands be so shifted as to disguise the correct time and to prove the genuineness of the reading. So the Spaniard's method of procedure is simply to ask for a hunting case watch, with a request that the setting of the hands be done optionally with the holder. While this is being done, he proceeds to blindfold his own eyes with his own handkerchief, which has been already prepared by folding, and as this lies across his left hand he adjusts two wads of cotton batting, ostensibly pads for each eye, and at once applies the bandage to his eyes and ties it at the back of his head. He is now ready to receive the watch in his right hand, face up, but case closed. He disclaims power to look through the works of a watch and, therefore, logically requires the face to be on the uppermost side. He receives the watch, holds it gingerly in a horizontal position between the index finger and thumb for a moment or two, then raises the hand, with watch between the same fingers, to such position that the watch is vertical and at a height about to his chin. After a moment he lowers the hand with a sweep, and in so doing lowers the watch to a horizontal position in the palm of his hand with the stem head resting against the ball or root thumb, and the hinge of the case against the ring and second fingers; simultaneously he exerts sufficient pressure by the ball of the thumb to spring open the case, which is covered and guarded by the flexed fingers. The watch case is opened but a trifle, perhaps one-half to three-quarters of an inch, and a quick glance is sufficient for the reading, and this made possible since the watch is held so low that a downward glance on the line of the cheeks, beneath the handkerchief, gives a perfect line of vision. This is facilitated by the cotton pads previously referred to, which when applied, rest on the brows, rather than directly over the eyes. Also "knitting the brow" and raising again, rides the handkerchief up and opens a line of vision, in which case the watch is seen with the greatest ease.

I have seen this man place his left hand to his forehead and by so doing almost imperceptibly raise the handkerchief to improve his downward line of vision.

A glance having been gotten at the watch, and the time noted, pressure by the ball of the thumb and at the same time, the fingers, press the lid closed. By this combined movement the watch is noiselessly closed; and, this accomplished, the watch is again raised vertically before the eyes and maneuvered back and forth as though endeavoring to get it to a certain focus. As the watch is raised to the last position, it is caused to lie flat on the open palm so that it may be visibly observed to be closed. This whole maneuver is so natural that suspicion is warded off and the back of the hand toward observers forms a perfect screen when the watch case is open.

This last maneuver is simply acting, and during the time consumed by it the Spaniard makes mental calculation for the "lapse" of time, and so, seemingly, tells the time as he sees (?) it just a moment before it is opened for comparison. For example, if the exact time is twenty-two minutes to ten at the moment he actually sees the face of the watch, he stalls by maneuvering and at the psychological moment declares the time as twenty minutes to ten and, though he might be thirty seconds out of the way, it is not of sufficient importance to note.

A personal trial of this experiment will convince the reader of the ease with which it can be accomplished.

I have had several sittings with Argamasilla, and at one of them I handed him a watch that was itself tricky to open. Consequently, he failed to tell the time by that watch. At another time, at the Newspaper Feature Syndicate office, 241 West 58th Street, I had the opportunity to stand at his extreme left side and from that position "I positively saw him open and close the watch." Of course he did not know of my vantage point because of his blindfold, as I looked over his left shoulder.

It is a rule with this man to stand back in a corner close to a window, for the beneficial play of light, also so that no one of the observers may get behind him, but my favorable opportunity clinched my suspicion.

This man is a very clever manipulator, and he acts his part in such manner as to insure misdirection.

Since witnessing his performance I have presented the watch trick and so far no one has been able to detect the movement unless knowing beforehand the trick of opening and closing the watch.

The handling of the boxes varies considerably from that of the watch — but that too, will be made clear by accompanying illustrations.

Giving first, attention to the silver box: A printed card or small slip of paper with writing, is placed in the box, lid closed and locked with one small padlock and the second hasp secured by the turn buckle. The operator holds the closed box by a hand clinching each end and in his maneuvering, twisting and slightly swinging the box from side to side, he manages to drop the left hand and by the aid of the thumb lifts up the lid at the left corner. See Figure 3. Just before raising the lid and during manipulation he manages to release the turn buckle so the hasp slips free.

The right hand is so placed as to expose that end of the box, at times by merely balancing the box on the finger ends. A firmer grip, when required, is obtained as shown in Figure 3. In course of maneuvering, the card is brought to a favorable position for reading by successive joltings of the box, the left end being lowered and turned away from observers. The fact that the box is opened is unobserved by them.

The view shown in Figure 3, is as seen by the operator himself. The audience, or observers, see the back of the box and its end only as held or poised on the fingers of the right hand. The box is also held at such an angle that the observers do not get a view of the top of it.

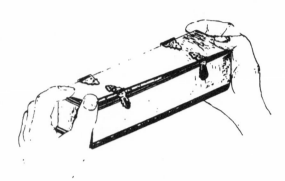

FIGURE 3

It should be noted that Argamasilla always chooses a position with the light behind himself, and such that observers are always "in front," facing him. He very adroitly guards against observers being at his side or behind him.

The box with sliding lid is handled differently, necessarily so, because of its particular form of construction. The casual observer on first examination, being unfamiliar with the mode of handling, is unprepared for a critical examination; consequently he does not notice that the metal of the lid is quite flexible and that the running grooves at the ends of the box are so free as to afford sufficient play by raising the lid—just a trifle, but "every little helps."

The runner flanges around three edges of the lid, and the projection lugs for attaching a padlock, would seem proof positive against the possibility of a trick, but the innocent observer has failed to note the fact that the bow, or shackle, is elongated a trifle, perpendicularly. It looks innocent enough when seen in its normal position (Figure 2, A), but that innocence is soon dissipated when viewed as shown at "B." This opening is made possible by the fact that the front edge of the lid projects a fraction of an inch beyond the front wall of the box, which affords a purchase for the left thumb without resorting to pressure on the lugs. The flexibility of metal and slight play in the runners makes the opening possible (Figure 2, B, is slightly erroneous in drawing. The horizontal edge could slant slightly downward both ways from the lug converging at the ends of box where held by the running grooves.)

The box is held practically the same as the silver box; reading of the card is made possible by variable deflection of light rays, and by proper manipulation of angles the eye has a range of practically the full bottom of box from front to back walls, the card being kept in left-hand corner of box. By turning the box upside-down it is an easy matter to slide the card out of the box enough for reading, and even at that it can be obscured from observation by the onlooker by the angularity in position of holding the box.

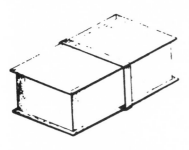

FIGURE 4

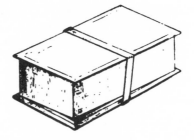

FIGURE 5

Figure 4 represents a Park & Tilford Nut and Fruit box made of tin; its lid has vertical flanges to fit into the box on all but the hinge side, and in lieu of a lock, the lid is held in place by an elastic band. This box is covered on all sides with colors from black to gold, the mass of color being black. Nevertheless, and notwithstanding the ban Argamasilla puts on painted metal, he did accept this box for a test, and safely so, because a casual examination shows the lid securely hinged, but the means of holding the lid closed is so "elastic" that the manipulation made necessary became identical with that for the silver box. However, Argamasilla took precautions to turn the box upside-down to facilitate reading, as shown in Figure 5. Under these conditions the possibility of reading is made perfectly clear by Figure 6 and by Figure 7, which represent the silver box minus trimmings. (Drawing slightly exaggerated as to distance opened.)

FIGURE 6

FIGURE 7

By successive joltings of the box, the card is sometimes brought to a vertical position against the back of the box (Figure 7).

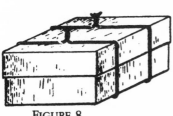

FIGURE 8

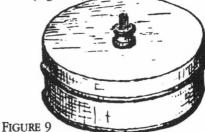

FIGURE 9

Figures 8 and 9 are boxes made of tin, unpainted, for testing Argamasilla's power for reading through metal. The square box was wired with two strands of copper wire soldered to the bottom of the box and twisted on top. The round box was simply bolted shut by a clamp bolt passing through the vertical axis of the box, soldered on the underside of the bottom, and the lid locked in place by a thumb nut. Insomuch as there was no possible flexibility to the lid of either box, Argamasilla failed by refusal to make a test in both instances, as undoubtedly he would have done with all the other boxes, if subterfuges and trick appliances had not been resorted to.

So said Houdini more than fifty years ago concerning one of the "phenomena" of his day. Now, I am not saying — nor should the reader infer — that Geller is using a box of his own design or construction, nor that he uses the same routine as described above. But a bit of research has shown me that any metal file-box I can purchase is capable of being used in much the same way. Study the illustrations (Figure 10) and you will see that, held in a similar manner, a regular card box can be levered open easily with one thumb and that a glance at the far corner of the box will reveal the uppermost face of the die. Figure 11 is taken from very close to the box, peeking through the small crack; this is a position that Geller could have easily attained if he could have handled the box at all — such as to shake it. But we are told in the "SRI Report" that the box was shaken "by one of the experimenters." We assume that Geller was not, then, allowed to touch the box. Any reasonable procedure would require this simple precaution, would it not?

So, to prove the possibility that Geller was able to do the old Argamasilla "peeking-into-the-metal-box" trick we need an indication that Geller was allowed to handle the box. Let's look back into the description again.

We have been told that "one of the experimenters" shook the box to tumble the die. Is it reasonable to assume that if Targ or Puthoff shook the box, the face uppermost would be unknown to Uri? Of course! Then additional shaking by Uri could not in any way affect the outcome, especially if he declared that he had to hold it to "feel for it," since we recognize that these "sensitive" persons must be allowed to develop certain liaison between the hardware and their super-senses.

Martin Gardner, a writer for *Scientific American,* and I, cogitating upon this matter for some time, and being unable to get a straight answer from the experimenters, decided that they would easily accept Uri's shaking the box at some point or other. And further inquiry directed at "Skip" Wilhelm, former *Time* magazine correspondent, verified that he was told by Targ and Puthoff that Uri *had* been allowed to shake up the die *after* one of *them* had done so! But why did they report that he "was not allowed to touch the box"? The reason is not hard to find, and it depends upon a semantic judgment.

Consider the "key-bending" trick Uri does so often. Since I have been doing it too, as part of my "in person" routine, I have verified that

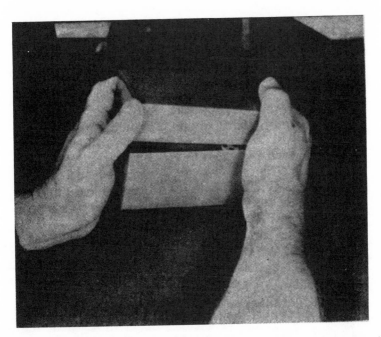

FIGURE 10. A metal file-box, such as Geller used in the SRI tests, can easily be opened momentarily, just enough to peek at the die, as Argamasilla did to fool the experts in Houdini's day. Photograph courtesy of Dennis Medina.

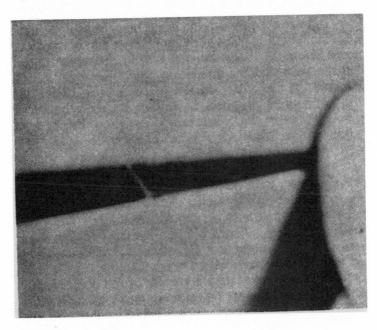

FIGURE 11. Close-up of the box as seen a few inches from the eye. It would be so held if placed against the forehead "to aid in concentration." Photograph courtesy of Dennis Medina.

people seeing the trick can easily be talked into declaring that it bent "while it was in my own hand!" Many times I've done the trick and heard the witness turn to a friend and say, "He bent it without even touching it!"—and mean this sincerely. And, taken generally, their statement is not a *lie*. It is merely incorrect. In the same way, the experimenters' claim that Uri "never touched it" can be translated into, "Uri never touched it in such a way that he could have seen inside it, to the best of our judgment." For I assure you, I cannot bend a key while you hold it, though I sure as hell can give the impression that I've done just that; so can Uri. So the spectator's statement re the key trick is not a lie; it is merely insufficient.

Is this the way that Uri did it in the eight-in-a-row success with the die in the box? We will probably never know. For their own reasons, SRI is not answering any questions on the subject. But bring into consideration this additional fact: We are not told whether, as is quite possible, Targ was the one who so carefully monitored Geller during the test. If this is so, we must consider the fact that Targ *is extremely nearsighted and wears very heavy glasses.* Therefore, under those circumstances, Geller could easily have gotten away with a quick peek inside.

Consider this: Very simple precautions would have sufficed to make this test into a truly scientific one. First, use a metal box with a lock on it. Second, do not allow Geller to touch, handle, move, shake, or in any way come in contact with the box. Three, insist upon having a positively declared, written guess of the uppermost face of the die made and witnessed before the lock is undone and the die seen.

And therein lies another interesting point. Just how *did* Geller "call" the face of the die? Three different versions exist. In one, we are told that he "announced" the guess. In another, he "drew the face of the die"; and in still another, he "wrote down" the guess. Just how *did* he do it? Or does *anyone* know? Or remember? Or care?

The evidence for Geller's success at the "die-guessing" trick is just so sketchy, so contradictory, and so badly reported that no conclusion can be arrived at other than that the experiment was no experiment at all, but the usual do-it-my-way Geller demonstration of chicanery.

And finally, as if there were not enough doubts about the procedure used to conduct this "test," *Time's* Wilhelm has reported that the set of tries with the die actually consisted of *many hundreds of throws,* the object being to get a run of consecutive wins. Doesn't it appear that Geller would be apt to get onto the protocol used in the test by this time? He was well experienced by the time he was able to start on his "miracle run."

Though we have far more striking similarities to make between Geller and other long-gone deceivers of the past in subsequent pages, the parallel between the Spanish Peeker and the Israeli Wonder makes interesting food for further thought.

The Old Broken-Watch Trick Revealed

> If you are desirous of obtaining a great name, of
> becoming the founder of a sect or establishment, be
> completely mad; but be sure that your madness cor-
> responds with the turn and temper of the age. Have
> in your madness reason enough to guide your
> extravagances; do not forget to be excessively opin-
> ionated and obstinate. It is certainly possible you
> may get hanged; but if you escape you will have
> altars erected to you.
>
> — Voltaire

On the evening of Friday, May 16, 1975, I found the perfect opportunity for testing a theory that I had held for some time concerning the
"wonders" that Geller had obtained by remote control via radio and
television broadcasts. Radio station WMCA, in New York City, far from
being inactive after midnight, features six hours of the Long John
Nebel/Candy Jones Show. John has been a close friend of mine for
many years, and I cannot count the number of hours we have faced each
other across microphones. I spoke with him about an experiment, and
he agreed to cooperate.

That night, the show featured James Pyczynski, a self-styled
"psychic" from Pittsburgh who had just returned from a visit to Canada,
where the *Toronto Daily Star* interviewed him and he was part of a startling demonstration on CBL radio. During the broadcast, people had
phoned in reporting that strange things were happening. And he was at
WMCA to see if the same results would be forthcoming. I was to arrive
an hour later to meet this boy wonder.

Pyczynski was one of those innocent victims of supernatural gifts
who didn't understand what was happening, but he told the audience
he'd had to drop out of X-ray school because weird things kept happening to the films and machinery and he was afraid of what might befall
the other students if he continued there.

Almost as soon as Pyczynski started talking, the telephone lit up on
all its six lines. Here is a list of some of the wonderful things reported by
listeners to that May 16 program:

1. A shower head bent out of shape.
2. A container of milk burst.

3. Several cats began howling and running about in an agitated manner.

4. A clock began running at superfast speed.

5. A television set turned on by itself.

6. Parts fell off a stuffed animal.

7. A refrigerator stopped operating.

8. Two mirrors cracked.

9. A clock, not running for years, had begun running when Geller was on television the day before; it had then stopped again. It started running once more as Pyczynski began talking.

10. Two reports came in of flickering lights.

11. Two calls reported loud noises, one saying a radiator had begun knocking though it was turned off.

12. A spaniel started sneezing loudly.

13. A window cracked.

14. A watchband fell off a watch.

15. A crucifix and a religious picture fell off a wall.

16. A light-bulb exploded.

17. An air-conditioner quit dead.

18. A toilet bowl was reporting gurgling for the entire time Jim was on.

19. Toilet paper fell off the roll.

20. In *one* report, a record turntable started going, a dog began howling, and a neighbor's chandelier fell.

21. All the lights in one house went out.

22. A radio tuner moved from another station to the WMCA frequency.

23. A piggy-bank cracked open and pennies rolled out.

24. An alarm clock was being wound, and the spring broke.

And much more.

When, an hour into the program, I made my official speaking entrance, the telephone board went dark instantly as I revealed the whole thing had been a hoax to prove a point. Jim Pyczynski is my full-time assistant, and had posed as a psychic.

It was now very evident how Geller had obtained such wonderful results with remote-control methods. First, people were calling in to "get in on a good thing." Second, some were reporting perfectly ordinary events that now took on the dress of supernatural happenings. Third, others were reporting events that had already taken place but had gone unnoticed until now. The cracked mirrors and windows were probably in this latter group.

The very next day, Jim and I were sitting in a New York restaurant eating breakfast when the coffee urn beside him gave a roar and expired with great bursts of steam and lots of hissing. Jim just looked at me with a shrug.

"Can't help it," he said, "these things just seem to happen when I'm around!"

I didn't humor him with an answer. But the following day, when my car lost its fan belt on the New Jersey Turnpike—while Jim was driving—I began to have second thoughts!

Early in 1975, the well-known magician and writer Milbourne Christopher, appearing on television and radio across the United States to plug his latest book, *Mediums, Mystics and the Occult* (Crowell, 1975) tried his own hand at creating havoc at home. Says Christopher:

> During a radio interview in Chicago on June 15, I announced that broken watches would start in many listeners' homes at my command. The response was immediate. Ed Swartz, host of the WIND phone-in show, was amazed. He took careful notes as twenty-two callers described what had happened. Not only had broken wristwatches been activated, but antique timepieces, untouched for as long as thirty-five years, started ticking, and a long-silent grandfather clock in an attic chimed. An excited man reported the pilot light on his oven had gone out earlier; his landlord refused to fix it over the weekend. "When Mr. Christopher said 'Start,' I ran to the kitchen, and the light was burning brightly!"
>
> Thirty-three calls reporting phenomena came to WGR-TV in Buffalo when I appeared on the midday news. One grateful listener thanked me during a show with David Newman at WXYZ-Radio in Detroit for repairing the broken fan-timer in his car. A caller told Mel Martin at WTOL-TV in Toledo that, as I spoke, the frame of his bicycle, which had been twisted in an accident, suddenly straightened.
>
> Forty-five watches started and twenty-six spoons bent in Cleveland while I was a guest on the WEWS-TV "Morning Exchange." Similar occurrences took place in the homes of Pittsburghers tuned to Jack Wheeler on WEEP-Radio and Marie Torre on KDKA-TV. A woman phoned Mike Levine at KDKA-Radio to report that when I said "Bend," her grandmother's golden wedding ring, misshapen for years, became round again.
>
> To date I seem to have triggered "phenomena" in more than a thousand homes. At the start of every show I stated emphatically that I was not a psychic and did not have any supernormal powers.

That last sentence is most significant. The believers were so desperate that they even accepted miracles by a confessed conjuror! I think the point is well proven by Mr. Christopher.

In *Der Spiegel*, a West German publication, the "remote-control" mystery has been further explained. I quote from a translation published in the *Hong Kong Standard* of March 4, 1974: "Human gullibility plays a major role in all psi-demonstrations such as Uri Geller's. This was clearly proven in another recent television program where an actor simply played about with a fork in front of the camera. Promptly from all over the reception area viewers phoned and wrote in with reports of knitting needles and false teeth being bent, piles of pennies falling over and cats getting excited—just as happened when 13 million television sets were tuned in to the Geller programme."

During May 1975, millions of television viewers in the United States saw Geller on the Mike Douglas show plugging his "autobiography." During the program, he ventured into the audience to bend keys, and without his even approaching the owners, some keys bent over. Though I'd appeared on the Douglas show some time before, to duplicate some of Uri's "miracles," I hadn't done anything like "remote-control" bending, and I was deluged with the usual let's-see-you-do-that letters and calls. Accordingly, I began injecting a spot in my college and personal appearance shows wherein I asked the audience to grasp their keys between their palms, repeat the magic words "Geller Lives!" and then examine their keys for bends. Fully one-tenth of the spectators report bends they were not previously aware of.

How come? Do I have the mysterious power to bend keys by some psychic force? I think not. If my reader will examine his or her keys, the probability is about 1 in 10 that a key or two will show at least some small deformation. The fact that Geller produces an occasional dramatic 30- or 40-degree bend under the same circumstances merely provides further proof that some people will go along with a good thing. Bending a key is, after all, not too difficult. I should know. I've been doing it for the past two years.

Geller's miracles travel well. On a whirlwind visit to Japan in February 1974, he taped a program for the Nippon Television Network in which he suggested that spoons would bend and watches start ticking again.

So swamped was the switchboard at NTV after the tape was played that its fuses blew out from the overload. Geller had called in live via long-distance telephone from Canada during the airing of its show, and when the local announcer declared, "His mind power is on," many Japanese viewers called in to say that their own teaspoons had bent and wrist watches long out of order had begun running again. But just as many other viewers called to say that nothing had happened to their spoons and watches; they called to say that Geller was nothing but an imposter.

But the television network was ecstatic. One of its officials raved, "Such a *great* show!" Ratings were 24.1 percent—the highest for that week. Japanese psychologist Soji Otani mused, "Whatever he does, the fantastic Japanese reaction underlines a very restless current state of Japanese mind."

One of Geller's latest wonders (though he was doing it long ago in his early Israeli stint, he has brought it back in full force now) is the old "starting-a-stopped-watch" gimmick. Mind you, that's not what he *calls* it. He says it is a demonstration of psychokinesis, whereby he can "fix" any "broken" watches. Can he, really? Let's see.

In May 1975, plugging his imaginatively titled book, *My Story*, Geller appeared on the "A.M. America" show on ABC television. I had been told that I would be given a three-minute telephone spot on the show (Geller insisted that no magician be present in the studio) and at the time I was told this—the day before—Geller had not been informed of the arrangement. Later that same day, I was called and told that my participation was canceled; Geller had threatened to do a walk-off if they went through with it. Again, Geller had bullied the media into doing things *his* way or not at all.

Since I was due in New York that day anyway on business, I dropped by the offices of ABC after the show to see what I could find out about conditions existing during his performance that morning.

The staff was full of wonder. Obviously they had never seen any of my television appearances (I'd been refused on another ABC show where Geller had appeared) and knew even less about my exposures of his tricks. I bent some keys for them, did some "telepathic" stuff à la Geller, and then made just one hand of a borrowed watch advance one hour exactly. They were impressed.

Then I asked them about the watches Geller had "fixed" on the show that morning. Where did they come from? There was a pause while everyone looked around.

One girl piped up, "We got them from around the studio." Another nodded in assent.

Then a third young lady offered: "Lots of people brought them in. They were really broken!"

But another interrupted with, "No, the prop department got them together."

There was eventual agreement that the prop men indeed supplied the watches for Geller to work on. But the important thing was this: No one really knew where the watches had originated! And they didn't seem to have made any effort to find out!

Later, playing a videotape of that same show, I heard the hostess say, "These have been gathered throughout the studio from a variety of sources." She was wrong, obviously, but quite innocently so.

Geller then tried "putting energy" into a watch after asking the hostess to assist by rubbing the watch with him. After a moment or two, he excitedly announced, "Yes! It's working."

The hostess was thunderstruck. She gasped and jammed it against her ear. "It's ticking!" she cried in a strangled whisper.

But then the host asking a bring-down question. "The big question here is, what was wrong with it?"

Uri quickly interjected, "These watches were brought by somebody else. They're not mine!" Then, "You see, it's very strange that they didn't start to work before *you* [the hostess] helped me."

Notice? Suddenly *all* the watches are said to be working, and at no time did anyone check to listen to any of them to see if they were already ticking!

"Now, there's no possibility that simply jarring the watch could, in a sense, cause it to wind internally without touching the stem?" the hostess asked.

"Well, let me tell you this," countered Uri. "Some people, mainly the magicians who are against me, say that if you shake a watch it will start ticking, or if you warm up the oil inside. It's really a ridiculous thing. But some watches—I mean—are with me—I mean, many of them. I don't know what was wrong with *this* watch. Maybe it has missing parts, or maybe it was totally broken inside, and it did start working! You see? So . . ."

The hostess interrupted. She had been picking up the *other* watches, and had listened to one. "This one is *ticking*!" she said, looking a bit bewildered.

"It started?" Geller exclaimed with an expansive smile.

She still looked as if she had missed something important in the process.

They were interrupted by a phone call from a viewer. But Uri wasn't to be put off. He hastened to take advantage of her discovery that a watch still on the table was already ticking.

"Let me see it. Look! This is totally—I mean, there's no glass on it—Ah—Ah—It's totally squashed in. You can see it yourself!"

No one looked very enthusiastic over the miracle.

(Later, the office at ABC informed me that this watch only ticked for a few seconds, then stopped.)

Finally the caller was on the air. She reported that a fifty-five-year-old watch she had been stroking had started ticking just then. She explained that it had been fixed about a year ago, but kept "quitting," and had been sitting in a drawer for six months. Now it was ticking!

Okay, how does he do it? A few questions of your local watch repairman would reveal the "secret" right away. Any watch that has been lying still until it stopped, or any watch that has the balance wheel and escapement intact, will start *ticking* as soon as it is jarred at all. Whether it will *continue* to work is a different matter altogether. Uri doesn't fix watches; he just does what any child can do by picking up the watch. It's that easy. He refers to them as "broken" and says they are now "fixed." Not so.

Notice that he tried to produce the impression that the first watch might have parts missing or be smashed inside. But on many television spots he has insisted that he cannot start watches that have missing parts and has become quite angry when supplied with such watches.

It remained for David Marks and Richard Kammann, writing for the official organ of the New Zealand Broadcasting Company, to properly test the watch nonsense. They reported in the May 17, 1975, issue of the *New Zealand Listener*:

> . . . we interviewed six jewellers in Dunedin. It turns out that many or most stopped watches and clocks are not really broken, but are jammed in some way. Perhaps the oil has flowed to one side, or there is dust in the oil, or there is some other minor fault that only requires a cleaning and overhaul. The watch-men told us that a little winding, shaking, rotating, and especially warming the oil by holding the watch in your hand may be all that is needed to get it going again—temporarily.
>
> These seem to be just the same physical things that a person would normally do when he got out a watch to concentrate on it, thinking "work, work, work" as Uri instructs him over the radio.
>
> We challenged the jewellers to see how many watches they could start this way, without opening the watch. In one week, and with over 100 watches, they reported an astonishing success rate of 57 percent. Could the jewellers have been exaggerating or using some special expertise? We sent out a few students to "fix" broken watches, and out of 16 watches tried, 14 of them started, and seven have kept going for at least four to five days.

I congratulate these two gentlemen. They have applied a little common sense and a few well-placed questions to solve a simple problem.

The "A.M. America" show, on ABC-TV out of New York, has used Geller as a guest frequently before. When the psychic superstar made an apearance on an earlier broadcast, Felix Greenfield of New York, one of Geller's major detractors, was consulted by the people at ABC-TV on how to design controls for the tests.

When a young lady named Donna, who was in charge of arrangements for the early-morning show, arrived at the studio at 5:50, Geller was already there! The show didn't start until 7:00, but Geller told her he wanted to supervise the "can" test, in which ten film cans were to be carefully sealed, one containing a simple object. Geller sat there while she taped the cans shut, and it was obvious to her that he knew which can was the special one. She excused herself and called Greenfield.

Greenfield's answer was simple. He told her to switch the special can, and retape them all, without letting Geller know that she had done so. She did, and when the program went on the air Geller failed to find the right can.

But there's more to it than that. You see, Geller was supposed to find all of the empty cans, one after the other. The drama in determining nine empty cans and ending up with the one full one is obvious. But the second can he pointed to and said was empty turned out to be the full one. Obviously a bad failure? It would seem so, but we have forgotten to use the convoluted logic applicable in these matters. You see, as a caller soon informed the host of the show, that had to be considered a *success* or more correctly, a "negative success"—because chances were very small that Geller would fail so early in the guessing game! Remember: When he wins, he wins; when he loses, he wins!

After all, if astronaut Edgar Mitchell can use this logic, why can't everyone?

On the Channel 9 (WOR-TV) "Straight Talk" show in May 1975, Geller "fixed" a watch belonging to co-hostess Fran Rothstein, who was wearing the watch at the time simply as a piece of jewelry. She gave it to Geller to use on the show, and sure enough, though the stem was missing altogether and the watch did not run, it began working regularly, she thought, after a treatment by the wonder-worker. Fran reports that she wore it for several days, and it continued to work for that period until she took it in to Sidney Siegel, a watchmaker in the area whom she knew well. He repaired it properly by installing a new winding stem and mainspring.

But doesn't that mean Geller actually fixed her watch? Hardly. Fran, under careful questioning, revealed that she didn't bother to determine whether or not the watch was ticking when she gave it to Geller, nor did anyone else. And when she put it on her wrist, it did the same thing it had been doing all along—it ticked intermittently, and stopped again. It was useless as a timepiece. Mr. Siegel explained: "As long as the escapement is free, as hers was, the watch will tick whenever moved or jarred. It will run for anywhere from a few seconds to half an hour, or, if the watch spring is broken at certain positions, it may run for half a day. This just happens all the time. It's no miracle at all."

The watch business posed no problem at all for Professor Juritz of Cape Town, South Africa. After the Geller episode there, he managed to do it himself. He had offered Geller a number of broken watches, as he'd been asked to, but Uri objected when he found they were really *broken,* and refused them. Before the test, he examined every one carefully, and finally accepted one he was satisfied with. He shook a *stopped* watch, and it began ticking. Then he quickly wound it a few turns surreptitiously and handed it over to be examined. Some less observant souls there were of the impression that he had *fixed a broken watch.* Not at all.

So the old watch trick is just that—the old watch trick. And not very good, at that. Ho hum.

Magicians can't really get much mileage out of the watch trick, but they are using the key-bending trick everywhere. Every magic shop sells manuscripts telling how to do it, and the kids vie with one another for a new way to "do a Geller." Ali Bongo, the English prestidigitator who has fought Geller in his country, recently came out with a bright idea that makes it a cinch for any amateur to perform key-bending as well as Uri ever did.

It is interesting to note that, prior to the Geller phenomenon, had one of the magic fraternity published a manuscript describing "How to Bend Keys for Fun and Profit," no one would have bothered to buy it. As a magic trick, used for performance purposes, it is a dismally bad item. The premise is bad, the whole conception is worse. It lacks all the charm and "story" of a classic illusion, and would have been laughed out of any of the conjuring periodicals as a failure.

Yet now, since Geller has clambered to fame over the ruins of a ruptured logic and in spite of at least a residue of common sense that must be left in the world of science, conjurors all over the world have rushed to get in on the glory, and catalogs that deal with mail-order wonders have been full of devices and methods of bending keys, nails, and spoons. But where even the ones "in the know" have failed is in assuming that there are "gimmicks" of a mechanical nature used by Geller to bend the metals and minds of his audiences. There are none, and even a supposed "secret chemical" (rumored to be a "metallic halide," probably mercuric chloride or mercuric nitrate) that can effectively soften metals is said to be used by the Israeli wizard.

There is one *possible* "gimmick." Geller had a huge belt buckle made in New York's Greenwich Village early in 1973, shortly after his arrival on this side of the ocean. It has slots at either side, suitable for inserting a key for bending purposes. It would have been excellent as a tool to assist in the key trick, but Geller seems to have given up wearing that particular buckle in recent months, perhaps because a chap at one of the television stations called attention to it off the air and made Uri a bit uncomfortable.

Concerning the "chemical" approach, I might say that if such a compound or process existed that would soften metals without heat, it would be worth literally millions, and we'd have been spared the entire Geller episode. He would have retired a rich man. Science has sought such a process for a century now, and the preposterous claims that mercury compounds are employed for this trick are easily dismissed when it is realized that treatment with such a substance leaves the metal coated with bright mercury and in the form of an amalgam, a crumbly grayish mass of completely altered metal. Again, uninformed persons who cannot produce a single real example of the phenomenon described are responsible for such misinformation. And Geller laughs himself silly at the stupid tack the investigation has assumed.

At the moment I write this, Geller has been reduced to only three claims to fame. One, he "fixes" "broken" watches; two, he causes things to happen in people's houses when he appears on television and radio; three, he rants, "Let the magicians perform under scientifically controlled conditions, like I did!" Well, it's time to come up with another set of miracles, Uri. We can fix the watches. We can make people go crazy at home. And we now know that you performed under anything but scientific conditions for the scientists. Can you still fool the journalists? Read the next chapter and find out.

13

He Didn't Fool Them in Israel!

Many a hoax, intended to have a fleeting effect or no effect at all, has attained gigantic proportions of influence. Though exposed time and again, it has refused to die; though interred at one time, it has been exhumed at a later date with confusing results or worse. Whether the public likes to be fooled, as the great Barnum declared, or is fooled for other reasons, it always has been. And it probably always will be.

—Curtis D. MacDougall, *Hoaxes*

In the February 20, 1974, issue of *Haolam Hazeh*, a well-known Hebrew weekly magazine published in Tel Aviv, the cover story was one that was designed to put Uri Geller out of business in Israel for good. In English the article's title reads: "Uri Geller Twirls the Entire World on His Little Finger; Only His Closest Acquaintances Know His Methods." With the permission of that publication, I obtained a translation by Dr. Sarah Feinstein of Chicago, who works with the Hebrew Alliance and is quite familiar with current use of the language. What follows is perhaps a bit stilted in English, since we have made every attempt to retain the same wording where possible and the identical semantic content as far as could be done.

How this article did not come to the attention of the Western press, I cannot tell; perhaps the fact that it appeared only in Hebrew was a good enough reason for its missing notice here. It is a shocking document, in that it reveals to just what extent Geller went in his own country to deceive his own people.

There are a few errors here that occur when descriptions of Uri's methods are brought up; some methods are just not possible, and others are less than likely. It is in the description of the personalities involved that the article has its greatest value.

The last section, "Geller's Eleven Tricks," which deals with the basic deceptions used by Shipi and Uri in their act, has been edited a bit (for clarity). Otherwise, the phrasing is essentially the same as that given me.

I don't think Uri and Shipi are going to like this.

Adolf Hitler had a Jew, probably the only one who merited being an exception. Hitler believed in him with a blind faith. This was the magician

Hirschmann* who changed his name to Erik Jan Hanussen. Hanussen used to perform before Hitler, the chief of police, and the nobleman Heldorff. He used to do all kinds of magic tricks and to tell them their future. He would also move objects from place to place across the room without touching them. Hitler himself was ready to vouch for these special gifts, which he considered to be supernatural. The three Nazis used to take counsel with Hanussen, and more than once he determined their courses of action.

Jan Hanussen succeeded in fooling the magicians of Germany who claimed they had special powers, until one day he made the mistake of his life. Twenty-four hours before the burning of the Reichstag [1933], he predicted this conflagration with much theatrics. When one of his Nazi customers heard this, he remembered that he himself had told Jan Hanussen the plan to burn the building. Several days later, Hanussen's body was found in the woods riddled with bullets; he had been executed in accordance with a personal command from Adolf Hitler. But Hitler continued to be a believer, even at the height of the war, and he ordered the performance of certain experiments in telepathy to examine the possibility of communicating with submarines in the midst of the ocean.

A Contrived Picture from Italy

When Uri Geller, the young Israeli described here, was twelve years old, his mother married for the second time an Israeli who at the same time opened a hotel in Nicosia, Cyprus. Uri went there with his mother and his stepfather and one evening his stepfather told him the story of Jan Hanussen. Ten years later, Geller turned himself into an Israeli version of Hanussen. He had many astonishing feats that he performed, and everyone who saw him, or who came in contact with him, immediately developed a certain respect and awe. However, when Geller began to exaggerate, and crossed the very fine boundary between legend and rationality, he defeated himself—exactly as his model, Hanussen, had done previously.

About three years ago, Uri Geller succeeded in dividing the Israeli people into two camps. There were detractors and believers. He saw in this tactic a very fine publicity stunt, and saw his fame increasing with every exaggeration. He also went to Italy, then sent from there to the [Israeli] newspapers a faked photograph, in which he is apparently seen in the company of the Italian motion picture actress Sophia Loren, in order to "prove" that he actually met her. This was the beginning of the end of the Uri Geller legend in Israel.

The man who was able to fill three assembly halls to the point where there was standing room only found within one evening that he was appearing in a second-rate nightclub. His admirers and his detractors agreed

---

* This conflicts with information from other sources, who say that his name was Hermann Steinschneider. But it is obviously the same man, regardless of what name he used.

that the era of Uri Geller had passed. However, an ambitious man like Geller, who had tasted the success, the publicity, and the easy profit, was not going to give up that easily.

A Student of the Shin Beth

Shortly after this, he left Israel for a while, and several weeks after that he again appeared in the headlines, this time in the headlines of the entire world. With this renewed fame on a very large international scale, Uri Geller returned to a prominent position in the Israeli newspapers as well. One columnist, Ephraim Kishon, a social critic for the newspaper "Ma'ariv," expressed himself sharply against all those persons who rejected this young man. Professor Amnon Rubinstein wrote in the newspaper "Ha'aretz" a series of articles in which he analyzed the image of Uri Geller, though he did not take a personal position or opinion on the matter. It was mentioned that the Israeli Ambassador to London during Uri's visit there prevented him from bending a fork, contending that it was the property of the State of Israel. This amusing item was covered extensively in the press.

In Israel today, however, his friends and relatives, his girl friends and his managers, and all others who worked with him are ready to swear by all that is dear to them that Geller is a cheat and a liar; and they are able to demonstrate with their own hands all of his tricks that he used in order to create his reputation. According to them, Geller learned personal data—special obscure details and information about individuals (both true and false)—which he used to support his claims to special powers of divination.

Uri Geller, born of a father who is an officer in the Israeli Armed Forces, told all who asked that he was born of a circus family and in one place claimed that he was born in Cyprus. But the simple truth is that he is an Israeli, and that is an indisputable fact. He traveled to Cyprus with his mother and his stepfather when he was twelve years old, and that was the first time he had left Israel.

Itzhaak Saban, one of Uri's close friends, has revealed that Geller used to use him as a confederate in the audience. He used to sit in the front row during Uri's performance and give him all kinds of signals, by means of motions, in order to make Uri succeed. On one occasion, hearing him tell so many lies about his performance, Itzhaak literally pressed him to the wall and forced him to admit that the entire performance was contrived. Uri had not bothered to tell anyone that some of these techniques he used were learned from the members of the Shin Beth,* who had been quartered at his father's hotel in Cyprus.

A Book About Magicians

Several times, Uri maintained in his interviews with the press that even as a young student in elementary school he had begun to feel his

---

* An Israeli intelligence-gathering organization like the CIA.

special powers and was able to read the thoughts of his teachers and his fellow-students. However, the actual truth about the beginning of this process in his life is told by his very close friend Hannah Shtrang. She is today an office worker for the Motorola Company in Israel.

"Uri was the counselor at camp of my little brother Shipi. The friendship between the two began shortly after that. My little brother always had very strange ideas, and Uri would tell him from time to time about a book which he had come across that told about magic and magicians, and the two boys decided to make a business out of it. Uri was then about twenty-one years old, and he was pretty depressed. It was only a few months after the termination of his army service. He had been thrown out of an officer's training corps and also from the paratroopers.* He was very deeply hurt by these defeats. He had been rejected and he took it very hard, particularly because his father was a famous soldier and his sole ambition was to prove that he could be as successful as his father.

"My brother Shipi was at that time only fourteen years old, but Uri believed in him and my brother brought him into our home, which is where I met him.

"There is a great deal of personal charm in him. He was a very good-looking young man. A romance started between us and has continued until this present time. When Uri left Israel to conquer the world, he took me with him. After several weeks I was forced to return to my job, which I did not want to lose.

"Uri and Shipi performed together all forms of tricks. The basis of all these tricks was that my brother used to sit in the audience and pass signals to Uri that they had practiced beforehand. They began their performances in small living-room parties, particularly of students. They would receive forty to seventy pounds. However, when they realized that the audience was very excited and enthusiastic, they decided to change this mere cooperative relationship between the two of them and to go into business.

"They turned to a manager, Baruch Cotni, the owner of a stage production company, and they auditioned for him. They convinced him that the entire country would be wild about the talented Uri with his 'supernatural' powers. Uri represented Shipi as his younger brother."

(Uri's father said that he has only one son, in speaking to the reporter of this newspaper.)

Little by little, the Uri Geller mania began to make waves with the Israeli public. As a result of publicity in a prominent newspaper, which praised him sky-high, he began to do three or four shows a day.

One of Geller's conditions for performances was that his "brother" would always get a seat in a front row or at least in the middle of the second row. So said Baruch Cotni. He went on to explain that once he caught Shipi making the agreed-upon signals and he pointed this out to Uri.

The next day, in addition to Shipi, a young woman appeared who was very cute but not really a beauty. Geller made a new condition now, that

---

* This is the article wording provided me by the translator.

this woman had to sit beside Shipi in the audience in a special seat. This woman was Hannah, Shipi's sister, and she began to be a part of the act, passing signals to Uri on stage.

Hannah, who was Uri's friend and still is (she says that the other girls in Uri's life have been mere decoys, and that he always returns to her), maintains that Uri has very special supernatural powers but that he also uses a great deal of trickery. "I used to help him with his tricks during appearances," says Hannah.

In the meantime, [Geller's] chauffeur admitted to many tricks that he maintained Uri had instructed him about. He said that Uri confessed, in a heart-to-heart talk with him, that everything in the act was just bluff.

"Uri is a good fellow. If he has driven the world crazy, then he is a very talented guy!" says his chauffeur. "I know all of his tricks very well, and I can even appear in his place if I wish to. But Uri has a very special, unique talent. When something does not succeed for him, he always manages to get out of it. He comes away clean from any situation and he controls people in a total manner."

Saban, Uri's very good friend, is one of the only men to whom Uri has [ever] confided that "all" of his performance was based upon fakery. "In front of all his other friends and even his parents, Uri has always maintained that he has supernormal powers. Among his very close friends, he claims that though he has supernatural powers, he sometimes uses some trickery."

To Explode the Balloon

Success gave Uri a swelled head. He used to go to his manager with continual demands for much more money than the contract called for. "He would come to me two or three times a week," says Baruch Cotni, "with demands of two or three hundred pounds for each performance. There was no end to it."

Uri's demands finally caused a rift between the two, and Uri found himself without a manager. He found a new agent, Micky Feld. Cotni, angered by all this, decided to expose the Geller mess once and for all. He searched about and found a magician, an ordinary magician who worked the bar mitzvahs. His name was Ayalon.

The recipe for success was exactly the same, and within a short period of time there was great excitement throughout the land. Not only had Ayalon mastered with fantastic success all the original tricks of Uri Geller, but Ayalon himself began to inform the newspapers that his story was similar to that of Geller's—that he was the real thing. This began to pose a threat to Geller's reputation.

There were those in the public, however, who would not "swallow the frog" of two supermen with invincible powers. They decided to explode this balloon by any means at their disposal.

Four young men, who were workers at a computer center in Jerusalem, used to come to every performance of Uri Geller and bring with them binoculars and telescopes. They would follow his every gesture and movement with great attention, and by these means they were able to discover his tricks. They began, then, to interrupt his performances by calling out from the audience. About this time there was a decision by the producer of the popular Israeli TV show "Boomerang" to build a program around Uri Geller, with audience participation. Somehow the Jerusalem quartet was able to infiltrate the audience on that occasion, and as soon as Geller began to play his guessing games—particularly the guessing of some writing on a blackboard that he had not been allowed to see—the four demanded loudly that the performance be conducted in the dark. This was so that no person in the audience would be able to signal to Geller the information written upon the blackboard. Uri Geller refused this condition, so the show disintegrated and was not telecast.

However, the greatest blow that Uri suffered came from [a] Professor Klassen of the University of Tel Aviv. He is a professor of physics and also an avid amateur magician so well accomplished in the art that he is looked upon by his friends as an excellent performer. Klassen was present at [a Geller] performance and was able to identify most of his tricks. He was incensed. "What I'm upset about is that there appears to be here a swindle of this audience," the professor said. "If Geller would say that he is simply a magician, I wouldn't care, because then he would be regarded as a fine magician. For him to claim that he has special divine powers is lying and cheating, and can bring about a great deal of damage."

Klassen invited the producer of Uri's show, Micky Feld, to his own house, where he performed for Feld all of Uri's routine. Feld, who was one of Geller's converts, was absolutely stunned and shaken. However, he refused, because of business reasons, to expose Geller.

At a certain point, Ayalon the Magician, Geller's "double," began to feel the ground hot under his own feet. He decided, therefore, to change his statements to the press, and at a special press conference which he called, he said, "I did all that I could in order to show Uri Geller to be a liar and a cheat." At the same time, he revealed that all of his tricks and those of Geller were nothing but simple tricks that one can learn from consulting a good instruction book for magicians.

The False Messiah

Danny Pelz, the showman who worked at this time with Uri Geller says, "Until the whole thing blew up for him, after the episode with Sophia Loren, Uri Geller had earned more than a quarter of a million pounds in Israel and purchased a brand-new Peugeot 404 and a luxury penthouse in the north of Tel Aviv. We, from our side, know all the lies. We have much proof of them. And we also helped him to perpetuate some of these lies.

"When Nasser of Egypt died, Uri was in the midst of his performance and we notified him of this news through the curtains at the back of the stage. The audience, naturally, did not know a thing about it. As soon as we conveyed the news to him, he exploited this information in most theatrical manner. He appeared to be fainting, and called for a doctor. A doctor volunteered from the audience and came up on the stage. Uri asked him to take his pulse right in front of the crowd of seven hundred people. Uri said to him, "I feel terrible. Very, very bad. I feel bad because I think Nasser is dying right now. Right this minute." Naturally, immediately after the performance the audience left the theater and found out about Nasser's death. Thousands of people were once again convinced that Uri Geller was a prophet."

This event is paralleled by one that took place at Stanford Research Institute in California when Geller had attempted to impress two scientists sent there by the U.S. Department of Defense, which had heard rumors of Geller's wonderful powers. Uri had excused himself from the lunch table and left the group. Suddenly he reappeared, looking very distraught, and warned them, "If any of you are planning your return to Washington today, don't do it! I have a premonition that there will be a serious plane crash!"

As the group left the restaurant later, they discovered that there had indeed been a plane crash. But the marvel was less than it seemed. It was pointed out that the news of the accident had already been reported and was even in the newspapers on the street at the time Geller left the lunch table. Even the scientists of SRI were lacking the charity to ascribe this "premonition" to supernatural abilities.

He [Pelz] explains, "Geller has several special attributes which help him to deceive his audiences. He has very powerful hands, and eyes like an eagle. He can see things at a distance and from the side that most men cannot. He also knows how to draw things in great detail after having seen them, briefly, but once. But such things can be studied and mastered without too much trouble."

[Pelz] also says that he served as "assistant" to Uri in the audience when the regular confederate could not be there to perform.

Uri's girl friend, Hannah, also had something to say about this. "Uri and Shipi used to train for long hours together, even after he was already famous, drilling together in the drawing and reproduction of certain objects after they cast only a quick glance at them. My brother Shipi knows, too, how to draw them exactly."

Saban [the chauffeur] is ready himself to duplicate all of Geller's tricks, and reacts with a wide know-it-all grin when mentioning the comments and decisions of the world-famous scientists who studied Geller. For the reporter of this newspaper, Saban succeeded during the interview in moving the hands of his wristwatch without touching it in any way. After doing it he explained that it was done by means of sleight of hand. "When I turn over your watch in the palm of your hand," he said, "I was able by quickness of the hand to move the hands of the watch secretly." This trick, which at the moment is driving the world crazy, he learned from Geller.

Note that even the Israeli reporter falls into the trap of misreporting what the performer has done! He says the watch hands were moved "without touching it in any way" — then reports that Saban turned over the watch *while handling it!*

Uri Geller announces that he has been blessed with a facility that is undisputed, and that is the ability to read thoughts. However, despite the protestations of the members of the Association of Parapsychologists of Israel, asking that he meet with them to be tested, he has always managed to evade them. There is the assumption that he is the greater authority on the subject, and not they. A Professor Bender, a parapsychologist in Tel Aviv, absolutely denies that this man has any sort of talent such as he claims. According to the professor, even those people who have this facility are not always successful in reading the thoughts of people, and only in certain situations and without repeatability.*

An additional talent which Geller was able to acquire is hypnotism. There is no doubt that he is able to hypnotize, but he does it in a very amateurish way, and his methods are even dangerous. The truth is that practically anyone is able to hypnotize another after some training, but not everyone should be authorized to do this, because it is possible to put the subject in some danger. At one of his performances, Geller asked for a subject to come up on the stage with the purpose of hypnotizing him and causing him to stop smoking. The subject came to the stage and Uri asked him, "Is it true that you want to stop smoking? Is it true that you get nauseous from smoke? Is it true that you will not smoke anymore?" To these questions the man answered yes, and when Uri gave him a cigarette he began to cough and to express distaste with it. He threw it away with revulsion.

However, a quarter of an hour later, one of the people in the audience called out to Uri that the man was smoking. And sure enough, there was the man sitting in the audience smoking with great enjoyment. This brought the audience to the point where they were booing Geller.

A special power that Uri claims to have is that of telekinesis. This means the moving and breaking of objects without touching them. Yet it is a fact that one of the forks that Geller broke during a demonstration in Europe was tested in a laboratory and was found to contain traces of special chemicals.† And the movement of the hands of the watch or clock are easily attributed to sleight-of-hand motion. The "fixing" of "broken" watches and clocks in the homes of many people who view him on television can easily be explained. Every watchmaker, even a beginning watchmaker, knows and will tell you that when you take a watch that has been inactive — not working for a long period of time — it will begin to function for a few seconds or moments as soon as it is jarred the least bit.

---

* Here's Rule #1 again!
† See the end of this chapter, trick number 8.

The promise that Geller made to the English in London to move the hands of Big Ben, the famous tower clock, remains in the realm of a promise.

Counterintelligence

In the heyday of Geller's performances in Israel, he performed his tricks before professors from the Weizman Institute. It was a regular type of performance, but when they asked if they could frisk him he refused. This fact, however, did not prevent him from claiming that he was fairly frisked by the scientists from the institute. Professor Klassen assembled the scientists sometime later and asked the young son of Amos Deshalit to give him, Klassen, his watch, and he caused the watch to advance by sleight of hand.

Again, a performance was arranged by the counterintelligence of Israel for one of their bases in Israel. This aroused the interest and enthusiasm of many people in the counterintelligence. Uri managed to exploit this very well. At a later time, he maintained that he had been frisked, and that he was checked out by the security people and was deemed to have divine powers.

He began boasting that he had been invited by the intelligence forces in Israel and by the Army to carry out certain tests "which no one else would be able to carry out." He maintained this before many of his audiences of thousands of people, for example, by saying that he had piloted a Phantom jet for the Army by means of mind power alone, without a pilot. The Security Department invited him for a short interview, and he was warned not to make these claims any longer. He understood the implications involved, and stopped doing it immediately.

Uri was able to fool the renowned scientists at the Stanford Research Institute in California in the United States. After several experiments which these scientists conducted, Geller continued to maintain that he had supernatural power and that [this] had been proven in an indisputable manner. The American newspaper the "New York Times" reprimanded these scientists and wrote, "Instead of conducting these experiments you should have brought regular magicians who might have been able to explain to you the secrets that are the basis of Geller's tricks."

Of all those persons close to Uri, it seems that only two of them really believed in his powers with an absolute trust. These are his father and his second wife. They say, "Uri Geller has special powers that no other man alive has. If only he would know how to utilize them and not be driven to using simple magic tricks in addition to the powers he really has, then he would have many more people who would believe in him without a shadow of a doubt."

Geller's Eleven Tricks

Here are the eleven basic tricks with which Geller fooled people in Israel and elsewhere.

(1) Reading Numbers Written on a Blackboard

Here Geller has a member of the audience write a two- or three-digit number in large script upon the board, so that it can be seen by the audience. Geller has been blindfolded with a black handkerchief. After the audience has seen the number, it is erased and Geller removes his blindfold, then reproduces the number exactly. It is done by means of a code transmitted by his confederate in the front row. Here is the code:

1. Touch left eye.
2. Touch right eye.
3. Scratch nose.
4. Lick lips.
5. Touch left ear.
6. Touch right ear.
7. Cover wristwatch.
8. Pull the chin.
9. Chin resting on hand.
10. Elbow resting on right leg.

If this is, indeed, the Geller code, it's a pretty bad one. Surely he and Shipi could have devised a better system. But if it works—and it obviously does—then it is quite satisfactory!

(2) The Blindfold Drive

In this stunt, Geller would drive a car around the streets while blindfolded with his handkerchief. [I cannot go into detail here though the original article did, since the method described is precisely that used by the professional conjurors. My readers will forgive me, I trust.]

(3) Moving the Hands of a Watch

Geller takes a watch and causes it to advance or turn back an hour or so. There are two methods described. First, simple sleight of hand enables him to wind the "hack" forward or backward as he handles the watch, after which he looks at it, keeping the face away from the owner, and "verifies" the time. After apparently trying several times, Geller suddenly succeeds, as the face-down watch in the owner's hand is shown to have changed. In the second method, which only works with certain electronic watches, a small magnet that he bought in a Tel Aviv watchmaker's shop is used from its concealed place in his sleeve. This magnet is sold to be used for this purpose by the owner of the watch.

(4) Bending and Breaking Rings

Geller asks for rings, warning his audience not to bring expensive rings to the stage, since they may break. About twenty young girls rush up, and the rings are placed on a chair, Geller selects one, and puts it in the hand of one of the girls. After several tries, he finally seizes the ring from her hand as she opens it, cries, "That's it!" and rushes down into the audience to show the ring. It is broken or bent. It is done by his very strong hands as he goes into the audience.

I disagree. Such a "move" to break a ring is impossible. My personal observation of Geller has shown me that the girl on stage does not have a chance to see the broken ring and that Geller switches the original for a broken one as he rushes down to the audience.

(5) The Lie Detector
While Uri is blindfolded, a member of the audience stands up and is seen by the crowd. With the blindfold off, Uri then asks many people up on stage, including the chosen one. He shuffles them about, finally selecting the one person from the crowd. It is done by the confederate, who signals Geller when he is near the right person.

(6) Snapping Chains
Geller learned the trick, which only works about half the time, of breaking small chains as one breaks wrapping string.

Nope, I can't accept this either. I would like to see someone do *that* surreptitiously! There are other easy ways of doing this, and getting to the chain in advance is the easiest. David Berglas, England's prominent mental performer, wowed a BBC audience using welded steel chain (which, however, had been carefully inspected beforehand) and *breaking it at the specific link called for*! Figure *that* out!

(7) Drawing an Object
[Here, the article seems very unclear. The best I can make of it seems to be that Geller is able to use a "photographic-memory" stunt to reproduce a drawing only glanced at. It says that he got the routine in "an English book from a magic shop." I fail to see just what the effect of it is supposed to be.]

(8) Causing a Rise in Temperature
Geller calls a young girl up on stage and places a rolled-up pellet of aluminum foil in her hand. He suggests to her that it is getting very warm, so that she cannot hold it any longer. And she opens her hand to release the foil with a scream. It is a well-known magician's trick done with a chemical.

Yes, it is a very well-known trick, and one that should be taken off the market around the world, since it employs one of the most dangerous chemical compounds known. It is a *highly* poisonous substance, which can be absorbed through the skin and cause crippling and death— *especially to the performer*! I shall not describe it here, but simply assure my reader that it causes the foil to get so hot that it cannot be held. It is what chemists call an "exothermic reaction." It is my belief, incidentally, that this part of the performance is responsible for the silly stories that have circulated about certain "special chemicals" supposed to have been used to soften the spoons and keys that Geller bends. It simply will not work that way, and no one has yet been able to verify this dumb theory.

(9) Identification of Objects

In general, Geller used to peek at the crowd before his performance, and note those who took out objects from their pockets; and later would recite the objects to their owners. After he was caught at this, he was embarrassed, and insisted that the curtain be open before his performance, so he could not be accused of peeking through it. He developed a scheme whereby a confederate would hang around the box office, noting objects as people paid for their tickets. These objects, from their pockets and purses, were noted by the spy and the exact seat noted, so that Geller could call out the number and say what objects were carried.

(10) The Bending and Breaking of Metal

Geller used to exploit, whenever he could, the great strength in his hands, so that he would bend the key or spoon before it was examined. When the object was given to him before he could prepare it, he used a special chemical that he could smear on it after he put his fingers into his pocket. After one of his appearances, in a town called Naharia, Geller invited his cohorts to supper in a restaurant called Fin John, and when the waiter presented him with the bill Geller said he was known as a "cheapskate" and if he could bend the fork without touching it, would they forego the bill? The waiter agreed, and Geller, who had the chemical already in his hand, bent the fork. But because this was not done in an open place, his friends who were sitting close discovered the funny chemical smell from the fork.

(11) The Prick of a Needle

[Here is described an unclear trick in which it is claimed Geller used "hypnotism" to cause a spectator to be insensitive to the stab of a needle. I have no idea what is referred to, nor can any one of my translators solve the description.]

14

Alan Spraggett Throws Down the Gauntlet, Then the Towel

Homo vult decipi; decipiatur.

I first met Alan Spraggett some years ago on the "Long John Nebel Show" when it was on NBC radio. Spraggett had just written a book titled *The Unexplained* and I had appeared to counter some of the claims he was putting forth for various wonder-workers. Spraggett seemed to believe, as do most psychic investigators, that he was quite qualified to detect any trickery performed in his presence. By the end of the radio program, we each understood that there was a wide gulf between us when it came to judging these phenomena, *and* the qualifications necessary to judge them.

Spraggett authors a newspaper column that is syndicated throughout the United States and Canada; it is entitled "The Unexplained" as well. He is well-known in Canada and conducts a television show on the Global Television Network, "E.S.P.—Extra Special People." I was invited to be his guest during a visit to Canada in November 1974. Since my friend Walter Gibson—a confidant of Houdini who, under the nom de plume Maxwell Grant, created "The Shadow"—was to be a guest as well, I gladly accepted. But I expected that I would come under some considerable fire.

Spraggett had, a few days before, attended the annual Houdini séance at the Houdini Magical Hall of Fame Museum in Niagara Falls. At that (as usual, fruitless) attempt to recall the spirit of the famous magician, some rather strange events had occurred. A vase of flowers on a bookshelf had toppled over and a book had fallen open at a page displaying a poster of Houdini asking, "Do Spirits Return?" Spraggett had been less than enthusiastic over the occurrence, evidently suspecting that I'd had something to do with the event. He was right, and this is the first time that I've admitted it. But he was wrong as well. I had "seen him coming," as they say, and really gave him a demonstration of how a victim is pulled into the net.

My good friend Moses Figueroa was with me, as he has been for many important events in my life, and between us we set out to put Alan in a position where he *had* to arrive at certain conclusions.

Early in the day, we spirited away (if you will pardon the expression) a vase that held a huge bouquet of gardenias and carnations. In our motel room, we prepared it with a plasticine partition down the middle, so that water could be retained in either section. A matchstick "plug" was inserted near the bottom of the plasticine, so that if water were in one side, removal of the plug would allow the water to leak slowly from that side to the other, changing the balance. We placed the vase back into its original position, balancing it carefully with water in the back section, with a book opened and perched in the flowers out of sight. A small string was fastened to the plug and thence to a bead hanging beside the vase.

As the television lights were being set up, we put the master plan into action. Moses obtained a length of thread and we made sure that one of the technicians saw him trailing it behind him. I figured that everyone would be questioned afterward in order to dig up evidence, and I preferred that a false solution (all laymen think tricks are done with threads, anyway) would be easily available. It worked to perfection.

At the start of the séance, I was scheduled to perform one of the Houdini tricks—the escape from a sealed can full of water. I used the original equipment Houdini used, and Moses and I figured that the audience would be so captivated by the show that he would have ample time to remove the plug in the vase via the bead and string. That's exactly how it happened. As I was emerging, to applause, from the curtained cabinet, Moses reached for my robe and pulled the plug. We knew we had at least fifteen minutes before the vase would topple.

It proved to be much longer. As I sat at the table and listened to the medium drone on, I felt the stupid thing would never tumble. Reporters kept on getting in front of it, though they had been specifically asked not to, and Moses had a heck of a time keeping them clear. Finally I saw it begin to tilt, and Moses gave me the high sign. A minute after the medium asked for the third time for a sign from the departed, there was a gasp from the crowd as the entire thing leaned forward majestically and fell to the floor. It was a beauty of a trick, if I do say so myself.

But Spraggett was outraged, and on radio that night he mentioned my battle with Uri Geller, challenging me to "put up or shut up." If I could do the act, then I had better do it, he said. And he invited me to appear on the show; I accepted, but said I would not give a performance.

That Sunday, I arrived at the Global studio soaking wet from a heavy rain and met Mr. George Owen, a parapsychological "researcher," there. He astonished me with an accusation.

"We caught you, Mr. Randi! We saw what you did on that Mike Douglas TV show. You made a big mistake!"

I asked him what in the world he was talking about.

He explained, "When you did the trick with the film cans [he was referring to the bit using ten aluminum film cans in which the performer identifies the one can that contains a hidden object] you used that chap, your assistant that you came to Canada with the last time! We recognized him! He was your stooge!"

I got Owen a bit calmed down, and found he was claiming that the man who had sealed up the hidden object in the film can was the same person I'd visited him with about a year before! I was stunned. The person I had visited Canada with was my foster son, who was about five foot eight, had a mop of curly hair, and was seventeen years old! The person who appeared with me on the Douglas show was Roger Miller, who is hardly seventeen, is *much* taller and heavier, and does not any more resemble the kid than Charlie Chaplin resembles Robert Redford! (And I'd never met Roger Miller before in my life!) Yet George Owen had come up with this fantastic solution to my performance and was convinced of it.

A bit shaken by all this, I was welcomed to the control room at Global and dried off a bit. An interview was already under way and I watched it on the monitors. I was not particularly apprehensive, since I was not under any pressure to perform, and was there only to be interviewed.

Spraggett finished that show (they were taping for later playback) and, upon being told I'd arrived, said that he would take me next. I entered the studio, and we started in.

Spraggett began by giving me a big build-up, and then headed into the Geller matter. Though I'd said that I wasn't there to perform, but might do a demonstration of something Gellerish, he tried to high-pressure me into the whole act. I was angry. He had no right to expect me to produce the same as Geller when I was not given the option of "passing" and when he was obviously out to trap me—since with Geller he had approached the matter already believing. I decided to pull some of the real goods out of the hat.

Now, there is a technique to the "con" game that involves winning a little, then losing, then seeming to be ready to lose very big, in order to reel in the victim. I launched the attack.

First, Spraggett took from his desk two large silver soup spoons. They appeared to have been well worn at the tips, and they were antiques. He challenged me to bend them.

While he held on the handles, I stroked the bowls. He discarded one, and we concentrated on the other. He agreed that at no time did I put undue pressure on them. After a moment, the spoon suddenly became plastic, sheared off, and broke into two pieces. But Spraggett was not amused.

He "explained": "The spoon was bent as you were picking it up— uh—and—uh—this is a phenomenon of course of—in previously bending it so that there is a stress point, and then with a little bit of leverage, it separates quite neatly."

Me: "You mean, that's the way Geller does it?"

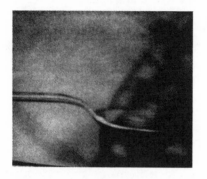

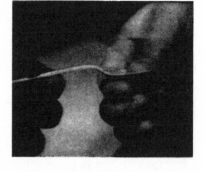

FIGURE 1

FIGURE 2

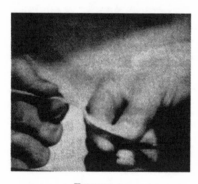

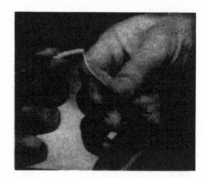

FIGURE 3

FIGURE 4

FIGURE 1. On the "ESP" show, Randi holds a carefully guarded spoon supplied by Alan Spraggett, the host. Note no fractures or kinks are visible in the spoon.

FIGURE 2. The spoon is lightly held by both persons; Spraggett's hand is on the left.

FIGURE 3. Rocked up and down and stroked lightly, the spoon is about to break.

FIGURE 4. The spoon begins to "melt" just above the bowl.

FIGURE 5. The spoon continues to bend plastically, held between thumb and forefinger.

FIGURE 6. The spoon finally parts, revealing a jagged fracture.

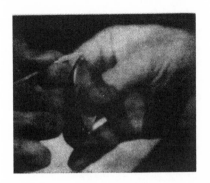

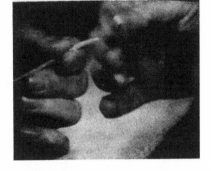

FIGURE 5   FIGURE 6

Alan: "No, but that's the way *you* did it!"

Me: "Oh, you say Geller *doesn't* do it that way?"

Alan: "Geller may—Well, let me put it this way. I have seen Geller . . . bend spoons and knives, and I said I was quite sure at the time, and have been ever since, that that was fraudulent . . ."

Then why, may I ask, if Spraggett was so convinced that the Geller thing was a fraud, did he ask me to try this "Geller test"? He said (see above) that Geller does *not* use the method he described, but that whatever thing he *does* do to the spoons is "fraudulent"! Pardon me if I'm confused at this point. Besides, Spraggett's description of the spoon trick I'd just done doesn't hold up when you examine the stills taken from the tape. (See Figures 1–6.) It would have been impossible to do what Spraggett described while he was holding the spoon, and he kept the spoons under *strict* control before and during the performance, of course.

I was ready now for Step 2.

Spraggett produced a nail from his pocket. Now those who have seen me on any number of television shows bending huge spikes and such will be confident that I could have easily done the same with the small nail Spraggett presented to me. It was a flimsy finishing nail about three inches long. But I had to swallow and look worried in order to get the hook in deeper. And it went in deep!

Spraggett explained that he had gone to a great deal of trouble "to protect myself, against people like you, who imply that all psychical researchers are nitwits . . ."

He said it, not me!

But I refused the nail, and he began to get back a bit of his color. He reached into his inner jacket-pocket and extracted what appeared to be a pre-stamped envelope, sealed with transparent tape. He described to me and to the viewers what he had done "to protect himself" concerning Geller.

"I went to great pains that he could not be aware of what was in the sealed envelope. I posted a guard at the door . . . He asked me to go away, anywhere I chose, use my own paper and draw something, put it in a sealed envelope and bring it back with me, which I did.

"Now, I've done the same here. He did not have any opportunity to eavesdrop. I posted a guard at the door. I used my own paper. I didn't even write on the desk surface for fear of some secret carbon. I was almost paranoid."

I commented, "Very good thinking!"

Spraggett continued, "I put it up against the wall and made the drawing. I put it in an opaque envelope and held the envelope up to the light [he demonstrated with the sealed envelope] to be sure it *was* opaque—and it *was*. Then, Geller took it—and I'm going to allow you to—and held it between his palms for ten seconds. Then I took it and put it in my pocket [he did this] and Geller reproduced the drawing virtually *exactly*."

Me: "In other words, you're saying that these conditions cover all the possibilities, and that your conclusion, therefore, is that—"

Alan: "No! No, what I'm saying is, let's see *you* do *that*. That's all I'm saying."

Me: "And if I *could* do it, what would you say?"

Alan: "I would be very impressed. I'd be *extremely* impressed."

Me: "But would you be impressed enough to say that I'm a psychic?"

Alan: "I don't know. I would have to consider that. But I would certainly say that you're a hell of a lot better magician than I *think* you are!"

Me: "Wait a minute. You say that Uri Geller is a psychic because he did this?"

Alan: "Well, let's see *you* do it!"

Me: "Now, wait a minute. I want to get a conclusion from you. You say that Uri Geller is a psychic because he did this. Now if *I* were able to do it, would you say *I'm* a psychic?"

Alan: You *do* it, and I'll say that the Amazing Randi has amazed me."

Me: "But you know, if I were able to do it, I would like to have a confession from *you*—that *I* have done as well as any psychic you've seen."

Alan: "Well, let's put it this way. Go away and think about it, and if you can come up with a modus operandi, I'd like to know about it."

Me: "How much time have we left?"

Alan: "If Geller duped me, I would honestly like to know how he did this particular trick. Now, I described it to a number of magicians, and they cross-examined me. I showed my awareness of some of the trick methods—"

Me: "Give me ten seconds."

The victim was impaled. He had evaded all my questions, was unwilling to allow that this test was capable of proving whether I was really a psychic, or whether he would have to re-think a lot of his decisions about the so-called wonders he'd witnessed. He simply could not believe that I could tell him the contents of an envelope that he had concealed in his inner pocket, drawn twenty-four hours before in the privacy of his own home, the only persons knowing the secret being himself and his wife. By his own admission, the security was as tight as it could be. He had brought to bear all the skill he could muster to be sure I would fail the test—unless I was really a psychic, and could divine the secret by supernormal means.

He now removed the envelope from his pocket and placed it upon my hand. I covered it with my other hand for ten seconds, and handed it aside. I asked for a pad and felt-tip marker. In full view of a television camera, I made a drawing, turned it face down, and asked, "Would you like to open the envelope, Alan?"

FIGURE 7. Randi holds the Spraggett sealed envelope between his hands for ten seconds. The envelope had been prepared twenty-four hours before in Spraggett's home and kept under tight security.

He did so, unfolded a small sheet of blue paper, and revealed a drawing of a tugboat with two decks, in the waves, with a single smokestack pouring smoke to the right.

I asked: "Am I a psychic if I've reproduced that, Alan? Yes, or no?"

Alan: "If you've reproduced it, you're quite extraordinary."

Me: "But I'm not a psychic?"

Alan: "You're extraordinary. I'd have to consider . . ."

I showed the drawing. It was *identical in every respect* to the one he'd drawn twenty-four hours before.

Me: "Am I extraordinary, Alan?"

Alan: "That's—quite extraordinary, Randi."

Me: "I feel so."

Alan: "Quite extraordinary."

Me: "Have I proved anything to you?"

Alan: "Look, we have to take a break . . ."

We took a commercial break, and when we returned, Spraggett finally answered a direct question.

Said he: "One thing I have learned is that it is a mistake to underestimate the prowess and ingenuity of a magician."

Later, he added, "I remain unrepentantly skeptical about your writing off Geller immediately. And give me two days and I'll drop you a line and tell you how you did this. Okay? It might take me that long to figure it out, although I think—I think I will have figured it out—probably in an hour. I did the numbers trick that you did at the séance. It fooled me for a moment . . ." Spraggett then commenced to give me an incorrect version of a prediction trick that I had performed in Niagara Falls. He was wrong, but I'm sure he is convinced he *has* the solution.

By the way, Mr. Spraggett, I waited around for "an hour" after the show, and you didn't have a solution. Two days later, there was still no communication from you. It has been more than a year now, and I haven't heard from you.

My reader, I'm sure, can see how directly this ties in with the Geller matter. Alan Spraggett is a highly respected investigator of the psychic, but simply lacks the expertise to confront possible trickery and expose it. The pros will get him, not with the limited list of tricks that kids buy out of catalogs in the belief that they are the last word in heavy prestidigitation, but with the *real* secrets that only get trotted out for the do-or-die occasions. And not every magician is going to be able to act in consultation on these matters. It takes a particular bend of mind for this work, and I've got it.

Uri Geller has it, too.

15

Geller's Major American TV Appearances

> The accused stood before the magistrate, convicted
> of a crime on the evidence of eye-witnesses. "Your
> honor," he exclaimed in astonishment, "how can
> you believe these five rascals who saw me do it,
> when I can produce a hundred people who didn't?"
> — Adapted from *The Supernatural?*
> by J. N. Maskelyne

By far the most prestigious of all American television shows for an act to appear on is the NBC "Tonight Show," hosted by Johnny Carson. My own shots with Carson have been worth more than I can estimate, and people who have never seen me on any of the hundreds of other shows I've appeared on *have* seen me on "Tonight." So it was no wonder that Geller's people aimed for a shot like that and hoped it would be a great victory for the cause. It proved to be the greatest comeuppance that Geller ever faced outside of Israel.

Geller's men had bullied and wheedled all sorts of loose conditions from other television shows, but when it came to this one they faced a host who would brook no nonsense from those claiming supernatural or divine powers. And the staff were with the boss: There would be no fakery except in the name of fun and entertainment. In spite of this stand by the Carson folks, perhaps Geller figured they put on that costume just for the public and that Johnny Carson would pretend to be blind to any deception he planned.

I was well assured that Carson would do no such thing, and in refusing to cooperate in such deception he set an example that equally well-informed hosts of other shows have failed to adopt. During an appearance a few days after the *Time* magazine article was on the stands, I chatted with Carson on the air and during the commercial break. He went into details about one young "mentalist" whose manager had sold him as the real goods and told me that he'd assured both the performer and his manager that if he, Carson, knew how the thing was done he would expose it. And he did just that. We haven't heard from that chap in some time now.

So when the Carson people reached me and asked for advice on how to decently control the props during Geller's stunt, I gave them a simple set of rules that they followed carefully.

With a number of immediate engagements of my own at the time, I was unable to jump to Los Angeles to supervise the precautions for the Geller appearance. Besides, I felt that if Geller discovered I was in the area he would get cold feet and do a walk-off. I didn't want that, but I didn't want him to get away with the tricks either. The Carson staff were just about the only people whom I knew I could trust to really follow suggestions about control conditions, and I spoke to them at length on the phone about it.

First, I told them they should get the spoons, watches, nails, keys, and film cans just as they would be asked to do by Geller. They were to be new items, previously unused if possible, and were to be purchased in just the quantity required—no extras or duplicates were to be available. Geller and his apostles were not to be shown the props before the show, except for a minute or two at a controlled distance of five feet. They were not to be allowed to touch or handle any props for any reason. They could not be left alone near them; in fact, the props were to be locked up in a prop cupboard before Geller and company got to the studio. Above all, *Shipi Shtrang was not to be allowed in the backstage area.* The props were to be set on stage in a position remote from Geller's entrance point, and while he was onstage with them—*particularly* when the camera was not on him (as during commercial breaks)—Johnny was to keep his eyes glued to Geller and the props.

All these rules were adhered to—the last to such an extent that I swear Carson almost got bug-eyed staring at the hardware.

AND THE RESULT WAS THAT DURING GELLER'S APPEARANCE ON THE NBC "TONIGHT SHOW" ABSOLUTELY NOTHING HAPPENED.

Well, not *quite*. When an actor on the show was directed by Geller to pick a spoon and caress it, there was a *very* slight difference between that spoon and the other two the staff had supplied to be used. It almost seemed like a partial "win" for Geller.

But luckily I had videotaped the show, and in replaying the tape I was delighted to see the evidence staring at me:

There were three silver spoons placed in a row on the table. The center one, in a close-up "pan" of the camera over the props, showed a slight difference *before* Geller even started talking with Carson. And it was the center spoon that Geller told the actor to pick up. Need I say more?

After the show, I called the prop man at NBC-TV. He told me of how they were in stitches watching Geller during the commercials. At that time, the band plays for the benefit of those stations across the country that merely put up slides with ads on them. The guests and Carson are not shown, and they are not "miked," so cannot be heard. Geller was literally stomping with all his might on the floor in time with the music, and it was obvious that he was trying to jostle the aluminum film cans. Such jarring can make the one with the substance (water, in this case) stand out from the others. A bit of experimentation proves this. In fact, the trick is now on the market in magic shops, in a dozen variations.

But Carson admonished Geller at that point, and though Geller bent down to the cans and tried everything short of blowing them over, he was unable to determine anything about them. I wonder if the cans had been made skid-proof by applying something to their bottoms?

Also, Geller showed no interest in trying to deduce the drawing they had sealed up in an envelope for him. A good decision, since it had been sealed away under lock and key in the briefcase of Fred DeCordova, the producer, who was seated at the foot of a television camera, as is his wont.

Geller blew it—and I think I know why. And now, so do you.

I really can't figure Mike Douglas. I must have appeared with his show a dozen times now, and we've always had an excellent rapport. Mike has done me up in a straitjacket and hoisted me over the streets of Philadelphia from a crane. He has played straight man for my magic tricks and even worked as a confederate a few times. I've caused him moments of some considerable apprehension, too, as when he and Jackie Gleason locked me up in a combination safe on one program.

But, because he's such a nice guy, Mike is unable to knock anyone. When Geller made his first appearance on the Douglas show, Mike was understandably deceived. He had no reason to disbelieve the claims of Geller and took him as he found him. The nail-bending tricks Geller did with guest Tony Curtis (see Figures 1 and 2) were as usual, the nails being tossed about and handed around for examination—with one exception, of course—the nail that seemed to develop a bend in Tony's hand.

Earlier, Hugh Downs had exhibited to the panel a key that Uri had bent prior to air time; then there was a sudden and obvious "edit" of the videotape, where the action took a sudden jump and the nail trick was in progress. I wondered about that defect in the tape, since edits in such shows are very rare, the producers wishing to maintain an "immediacy" that will keep the illusion of a live show. When I appeared on the show a few months later, I decided to ask about it.

Douglas and I were standing backstage in conversation, before making our entrance before the cameras. I brought up the subject of Geller and asked about what he had done on the show. One item surprised me: I was told that Geller had done the trick with the ten aluminum cans. I assured Mike that it hadn't appeared on the aired version of the show, and he was quite surprised. Geller, he said, had *tried* the trick, but it had failed badly.

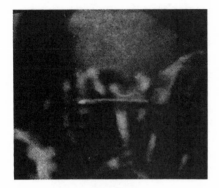

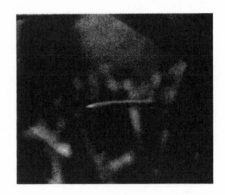

FIGURE 1   FIGURE 2

FIGURE 1. On a "Mike Douglas Show," Geller holds up a previously unexamined nail that he has "bent" while it was held by Tony Curtis. The bend appears *very* slight.

FIGURE 2. Note that, one second (28 video frames) later, Geller has raised his hand slightly and rotated the nail to produce the illusion of a greater bend. The illusion created is that the nail visibly bends. At this point in the performance, Geller declared, "It keeps bending, if you watch it very carefully!"

Then I remembered the edit. I told Mike that the can trick had been edited out, and he declared that his shows were never edited. A quick consultation proved that *without Mike Douglas's knowledge* the segment showing Geller's failure *had* been cut out!

Douglas was annoyed at this disclosure. It seemed someone wanted Geller to look good. Was this another example of the bullying techniques of Yasha Katz to help preserve Uri's image?

My appearance that day was to refute the Geller miracles. Before the show, I'd asked Roger Miller, the well-known musician, to select one cough drop from a box of assorted flavors without knowing the flavor of the one he'd selected and to seal it, wrapped in paper, in any one of a dozen aluminum film cans. He had already done so, when he received a visit from the associate producer in his dressing room. He was told to switch cans, so that there was no chance that I could know which was the right can. The whole set of cans was then covered up and locked away in a room, inside a locked metal filing cabinet. It stayed there until I went on the show.

This was a bit different from one episode on ABC-TV, where the producer, having given strict instructions to his secretary that Geller was not to be allowed to come *near* the cans, discovered this same young lady in her office with Geller poised over the cans, holding her hand! She explained that Uri was testing *her* psychic ability to find the right can—and she saw nothing amiss in that at all! I wonder if she wants to buy some lunar real estate?

I had also asked Miller to make a drawing in the privacy of his closed dressing room, seal it in three envelopes, one inside the other, and keep it in his coat pocket until show time. He had done so, with great security procedures, again supervised by the associate producer.

On the set, Mike introduced me as a frequent visitor to the show who was claiming that he could duplicate the Geller tricks.

The cans were brought out, still covered, and in true Geller fashion I concentrated mightily, eliminating the cans one by one until only one

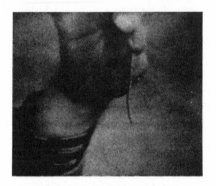 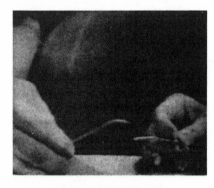

FIGURE 3   FIGURE 4

FIGURE 3. On a subsequent Douglas show, a nail bent by Randi while in the hand of Roger Miller. Note the very definite bend.

FIGURE 4. A moment later, Miller's hand still holds the nail, this time beside a hotel key that bent in the hand of Jaye P. Morgan. Note the different amount of bend visible when the nail is presented from a different angle.

remained. I asked Mike to open it, and inside he found the wrapped cough drop. All the others had been opened and found empty. Without my looking at what color the cough drop was, Mike popped it into his mouth, and I announced that I thought it was an orange one. I was right.

Then we moved on to the nails. They had supplied me with a box of ten-penny nails and we looked them over to find a couple of straight ones. Then there followed an exact duplication of the Tony Curtis nail trick, using Roger Miller this time. Jaye P. Morgan showed us her hotel key, which I'd made bend while she held it in her hand.

We were about to get to the envelopes, when it came time to take a station break and then go outside to the street for a blindfolded-drive demonstration. I had given Mike and Roger a black-cloth blindfold lined with sheet aluminum and a heavy, double-layered black cloth bag, which they'd examined and tested thoroughly. The prop department had obtained some raw pizza dough and Mike jammed this into my eye sockets, then put the blindfold in place. The bag was then pulled over my head and tied around my neck with a length of rope. I was led to my car and I slid into the driver's seat.

We had arranged to have pylons set up in the street as I was being blindfolded, with the personnel of the show standing in as human pylons as well. But just before Roger got away, I asked him, "Roger, the drawing you sealed up—was it a drawing of your own left hand?"

He was a bit stunned. "Yes. Yes, it was!" he replied, and hastened out to join the pylons as the bystanders laughed at his astonishment.

I put the car in gear, turned it around, and drove through the maze of a dozen pylons accurately. I had about one foot to spare between two of the human obstacles, but we all survived. I parked the car at the curb, and Mike removed the stuff from my head, helping me pick gobs of pizza dough out of my eyes as well.

It was the close of the program, and Mike commented to his audience, "Believe me folks, what this man has done is just impossible! We blindfolded him, and it's just impossible!"

Well, almost, Mike. Almost.

I must point out that what I did was a bit more involved than the blindfold stunt Geller does. Andy Tobias of *New York* magazine had reported that Geller had his scarf tied over his eyes several times until it was to his liking and he was able to get a chink to peek out of. All I'm really trying to prove is that a magician cannot only do as well but often much *better*. Anyone who has seen England's David Berglas perform his sensational blindfold work will go away convinced that Berglas has another set of eyes in his fingertips.

Geller made another appearance on the "Mike Douglas Show" early in 1975 to plug his new book, *My Story*. At that time, he did the watch stunt and some key-bending took place either behind his body or when the commercial was on. And the kids who rushed up to him with bent keys weren't very convincing.

Uri has very little left that hasn't been exposed now. He's run out of material.

But not out of disciples.

Barbara Walters is certainly one of the best-known persons in American television. She turns out a prodigious amount of work each

FIGURE 5

FIGURE 6

FIGURE 7

FIGURE 8

FIGURE 5. On the Douglas show Randi has pizza dough pressed onto his eyes by Mike, preparatory to driving his car.

FIGURE 6. A previously examined and tested, opaque blindfold is strapped on next.

FIGURE 7. A bag of double-layered black cloth—thoroughly tested by Roger Miller—is pulled over Randi's head and tied about his neck by Mike.

FIGURE 8. Randi drives his car while blindfolded between Roger Miller (left) and Mike Douglas (far right) after negotiating a maze of pylons and people standing in the roadway, then parks at the curb.

FIGURE 9

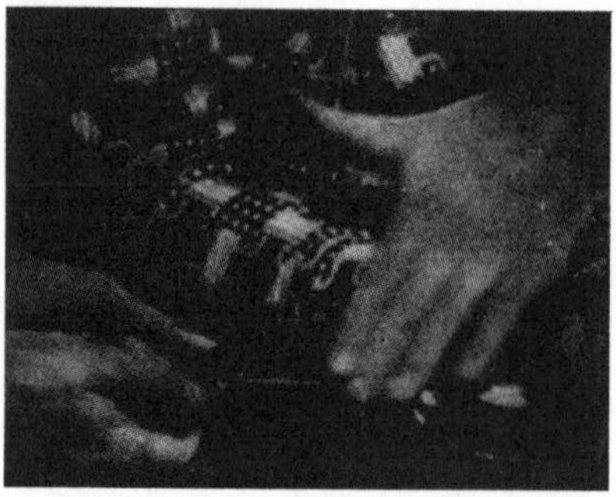

FIGURE 10

FIGURE 11

FIGURE 12

FIGURE 13

FIGURE 9. Barbara Walters of the "Not for Women Only" show holds two spoons; the one in the foreground has been examined, the other has not. Note the distinct "bump" fracture where the bowl is riveted to the shaft (arrow). It is *this* spoon which is retained for bending. The bowl is already bent away from the handle more than that of the tested spoon.

FIGURE 10. Geller strokes the spoon, covering the fracture with his left hand. Note that he has grasped the tip of the spoon with his right hand, levering the bowl downward. The breaking has begun.

FIGURE 11. The spoon is displayed. Note that the breaking is taking place right where the "bump" fracture was located.

FIGURE 12. Now the spoon is effectively broken, held by Geller. It is holding together by the thin skin of plating, and is ready to tear loose.

FIGURE 13. The bowl of the spoon drops off as the plating gives way and it falls to the table (arrow).

year and has been exposed to more major personalities than almost any other media interviewer. So it was no surprise when she came upon the Israeli "superpsychic" on her "Not for Women Only" show for the NBC network. Geller worked his wonders on her and got predictable results: She was convinced.

Let us examine his "telepathy" test with her. Here are the exact words she used.

Barbara: "I made a drawing before we went on the air, when Uri was not in the room. We've put it in—It's in two envelopes, is it? (*Turning off-camera for verification*) I think—"

Uri: "Keep it in the book."

Barbara: "Keep it in the book. It's in two envelopes. No one has touched it but me. It's sealed and it's in a book. I did it about a half-hour ago."

Hold on. Look back at that statement. Barbara has said, "No one has touched it but me," yet she says earlier, "*We've* put it . . . ," and then she expresses doubt as to the number of envelopes! Obviously she was not a witness when it was sealed up. And whoever verified that there were two envelopes was obviously not in on *all* the handling, either, as we shall see. So there were a number of persons who handled the sealed drawing—*or a packet that looked like the original!*

And note that the drawing had been kicking around for at least half an hour.

Geller then went through the usual heavy histrionics to develop the drawing, and Barbara did her best concentrating. When he finished, she declared it to be a "hit." Applause.

Barbara: "And it's not the easiest drawing. It's in *three* envelopes, and we said nobody has touched this but I. [*At this point, the original drawing is shown to the audience, with many oohs and aahs.*] As I say, I don't believe—If it is a trick . . . It's a fan—I—can't possibly imagine— The envelope has not been touched, three envelopes in the book, I did the drawing in front of our executive producer, who is standing there, who is the only one who saw me do it and there it is . . ."

Uri: "I do this as well under very controlled conditions."

Now we have *three envelopes*! Where did the third one come from? May I suggest that it was the idea of Geller or one of his cohorts (Shipi was there, too) to put the additional envelope into play? If so, it is an ideal opportunity to either switch the original out, or, if this has already been done, to switch it back in again. It begins to develop that no one really knows just what happened to the drawing in this period! And again Barbara has repeated that no one has touched it but herself!

I'm amused to hear Uri's statement about "very controlled conditions." Apparently he doesn't consider *these* conditions to be very controlled . . .

To continue:

Barbara: "When you say that you've been tested under scientific scrutiny, how is that done?"

Uri: "Well, for instance, what I did with you, for instance, then, I'm not, for instance, I'm not at all at the Institute when they do the drawing."

Barbara: "At Stanford Institute were you alone in a sealed room?"

Uri: "Exactly. Yes. And then they have a hundred drawings and they are all sealed up, and actually nobody knows which drawing they pick out. So the experimenter himself doesn't know what's in the envelope."

Come on, Geller! You failed to mention a very important point here. *When you did those tests at SRI, you failed them 100 percent— because they were designed and conducted by a real scientist, Dr. Charles Rebert!*

Barbara mentioned Geller in her discussion on the next day's program:

Barbara: "He said, 'Look, I'm picking up certain things from you.' And I will tell you what some of them are, and I will come back and tell you if any of these turns out. A long yellow dress—which I don't own— a new house, something political—people talking about you politically, the number 27, the month April, and a man—and he described the man, and a lost ring. None of these has any meaning to me."

No, they don't, Ms. Walters. And if you were to come upon just one yellow dress, or a number 27, or anything unusual in April, you'd be apt to think Geller was a wonder. But as it is, he has made seven predictions. Are you liable to do another show on how none of these prognostications turned out to be true? Of course not—and Geller knows it.

My opportunity to convince Barbara Walters of Geller's tricks came a few months later when I appeared on "Not for Women Only" in the excellent company of Doug Henning, star of Broadway's "The Magic Show," and Mark Wilson, prominent American magician. The program was on "Magic and Magicians."

When it came time to test my powers of "telepathy," Barbara made this statement: "Just before the program, I did a drawing. I put it in three envelopes in this book. We have not had this envelope out of our sight. Randi has in no way been close to it. The closest you've been to it, to my knowledge, is right now. Reproduce it."

Randi: "Would you put it back in the book. I want to be sure it's under control."

Now Ms. Walters's statement is *totally true*. There are no mistakes here. You have my word on it. I had to do it the hard way, but I produced a drawing of a house with a little girl standing inside, a chimney, smoke coming therefrom, and a doorway. Miss Walters's drawing was the same, except that her little girl was outside the house.

On the same program, I bent her key—on-camera, while she held it in her own hand—to precisely the same angle that Geller had bent another identical key. The two keys were compared carefully. And I also made her watch advance an hour as she held it.

After the show, Barbara expressed her surprise and disillusion. She said that she had based the whole past year of her life on the reality of Geller's tricks. But one thing struck me very hard: Barbara Walters didn't take insult from my performance, as many people have done. She's a real lady.

I noted that when Barbara interviewed Geller on the "Today Show" later, she was a mite cold—and Geller didn't feel like bending or telepathizing. Isn't that surprising!

16

Geller in England

> The six witnesses had given damning evidence
> against the defendant. It looked pretty bad for him;
> each had seen the crime committed. He stepped
> before the judge, outraged. "But your honor, how
> can you possibly believe these six rascals who saw
> me do it, when I can produce a hundred who didn't?"

In November 1973, while Geller was very much in the news in England, columnist Richard Herd of the *Daily Mail* called conjuror Billy McComb and asked him to visit and assess the Geller performance disguised as a reporter. They paused at a pub across from Geller's hotel; and, while Herd stayed behind sampling the local brew, Billy and a *Mail* photographer intruded upon an interview Geller was already involved in, in his room, with a woman reporter from the *Daily Telegraph.*

Billy professed total ignorance about the appropriate procedure, and Geller was quite annoyed with him. Commenting that no one had invited Billy, Geller tried his best to ignore him. But Billy was right in on the action.

"Geller rubbed and rubbed at a fork that I'd brought along from the pub," McComb reports. "He rolled it about to make it appear as if it was getting soft, but nothing happened until the photographer began to reload film. Geller quickly brought the fork down beside him, and it was then lifted up under cover of his hand, and shown to be bent." The preliminary photos had already been taken, and now those the photographer got showed the bend. "He seemed to make a 'move' every time the reporter looked down to write her notes."

For Billy, Geller tried and tried with no success—until he suddenly stood up, at which time Billy saw him depress the fork on the arm of the chair.

Geller acted quite thrilled to discover the bend in the fork, and threw it on the bed, exclaiming, "Look! It's still bending!"

Billy's reply to this was a succinct "No, I don't feel so," and thereafter Geller was less than cordial, so Billy took his leave.

McComb returned to the waiting reporter across the street and made his assessment. "The man's a fake," he said to Herd.

When David Berglas, the well-known British mentalist, first met Geller in London, Uri was all prepared for the encounter—or so he thought.

Geller walked up to Berglas, took his hand in his most sincere manner, and, looking into his eyes, soulfully declared, "David, you will find that I'm genuine. I don't use a radio in my tooth, chemicals on my hands, laser beams, magnets, or special belt buckles to do these things." Then he turned abruptly and walked away.

Berglas was nonplussed. Turning to those about him, he exclaimed, "Come to think of it, neither do I!"

How Geller can assume that the top-flight professionals are unaware of his methods is hard to understand. Perhaps it is because so many of the amateurs in the field have fallen for his tricks. In Atlanta, Georgia, for example, a member of a prominent conjurors' organization gave the Gellerites a two-page endorsement of his feats after being easily bamboozled in the dressing room after a television show. The parent body, as well as other prominent members of the society, were appalled at the member's action.

Berglas also discovered an interesting addition to the act that Geller used in both Manchester and Birmingham. Feeling that he could get away with almost anything in England, in each city Geller had performed a trick on television with a pile of "borrowed" watches. Shown in extreme television close-up, a watch was seen to be racing ahead visibly at hundreds of times a normal rate! Berglas investigated, and found that, in each case, after the program the super-watch was no longer to be found among the pile of watches used. When he told the producers that this watch had not been added to the pile, they admitted that this was certainly possible under the loose conditions that prevailed. From a professional standpoint, Geller left himself open to being caught outright in these cases, but evidently didn't figure on David Berglas being present.

One episode in England had everyone guessing. When Don Coolican, feature reporter for the *London Daily Express,* looked into the Geller matter, he thought he should pursue the possibility of a chemical being used to soften the keys and nails. To this end, he consulted Dr. Philip Carter and Ian Burgess of St. Dunstan's College. These gentlemen helped him produce a chemical mixture that he presumed would soften metals; he claimed in an article in the *Express* that it did just that "in seconds." So it seemed there was this possibility for the Israeli wonder's metal-bending feats. A short time later, Coolican again appeared in print to retract his chemical explanation. He'd traveled to Copenhagen to test Geller, and Uri had performed after washing his hands! This disproved any chemical explanation.

The chemical explanation doesn't *need* to be disproved. There is simply no compound that will work the way Coolican claimed, and I defy him to produce such a substance. Further, when Berglas questioned him in some puzzlement about his contradictions, Coolican told all.

After the publication of the first Coolican article, Yasha Katz,

Uri's manager, had approached the *Express* management threatening all kinds of actions if a retraction was not printed. The editor called Coolican in, and instructed him to correct the situation. Coolican complied. So we have here an incorrect solution to a simple conjuring trick followed by a forced retraction of the wrong conclusion. I trust the reader follows that.

David Berglas has a response to all this nonsense. He has offered the fine sum of £5,000 ($11,300 U.S.) to any psychic who can claim it. He will gladly outline his conditions upon request. His money has never been safer.

England had fallen so hard for the Geller farce in 1970 that the perpetrator was taking a lot of chances. On one occasion, he confidently predicted to Daniela Bravinsky, secretary to a popular English television personality, that she would have a baby girl in three days time. She had the baby, all right—a boy, a month later. Determining that the lady was expectant was all that Uri had done. And just about anyone can do that, at that stage! But what if he'd been right? The press would have trumpeted it to the world. As it was, no attention was directed to the prediction.

My visit to Britain in 1975 provided me with an opportunity to quench another Geller claim to authenticity.

Geller has repeatedly ranted about how he has been "approved" by scientists. To quote him on a television appearance in the United States: "Look, if the magicians think they can do these things, let them go and do it for the scientists, in a laboratory! Just like I did!" Okay, Uri, abandon that as a valid argument. It's been done.

On July 11, I was privileged to do a demonstration before a group of prominent scientists at the Biophysical Laboratory of King's College, London. One of their bright young men, Farooq Hussain, had been introduced to me by Dr. Joe Hanlon of *New Scientist* magazine, and Farooq had arranged to get together a committee that consisted of Dr. Maurice Wilkins, Nobel Prize winner for his work in discovering the DNA molecule structure; Dr. Christopher Evans, of the National Physical Laboratory and author of *Cults of Unreason*; David Davies, editor of *Nature* magazine; Roger Woodham, also of *Nature* magazine; Ted Richards, Ph.D.; and Farooq Hussain. These men, in fields ranging from biophysics to psychology, were all sober, intelligent observers of considerable prestige. Many more had wanted to attend, but the audience had to be kept down, due to limited space. They supplied a collection of cutlery, a pair of Geiger counters, and some keys. We gathered about the table and began the show.

I asked Dr. Wilkins to hold one of the spoons (which *they* had supplied) at each end, horizontally. I grasped it at the center, between my thumb and forefinger. I slowly and gently began rocking it up and down.

There was a perceptible plasticity to the spoon as it began deforming. Inside of thirty seconds, it was bending up and down at about 45 degrees each way. Suddenly there was a grinding, crackling sound and the spoon parted into two pieces.

If only I'd had a camera there to register the expression on Dr. Wilkins's face! Then he broke out in a wide smile.

I quickly followed this up with some key-bending, made the Geiger counter cluck like a mad thing as if I were radioactive in some way, and made a compass needle deflect by some 15 degrees while I stood six feet from it. All in all, it was a replication of some of the outstanding tests Geller did in British labs for far less critical audiences of scientific men.

A couple of the group were now called away to another meeting, to which they were already half an hour late. They promised to return, and meanwhile I mentioned the scientist J. C. F. Zöllner and his tests (see Chapter 17) of a century ago, wherein Henry Slade, a medium, had caused knots to appear in a controlled length of cord.

One of the committee found a piece of string and, searching in a desk drawer, a small glass tube. He poked the string inside and marked the tube with a secret design. Slowly I passed my hand over the tube. The man nearest then fished out the string. There was a knot in the middle of it. Some amazed looks were exchanged.

Later, in Dr. Wilkins's office upstairs, I asked one member of the committee to choose any word from any page of a book he himself decided upon from the office shelf. He opened the book only after I was across the room, my back to the wall. After he decided on the word he wanted, he closed the book and held on to it. I took a piece of paper from the desk and, in his full view, wrote out a word. It was "intended" — the exact word he'd only *looked* at! Nothing had been written, sealed in an envelope, or any such other thing. He had selected the book from among hundreds on the shelves, and I had only just met the man an hour before.

To complete my gamut of Gellerisms, I caused a couple of borrowed watches to advance several hours while held in the hands of their owners; then bent several short, thick cabinet keys held by Professor Wilkins's dazzled secretary.

I refer the reader to the Appendix at the back of this book. It contains a statement by the committee mentioned above that should put to rest once and for all the "authentication" that Geller claims from men of science. If I could perform his "miracles" for these men — who are sober, observant, well-educated, and intelligent — why couldn't Geller?

We're *both* good at chicanery.

One statement by Dr. Wilkins particularly interested me. He and the others had observed a series of phenomena for which they had no immediate logical solutions. Dr. Wilkins said to me: "I'm in a quandary. You've told us that what you did was accomplished by trickery. But I don't know whether to believe you or to believe *in* you!" Of course he was speaking in jest, yet the message was clear: What he had just witnessed was outside his experience as a scientist, yet he did not jump to the conclusion that the committee had just seen supernatural occurrences. As he and the others have said in their letter (in the Appendix), such demonstrations *must* be attended by a *qualified* member of the conjuring profession or the value of them as tests is nil. What a refreshing attitude, in view of the outrageous conclusion-jumping done by other British scientists!

Certain prominent American scientists have said, concerning the criticisms of their acceptance of Geller, that their detractors are either calling them liars or fools. Neither is correct, so far as I personally am concerned. I call them simply "unqualified" — in this particular field — to pass judgment on such matters.

Of all the persons who have ever sat in judgment of a possibly "paranormal" event, Dr. Maurice Wilkins is certainly most prominent and qualified. As codiscoverer of one of the most astonishing conceptions in science — the DNA molecule — Dr. Wilkins is outstanding in his field of biophysics. And biophysics is precisely the specialty that should be involved in attempting to prove whether there *is* anything to this psychokinesis matter. Persons whose callings range from mathematics to laser physics are, instead, studying the purported wonders.

While Geller and Shtrang laugh!

The Geller matter was well covered in Britain by one of the nation's highly specialized newspapers, the weekly *Psychic News.* The main thrust of this paper at present is the support of spiritualism and psychic healing, and the advertisements that fill its pages every week are mainly concerned with weaning believers from one "church" to the other. In order to show how easily a conjuror could launch a career as a miracle-worker from appearing in such a publication, *I* set out to get a write-up as the real thing myself.

Dr. Joe Hanlon suggested that a Mr. Peter Jones* would be most likely to interview me, and I felt that it would be necessary to prepare the ground a bit. To that end, I had Hanlon call Jones and suggest that I'd bent a few keys for him in a manner he could not fathom (I had) and that he was too busy with other matters at *New Scientist* magazine to cover the new wonder-worker. Jones was given my number and my other name, Zwinge.

He called many times over the period of a week, but I purposely did not call him back, so that he would be a bit more anxious to see me.

---

* This is not his real name. I have changed it to save him embarrassment.

He was told by conjuror Billy McComb that I was "being tested at a lab" and would call him when I was free.

Finally, on a Wednesday, I was "free," and called Jones. He was ready to see me almost right away, but I again put him off till that afternoon. Finally I showed up—mounting several sets of stairs to Jones's office—dressed in blue jeans, bright yellow shirt, and bat-shaped belt buckle. Such a costume is bound to throw anyone off.

The miracles began. In all, I made his own teaspoon get plastic and finally break while he held both ends, I bent another spoon while a woman in the next office had it beside her teacup, made a paper-knife in the other room assume an S shape, ran two clocks ahead two hours, made two keys in filing cabinets bend some 30 degrees, bowed a steel fork; and finally we discovered that one piece of the broken teaspoon had adopted a severe 40-degree bend while we weren't looking. Jones was impressed, as were the women in the next office.

I filled their heads with all manner of appropriate stories about my wonderful childhood. They ate it up. To clinch matters, in case there was any doubt about my authenticity, I left behind on the floor a half-sealed letter directed home. It contained drivel about the wonders the British scientists were discovering about me and how pleased I was to be going to an interview with *Psychic News*. I figured that if it were found and peeked at, it would put the final nail (a bent one, of course!) into the coffin.

Psychic News's press deadline was Tuesday. I wanted to keep my identity under wraps until the article saw print, since I had several other persons to see while still "in disguise" as either a psychic or a reporter. David Berglas could of course have done this whole swindle himself, except that he would be instantly recognized in his own country, whereas I had changed so much in appearance since my last professional visit to Britain that I could get away with it easily.

The article did not appear the following Tuesday, and when I called Mr. Jones, as Zwinge, he explained that there had been heavy coverage of some sort of spiritualist conclave or other and that he would probably run it a week later. I worried that perhaps Bastin, now well aware that the Enemy was at the gates, might inform *Psychic News* I was in the area—and that they would put it all together. In that case, I risked never seeing the piece in print. Feeling that there was little chance of the imposture running full course, I returned to the United States to continue work on this manuscript.

Then, on the morning of July 24, I called home routinely and Jim, my assistant, was in a flap. Dr. Christopher Evans had called from London to announce that a new psychic star had been born. Zwinge had bamboozled *Psychic News*!

I waited until the following Monday for the paper to reach me in the mail. When it finally arrived, I was stunned. I was featured, grotesque picture and all, smack on the front page! The headline announced, "Sceptic Sends Psychic to Put PN in a Twist."

Jones began with a description of how the "arch-sceptic" Joe Hanlon had brought me to his attention as Zwinge, saying that Jones was probably better suited to handle these matters. He suspected what he called a "send-up" (we'd say "put-on") but was reassured when called by another magazine, as well, about my mysterious powers. He continued:

Having established the ground to my satisfaction I then sought Jim Zwinge. It was not easy. He too proved elusive. After several phone calls and messages left round town I waited.

Again my patience was rewarded. Zwinge called. I invited him to my office to be "investigated." He agreed.

An engaging extrovert, with grey beard and intense eyes, he seemed to radiate a magnetic aura.

Before asking him to demonstrate his power, I asked about his background. A freelance writer for "Time" magazine, he lives in New Jersey, U.S.

Poltergeist disturbances happened at his home near Toronto when he was 15. Wine bottles exploded mysteriously, alarming his family.

"My father used to make his own wine. These bottles would explode spectacularly. A piece would break off into a long slice."

Prof. T. K. Lawson of Toronto University investigated the phenomenon. He took Zwinge to his laboratory for scientific tests.

Breaks in Two

Now Zwinge is making his own investigation. He approached Hanlon in London "and bent a couple of things for him, mostly keys. He was busy and mentioned PN as being my best bet for testing this ability."

The action then began. I did not realise what PN and "Two Worlds" offices were in for!

I collected a teaspoon from "Two Worlds." As he stroked it lightly Zwinge told me he "gets a sticky feeling. It's like running your finger over clear glass."

I touched the spoon ends as he stroked it. Suddenly it seemed to shudder. Then it broke cleanly in two.

I was impressed. Next we were summoned into the adjoining "Two Worlds" office. We found the occupants, Lilian and Mary, excitedly proclaiming, "Look at the paper knife."

Lilian had used it that morning to open the mail. It was perfectly straight then. Now its handle had curved an astonishing 45 degrees.

All could vouch Zwinge had not been near it. Up to that point he had not entered their office.

Later another "Two Worlds" employee, Mona Bethune, announced, "My tea spoon has bent!"

It was perfect when she stirred the tea a few moments earlier.

By now the excitement was growing. These supernormal incidents seemed to galvanise Zwinge. He leapt enthusiastically round the office seeking articles to bend.

We became alarmed. Would our typewriters suddenly cease to function? Could he snarl up the PN production line?

A colleague hastened to the editor to declare, "They are going great guns upstairs!"

An explosive remark of some validity!

By now further malfunctions were discovered. Mary noticed her clock had suddenly gained two hours. It had been correct earlier.

A glance at my office clock showed it fast by 2½ hours! Certainly Zwinge had no opportunity to interfere with them. He had been under constant surveillance.

Twist Is Delayed

I had not left his side, or taken my eyes from him, for one second. I was determined to be an objective reporter. I was fully alert to any suspicious moves. But Zwinge made none.

At one stage he stroked a fork. He seemed unable to make any impression. But after he left I discovered it had twisted noticeably.

Mary also found a filing cabinet key had bent in the lock.

Zwinge told me: "This supernormality doesn't happen in my home. It's always elsewhere."

I will not attempt to list the gross errors in this account, except to mention that Mr. Jones did *not* invite me to his office—he asked me if we could meet somewhere, and *I suggested his office*! You may think this a small point to make, but it is only an indication of how he did things *my* way after I'd made it so difficult for him to reach me; he was very anxious to interview me, and I had agreed to a meeting in spite of my very busy schedule.

Why was this imposture so readily accomplished? Peter Jones is a man of intelligence, one not apt to fall for such a "send-up," we would imagine. But it is just such a person who falls for the confidence man, given good enough reasons to believe in the bona fides of the perpetrator. When I sat down to be interviewed by Jones, I knew that I would have to give him ample evidence, not only of my paranormal abilities, but also of my past history.

I combined just about every acceptable story I'd ever heard and came up with poltergeist beginnings, followed by my own bewilderment at these wonderful happenings. I differed just enough from the standard stories to make it sound original and threw in just enough new stuff (the metal felt "sticky" when it was preparing to bend) to freshen it all and make it appealing.

So what now, believers? If you had read that issue of *Psychic News*, you'd have snapped up this new discovery easily! And you'd have used the account as glowing, incontrovertible proof of psychic powers! What makes this evidence any less valid than other similar evidence? Simply the fact that *I* tell you all these wonders were done under those "rigid" conditions by sheer fakery! It was tricks and nothing more.

At this point I want to assure my reader that, in my opinion, Mr. Jones is a thoroughly honest and honorable gentleman. I should feel badly if anyone got any other idea from this account. He accepted what he thought was a forthright account from a genuine psychic and had ample reason for doing so. I happen to be rather good at my business. And I am assured of this opinion of his honesty when I observe the letter that I had planted in his office, and which eventually arrived at my home in the United States, with correct postage affixed. I had prepared it in such a way that I could tell if it had been opened. It had *not* been opened, and it would have been easy for Jones to have done a bit of snooping. He is as honest a man as I've ever met. I doubt that *I* would have resisted the temptation to peek. But then I've never claimed to be honest either.

Consider, then, how easy it had been for Uri Geller to flimflam reporters in similar circumstances! He arrives thoroughly authenticated by the press and a few minor scientists, or so it seems. The rest is a piece of cake, since he is an experienced conjuror. The conclusion is inescapable: *any person with conjuring ability and any sort of a good story or reputation can become a "psychic" overnight.* It is evident that I myself could have launched a career as a genuine psychic marvel on the strength of this front-page article in *Psychic News.* Of course I'd not intended to do so, but it was certainly within my grasp at that point.

I was flattered to appear in this particular issue of *Psychic News,* which also revealed to us the wonderful empty overcoat that walks the streets of Cairo, advertised the highly useful "thought bricks," and celebrated the happy circumstance that such messages are being brought to "those who live in darkness." Thank you, I'll take darkness.

My apologies, Mr. Jones, and to the ladies as well. Perhaps the next time someone tells or shows you something impossible, you will all think more than twice. There is no Santa Claus.

I refer my reader to the Appendix of this book. There are two newspaper articles reproduced there that date from 1950. The "psychic" referred to is myself, and I was twenty-two years old at the time. I was to drop the entire pretense of being the real thing shortly after this run of articles appeared (there were dozens more), because I could not picture myself becoming a religious figure, as was bound to happen. In these interviews, I followed the same procedure that I did in England for *Psychic News,* the same method used by Geller and Shipi to confound news people today. As you can see, it is very successful.

I, too, could have become a Geller. But I have too much respect for myself and for my fellow human beings to assume divine airs.

17

A Century Ago: Same Game, Different Personnel

> Glendower: I can call spirits from the vasty deep.
> Hotspur: Why, so can I, or so can any man; But will they come when you do call for them?
> —Shakespeare: *Henry IV,* Part 1

Uri Geller is anything but unique. His kind have flashed on and off the world scene for centuries. But the Cagliostros of recent history are more easily discussed than those who held forth previously, since their impact on mankind has been better documented. Certainly no practitioner of the elusive arts has been better recorded than Geller, however. Every trivial feat he has ever performed is carefully set down by his admirers, though not every exposure is so carefully noted.

Let us consider his antecedents. Back in the 1870s, a sensation was being created by one "Dr." Henry Slade, an American whose career runs such a very striking parallel with that of Uri Geller that it will serve us well to look into it for research purposes. We will discover a score of rather remarkable similarities between the trickster of a century ago and the space-age Israeli of today.

Henry Slade was a "spirit-medium." For those of you not versed in the very specialized jargon of spooky stuff, this denotes a person who is able, through special "divine dispensation," to act as a conductor, or medium, between this humdrum world and the next (much more exciting) sphere of existence. Much sitting about in darkened rooms holding hands and singing "Rock of Ages" is usually required to conjure up shades of departed loved ones through these channels.

But old Henry had a somewhat different gimmick. He claimed (though he was not unique in these claims) that he could cause the ghosts to write their thoughts and messages upon common school slates. It was found necessary to have the slates in such a position that they could not be seen (spirits being such shy critters, as you may have suspected) and usually Slade would hold them beneath a table, from where scratching noises could be heard. When the slate was then exposed, lo! there were inspiring messages from beyond to be seen and marveled at.

Slade attracted the attention of more than one prominent scientist of the day, and these men fully supported his claims in the face of damning

191

proof against the medium that only a simpleton could deny. Slade was so very convincing to one scientist, a very respected Austrian astrophysicist named J. C. F. Zöllner, that the man wrote an entire book, *Transcendental Physics,* about the Slade tricks. In it, he declared Slade to be absolutely genuine.

The medium eventually was caught red-handed several times at his business, and finally signed a confession. He died in disgrace—that is, in disgrace to all but the woolly-brained confirmed believers, for *nothing* will serve to convince them that such a performer is without special powers. Nevertheless, I feel that my reader is beginning to recognize the territory, if not the story, so let us consider the many points of close similarity between the careers of "Dr." Henry Slade (deceased) and Mr. Uri Geller (very much with us).

I will outline the parallels individually, discussing Geller's case along with the Slade details.

A group of scientists working as the Seybert Commission was organized by the University of Pennsylvania, following the Zöllner book, to look into the Slade matter. It turned in findings that damned Slade as an outright imposter and fraud. They found not one of his tricks that they could not solve. In the book *The Supernatural?,* by Dr. Lionel A. Weatherly and J. N. Maskelyne (the famous British conjuror) the details of the exposure are outlined. The account goes on to say:

They also went to the expense of sending the Secretary of the Commission, Mr. George S. Fullerton, to Germany, to inquire into the real facts of the famous investigation made by Professor Zoellner of Slade and his slate-writing, and of which so much has been made by the Spiritualists. In summarising the conclusions at which he arrived, Mr. Fullerton says:—

"Thus it would appear that of the four eminent men whose names have made famous the investigation, there is reason to believe one, "Zoellner," was of unsound mind at the time, and anxious for experimental verification of an already accepted hypothesis; another, "Fechner," was partly blind, and believed because of Zoellner's observations; a third, "Scheibner," was also afflicted with defective vision, and not entirely satisfied in his own mind as to the phenomena; and a fourth, "Weber," was advanced in age, and did not even recognise the disabilities of his associates. No one of these men had ever had experiences of this sort before, nor was any one of them acquainted with the ordinary possibilities of deception. The experience of our Commission with Dr. Slade would suggest that the lack of such knowledge on their part was unfortunate."

Thus exit the celebrated Zoellner investigation.

Slade turned to drink following a full confession of his chicanery. The *English Illustrated Magazine* of January 1895 reported, "The famous 'Dr. Slade,' who created such excitement in London in 1876 and made so much money with his slate-writing, was recently taken to a workhouse in America, penniless, friendless, and a lunatic." He died there, in 1905.

There are sixteen points about the Slade case that agree with Geller's case; the seventeenth has as yet no equivalent with Geller. I will list these points for comparison:

(1) THE EXPERIMENT IS NOT PERFORMED WHEN PRESENTED. IT IS SUCCESSFULLY COMPLETED ONLY AFTER SEVERAL TRIES. Zöllner mentions frequently throughout *Transcendental Physics* that Slade seems seldom to have performed the tests planned when first presented with them.

One classic test involved knots in strings. Zöllner had postulated a simple but beautiful idea to account for all of the Slade miracles. He outlined a fourth-dimensional theory that need not concern us here, but which required that the performer be able to do such things as tie a simple knot in a piece of string while both ends were under control. Zöllner set out to arrange for such a test.

He cut some lengths of string and in each he formed a closed loop by tying the ends together. Each knot was then encased in a blob of sealing wax and Zöllner's personal seal was impressed therein. He proposed that Slade attempt to tie knots in the body of the string, leaving the wax intact.

For many days, the experiment was tried. At the end of each session, the cords were left in a drawer nearby, and brought out again the next day. Zöllner kept no record of how many cords were prepared, nor were they counted again at the close of the experiments. But after a number of days of fruitless experiment, Slade finally sat at the table with the loop hanging into his lap, the seal under his thumbs. And when he again showed the loop, there were several knots tied in it! Zöllner marveled, and declared the case proved.

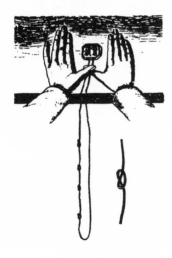

FIGURE 1. The arrangement of the sealed loop of string as Slade attempted the "4th-dimension" demonstration.

Several critics of Zöllner have pointed out that Slade had ample opportunity to steal one of the loops, then either open the seal or duplicate it by familiar means after tying the knots. It would have then been simple to substitute the loop while seated at the table for the test. The important point, however, is that the *time* of performance is of Slade's choosing.

As for Geller, his propensity for the same procedure is becoming legend. Almost all his supporters note that he seldom does the test at the time it is expected, hurrying away to other matters and causing great chaos and distraction by so doing. At SRI and at Birkbeck, reports tell of experiments being discontinued, and then resumed the next day—with great success. The delay enabled him to familiarize himself with the equipment and with the protocol to be applied.

I must mention that I performed the string business while at King's College in London, but did so only at the suggestion of the experimenters, after they found a tiny glass tube and a scrap of string for me in the lab. They themselves jammed the string into the tube, marked the tube with a special symbol, and only allowed me to place my empty palm over the tube. Within *five seconds*, they picked the string from the narrow tube, and discovered a knot in the center! There was no chance for me to take the tube home or duplicate it. So there are other ways, as well . . .

(2) THE PERFORMER DISTRACTS ATTENTION AWAY FROM THE REQUESTED OR INTENDED TEST WITH ACTIONS OR SUGGESTIONS INTENDED TO RELAX OBSERVATION OF THE ORIGINAL INTENDED ACTION. Both Slade and Geller developed a dodge that magicians down through the ages have used. Slade was forever distracting the sitters at his slate-writing séances by upsetting things from the table, opening the sealed slates repeatedly to examine them for results when there were no results, and otherwise had his victims looking all over the room—except where the tricks were taking place. Geller achieves what has been described by observers as "sheer disorder" when being tested, and he is allowed to get away with it because he threatens to lea e if annoyed by objections. Geller almost consistently will pass up a key offered for bending, turning to another one or an entirely different test, allowing attention to be taken from the original intent. Then when the first key is examined, it is miraculously found to be bent. The action has taken place during the distraction.

(3) THE ORIGINAL GOAL IS SWITCHED AND THE NEW GOAL IS ACCEPTED. Slade frequently managed to switch the goal intended, and gained acceptance of the experiment as modified. For example, when Zöllner had two wooden rings prepared, each of different woods, he intended that Slade—through his obviously good connections in higher levels of existence—should cause the two to link. He gave the rings to

Slade, who sat at a small pedestal table and held them below the top. To the surprise of the experimenters, the rings ended up around the pedestal of the table! (See Figure 2.) Says Zöllner, in *Transcendental Physics*:

> From the foregoing it will be seen that my prepared experiments did not succeed in the manner "expected" by me. For example, the two wooden rings were not linked together, but instead were transferred within five minutes from the sealed catgut to the leg of the round birchen table. Since the seal was not loosened, and the top of the table was "not at any time" removed—it is still tightly fastened—it follows, from the standpoint of our present conception of space, that each of the two wooden rings penetrated, first the catgut, and then the birch wood of the leg of the table. If however, I ask whether, in the eyes of a sceptic, the experiment desired by me, or that which actually succeeded, is most fitted to make a great and convincing impression, on closer consideration every one will decide in favour of the latter.

FIGURE 2. The wooden-ring test that fooled Zöllner.

This last statement is, of course, pure drivel!

Uri, too, has discovered this useful gimmick. Often he will select a key from among many on a ring, and though the chosen object does not respond to his psychic urging, another key on the ring does. When he tries to "project" a number or word to a person in the audience, that person may not "get" it, but anyone else who agrees with Uri's choice is declared "psychic" and credited with a "hit." And of course Geller takes credit for another "win."

(4) THE PERSON TESTED IS ALLOWED TO SUGGEST TESTS AND CONDITIONS FOR TESTS, THUS SETTING LIMITS WITHIN WHICH HE CAN OPERATE. "Dr." Slade suggested experiments, as well as procedures during these experiments. He would get messages in his head from the "higher planes," which said it would be preferable to have the slates across the room while the messages were developing. Often he would feel that the

very room they were in was not suitable, and he'd have to leave, slates in hand, to try elsewhere. These distractions were necessary so he could work his tricks, and the suggestions were later looked upon as quite legitimate and ingenious. Geller as well has made very useful innovations in scientific procedure and can be counted on to come up with wonderful ideas for new tests, all of which work, of course.

(5) PROPS ARE NOT ACCOUNTED FOR AFTER THE TESTS. When Slade was tested by Zöllner, many duplicates of props (like the sealed string loops) were left about unused. After the test had apparently succeeded, no accounting was made of the unused props. In a similar fashion, when Uri was tested at SRI, the dozens of unused envelopes in the clairvoyance test were not opened and checked afterward to see if they were the same ones that were sealed up. No one bothered, because the tests were over with! But therein might have been the solution to the Geller performance. We will never know, for sure. Science has seen to it that the case is closed.

(6) ACCOUNTS OF THE TIME INVOLVED TO COMPLETE TESTS ARE NOT GIVEN, WHEN THAT FACTOR COULD ACTUALLY BE VERY IMPORTANT IN ANALYZING THE TESTS. Similarly, for both the Slade and Geller tests, the time element is very difficult to determine. At SRI, we are told only that the tests varied "from a few minutes to a half-hour." With Zöllner, even less information is available. Of course, I do not expect to obtain Zöllner's information. He is very much deceased. But from SRI, which spent so much money and time on the Geller tests just recently, we might expect an answer. We have none; at least they will not in any way communicate with me on the subject. Perhaps they have excellent reasons for not giving me that information.

(7) PARTICIPANTS ARE CREDITED WITH PARANORMAL POWERS AND ARE SAID TO HAVE CONTRIBUTED TO THE SUCCESS OR FAILURE OF THE DEMONSTRATION. The lay participants in the performances are often given the notion that they, too, can perform the miracles. Slade many times remarked upon the wonderful powers possessed by the sitters, and gave them credit for the results. Bear in mind that people so flattered are apt to get a bit gushy and relax just a mite more than ordinarily. Blame for a failure can be assigned to them by the same token.

Geller has a great trick when he appears before an audience on stage. He says he will "project" an image to a person; if the person fails to "get" the correct image, Geller is faultless. The receiver is the dope; he wasn't concentrating enough. On the other hand, if the test works, both Geller and the goof are happy.

(8) OTHER SUPERNATURAL FORCES DICTATE CONDITIONS AND INSTRUCTIONS; THUS THE PERFORMERS ARE NOT RESPONSIBLE FOR ERRORS OF INTERPRETATION. I have already mentioned that Slade claimed that spirits suggested many of the conditions for tests through their almost

constant communication with him. Geller has the equivalent in the voices from Hoova, a fictitious planet from which come flying saucers, untold wisdom, and voices recording themselves on tape cassettes that then either erase themselves or dematerialize. How convenient! Seems the Watergate evidence did the same thing. Who's copying whom?

(9) IF AMATEURS, WHO ARE NOT TRAINED CONJURORS, CAN DO THE TRICKS, THEY ARE THE REAL THING, AND THE REALITY OF THE PHENOMENON ITSELF IS ESTABLISHED. Slade's efforts at spirit slate-writing were deemed the real thing by Zöllner because he discovered that two innocent ladies could also do it! As Sir Oliver Lodge, the prominent British scientist, was to say some years later about these matters, "As regards collusion and trickery, no one who has witnessed the absolutely genuine and artless manner in which the impressions are described, but has been perfectly convinced of the transparent honesty of all concerned."

Apparently, the idea is that if amateurs can do it, it must be genuine! The same philosophy is reflected today by Professor John Taylor of King's College, London, who wrote the book, already mentioned, on the subject of children who bend spoons and strips of metal à la Geller. He says he trusts them even to take home a spoon, then bring it back bent—and he believes them when they say they did it by some supernatural force! Why? Because they are not professional conjurors, so could not deceive? On this premise rests much of Taylor's belief in Geller, aside from the fact that he is a very bad observer when Geller is working with him.

(10) CHEATING BY THE PERFORMERS IS EXPECTED AND EXCUSABLE. THEY CAN'T HELP IT. (This is our old friend, Rule for Psychics 2!) If the performers have been convicted of, or caught at, fraud, does it make any difference to their believability? Of course not! Sir Arthur Conan Doyle, prominent dupe of spiritualists, stated: "That mediums I have recommended have been convicted of fraud; any medium may be convicted, because the mere fact of being a medium is illegal by our benighted laws, but no medium I have ever recommended has been shown to be fraudulent in a sense that would be accepted by any real psychic student. This same applies I believe to mediums recommended by Sir Oliver Lodge." Well, Sir Oliver wasn't too bright on the subject either!

Slade was caught cheating in England. He was taken to court on a charge of fraud, convicted, and sentenced to three months at hard labor. On a technicality in the wording of the charge, he was freed again, and before new warrants could be issued he and his assistant fled to France, never to return to England. Though this was not the only time he was caught, it was certainly the most serious fall he took. Was Zöllner fazed by this? Not at all. In fact, it bolstered his belief in the man Slade:

It has been alleged as a characteristic of "all" such mediums, that notwithstanding the most wonderful occurrences in their proximity, they

198 THE TRUTH ABOUT URI GELLER

have yet the inclination to deceive, that is, when opportunity offers, to produce the desired effect by such operations as they consciously endeavour to hide from observation. Having regard to the great danger of such attempts to the medium, and to the entire disproportion between the effects which can be so produced by an inexperienced trickster and those resulting from genuine mediumship, the question arises whether, when this is the case with a medium who has been proved with certainty to be really such, the same consideration does not apply as with persons suffering under so-called kleptomania? It is asserted that a well-known and highly-gifted lady in distinguished circles of Berlin society suffers from this disease. For example, after making large purchases at a jeweler's shop, she will secretly abstract an ornament, which, when she had got home, she will return by her servants to the proprietor. Sometimes a similar perversion of the moral instinct appears with women in the state of pregnancy. In all these cases we do not hold the persons in question morally accountable for these proceedings, since the end attained thereby is out of all proportion, considering the innocent and suitable means at hand. Although I never, during my thirty sittings and other intercourse with Mr. Slade, perceived anything of such perverse methods, yet I ask every unprejudiced person whether, if this has been the case elsewhere, the above morally and legally admissible judgment in relation to kleptomaniacs is not here also exculpatory, considering the certainly anomalous physiological constitution of such mediums.

And Geller? In Israel, as we have seen earlier, he was also charged and convicted. He has been caught many times cheating, yet believers just smile and sigh that he is compelled to cheat in order to convince the ignorant of the reality of his powers! Geller himself gave a good insight into this angle when he said, after a technician for Thames TV in London saw him bending a large spoon (while the film was being changed, as we might suspect) that, "Oh, sure, there's always someone who says they saw me cheating!" That's right from the horse's mouth, folks.

(11) FAILURE IS PROOF OF GENUINE PARANORMAL POWERS, WHICH ONLY WORK IN A SPORADIC AND UNPREDICTABLE FASHION. Re Slade, Zöllner says, in *Transcendental Physics*:

The question will moreover be asked, why just here in Leipzig the experiments with Mr. Slade have been crowned with such splendid success, and yet the knot experiment, for example, has not once succeeded in Russia, notwithstanding so many wishes. If it is considered how great an interest Mr. Slade must have in seeing so simple and striking an experiment everywhere and always successful, every rightly judging and unprejudiced person must see just in this circumstance the most striking proof that Mr. Slade is no trickster who by clever manipulations makes these knots himself. For such an one would evidently be at trouble so to increase his expertness, by frequent repetition of the experiment, as to be able to rely with certainty on his art to deceive other "men of science."

It seems that (see Rule for Psychics 1) consistency in performance is a sin. Slade was certainly judged by this rule, which allowed him many failures. Geller? Of course the same rule applies. The experts have already been quoted here as saying that his many misses prove his reality. If he were always successful, he'd be suspect!

(12) THE FEATS AND COMMUNICATIONS OF HIGHER POWERS APPEAR TRIVIAL TO US MORTALS BECAUSE THEY ARE TOO DEEP FOR OUR PRIMITIVE INTELLECTS. Many complaints came to Zöllner about the trivial nature of the messages that Slade was able to cause to appear on the slates. They were inspiring things like, "Be of good heart. Better lies ahead," and, "The roses of spring wither only to grow again." But Zöllner had seen through that mystery, too. Replied this great thinker:

It has further been asked, why the communications which are written for Mr. Slade on his slates, as is supposed by invisible spirits, are for the most part so commonplace, and so completely within the compass of human knowledge; high spirits must yet necessarily write with more genius, and also spell properly. A private teacher of philosophy at Berlin having made this objection to me personally, on his visit to Leipzig, I observed to him that any communication transcending the present horizon of our understanding must necessarily appear to us absurd and incomprehensible, and I quoted to him the following words of Lichtenberg: "If an angel were to discourse to us of his philosophy, I believe that many propositions would sound to us like '2 and 2 makes 13.'" Far from understanding me, that young philosopher asked me quite seriously, and with an expression of the highest curiosity, whether such propositions, then, ever appeared on Mr. Slade's slates to attest their angelic origin. Completely unprepared for such a naïve question, I was silent, and looked with some astonishment at my young philosopher, who had even already published a book on the new theory of space. Without replying, I thought, "Only wait; soon thou also wilt be at rest" ("Warte nur, bald ruhest auch du"), as regular professor of philosophy in the bosom of some famous German university, and then will it be with thy students just as with us "if an angel discoursed to us of his philosophy"; for Lichtenberg says, "We live in a world where one fool makes many fools, but one wise man only a few wise men."

When some have objected to the trivial things Geller does, such as key-bending and other infantile pranks, Puharich is not at all unable to explain. Even the words of "M," who speaks from a medium's mouth, are drivel: "M calling. We are Nine Principles and Forces . . . working in complete mutual implication . . . Peace is not warlessness. Peace is the integral fruitage of warlessness . . . now that the increment in the mass is exactly to the range of seven by an approximation of ninety-nine percent to the velocity of light, that is a kind of indicator . . ." and so on. Puharich tells us that we are not yet ready to have the deep knowledge that is contained in these pronouncements. Even a rapt believer like Professor John Taylor was left out of the race when he examined these messages from beyond. He was particularly shocked at the equations given Geller from the flying saucers. Says Taylor: ". . . they were simply *wrong!*" Here, I believe him. Because he is a mathematician.

(13) VOICES COME FROM BEYOND TO COMFORT THE RIDICULED PROPHETS OF THE NEW TRUTHS. Zöllner received a message from the spirits via Slade which said:

> Perservere firmly and courageously untroubled about thy opponents, whose daggers drawn upon thee will turn back upon themselves. The scattered seed will find a good soil: the minds of good men, although lower natures are not able to value it. In what you have witnessed, others later on will discover new beauties which escape you at the time. For science it will be an event of unprecedented significance. We rejoice that the atmospheric conditions have been favourable to us, for the conditions must be present, and, in part, prepared. They cannot be explained any more than those, for example, which must immediately precede the falling asleep. Neither in the one case nor in the other can they be compelled. Many enemies of the movement will be its friends, as one of the most important—Carpenter, whose antagonistic disposition has been already now, through thy labours, somewhat shaken, and who later will be thy fellow-labourer in the same field . . .

Isn't it nice to know that the spirits are encouraging the poor besieged scientist? Wouldn't it be nice if the Voices from the Intelligence in the Sky would do the same for poor beleaguered Puharich. Ah, but they do (in *Uri*):

> What you are doing is just the right thing. Struggling a little, getting creative imagination into exertion, awaiting a certain little point for guidance. We are satisfied that every step is being taken in intense sincerity. Failure and success is in your hands. But we also have to do these things. You have to do them, we have to do them—putting up the very best effort in intense sincerity. It's so pleasant to be deluded and to be surprised and to be flabbergasted. All these things are very pleasant and necessary. But if we were not pleased, if we had detected that you are making enormous mistakes or failures, I would have told you before.
>
> We were to look upon this as a long-term contract between you and us. Your cooperation is so very urgently needed. If we develop these techniques, we shall have taken long strides, because what we can do is just this much: indicate the formula and the method—but we understand how much labor, application, patience, it involves to get into operative focus. We have full realization of how much you have to work. So our plans are definite. We feel that you must put in some real effort. We shall cooperate, but your will has to exert itself. On a long-term basis, together we shall achieve some wonders, capital "W."

So, go in full trust and in full hope toward us and more toward yourself that these things definitely come out, and no matter what other things happen, they will only help the cause.

Makes you want to cry, doesn't it?

(14) PERSONS WHO ALREADY BELIEVE IN STRANGE CULTS AND ARE SOMEHOW PREDISPOSED TO ACCEPT ANYTHING THEY NEED TO BELIEVE IN ARE THE BEST PERSONS TO BE TESTED BY. Fechner was *very* nearsighted; Targ is *very* nearsighted. Such men are not, by definition, the best observers. The scientists of Slade's day were believers in far-out and preposterous pseudo-religions and cults. Puthoff, for one of Geller's present supporters, is an adherent of Scientology, a nut religion originated by a science-fiction writer.

(15) THE ENGLISH WILL BELIEVE ANYTHING. GO THERE AND PROSPER. Interestingly enough, both Slade and Geller reached their highest point of success in England. It seems that the ground there is fertile for what they call "nut-cases." English newspapers abound for advertising spirit churches, healing, and miscellaneous wonders—even today.

(16) USE THE OLD COMPASS TRICK. IT FOOLS THEM ALL. Slade was able to cause a compass to deflect; it convinced his scientist friends. Geller has made a compass deflect; it sold *his* scientist friends. The fact that this trick has been done by conjurors for over a century does not mean a thing to these scientists. A simple search of the conjuror's body by means of a probe would establish whether it's a trick or not—but this is not done. Such a search would annoy the "sensitive" so it is beyond consideration. Oh yes, Geller's *hands* have been searched—but so were *my* hands searched carefully when I also deflected a compass; *and I stood at a distance to do it, and did not use any confederates,* at King's College.

(17) On November 4, 1882, "Dr." Henry Slade, spirit slate-writer *extraordinaire,* was exposed fully for the last time, and in order to avoid being arrested for his fraud, signed a full confession and promptly went out of business.

And Geller? Well, he has said that he doesn't mind what people say about him, so long as they spell his name right.

His name has been spelled correctly all through this book.

18
The Magicians' Attitude and How It Changed

The devil can quote scriptures for his purpose.
— Shakespeare

When my name was first mentioned in connection with the Uri Geller matter, I became the target of much criticism from leading writers in the magic business.

We magicians have our own publications that the public seldom, if ever, will see. They are often obtainable only by subscription and frequently only go to members of organizations like the Society of American Magicians, the International Brotherhood of Magicians, or the Magic Circle of London. One such periodical is a small pamphlet called *Magick*. It is edited by Bascom Jones, who was very severe in his censure of me, though he was not the only one. His suppositions about my comments on Geller included the notion that I had set about to expose the secrets of the magicians and that I already had done so. This was not true, but the idea spread. I've never received an apology in *this* matter, though one was certainly due.

Soon I was assailed by a member of the Magic Circle (in which organization I proudly hold membership) and I felt it was time to reply. Upon my reply being published, the gentleman in England wrote to apologize and admitted his error of assumption. *None* of the American periodicals knew what I was getting at, let alone felt that an apology was due.

But the tide has turned. Geller became more of an obvious "hype," and soon legitimate magicians were having to answer for his claims to divine origin and occult abilities, though I must say that many of my fellow-performers are still claiming they can do the real thing, against what I feel should be a more respectable code of ethics for magicians.

In the following letter, written to one Alan Kennaugh of *The Magician*, a conjuror's periodical that railed against me and against Ali Bongo, a highly ranked fellow-member of the Magic Circle, the situation is outlined in terms I can hardly improve upon. The author of the letter, Sam Dalal, who lives in India, has been a correspondent of mine for years now and is not only a respected magician but editor of another publication called *Mantra*. Sam is familiar with Indian "versions" of Geller, and expresses himself rather well here. But I'll let him put my case for me:

202

An Open Letter to Alan Kennaugh

Dear Mr. Kennaugh,

I enjoy reading your columns in "The Magigram," and the column in the Feb., 1974, issue which arrived last evening was no exception. I often disagree with what I read, but that is a solitary and perhaps inconsequential opinion of no great importance.

But this time I feel compelled to disagree in print because sometimes views such as expressed by you in tolerance and good faith can have very serious consequences. People respect your views—and form opinions to concur with the trends of thinking which are expounded by their favourite columnists. When this thinking has certain basic errors, it is essential that these be pointed out to allow people at large to form a balanced and unbiased opinion.

The sum and total of your column is that you defend Geller, and say he is a "creditable happening" while people like James Randi and Ali Bongo, who have "exposed" him for a mere trickster, have really done no creditable service to Magic or laymen.

In support of your contention you have made the following points:

1. That Geller caught the imagination of the ordinary people like no magician has been able to in recent times.

2. That if people like Randi and Bongo start a debunking chain—it could harm every good and popular performer from Warlock and Harbin* onwards.

3. You make a balanced case as to whether Uri is a genuine phenomenon, or not, using a couple of Uri's quotes and those of professor John Taylor against those of Randi and a Beersheba ruling! (In the total context of your article . . . it tips the scales in Uri's favour.)

4. Your chief contention is that Uri has ENTERTAINED a vast audience—and the claims he makes are of little consequence in view of the total impact he has made on the public.

Now . . . let me point out why each of the above is either incomplete, or fallacious.

1. By itself, catching the imagination of ordinary people is not necessarily creditable. Hitler, for one, inflamed a whole country . . . with consequences that are a disgrace to mankind! But let us speak only of Magic and Mystics. Perhaps you have heard of Maharishi Mahesh Yogi . . . or Satya Sai Baba. Both are recent phenomena—WITH A FAR WIDER FOLLOWING THAN GELLER! Satya Sai Baba has had more than one book written on him by "devout disciples" from the West. He is no better than Geller in that his bag of tricks consists of materialising rings and charms, and heating silver foil and producing ash. He has a GREAT FOLLOWING . . . just by playing "Superman" in real life. Perhaps you will ask what he has to do with Geller? Let me quote from an "open letter" of Randi's re Geller which appeared in "ARBA" #1462.† "I know a bit more about this

---

* Two well-known British conjurors.
† An English conjuring periodical.

young man than you chaps do over there; for one thing, he is intending to enter the 'Psychic healing' field 'soon,' and when he starts into that racket he can kill people. He is well on his way to becoming a religious figure, and he is ruthless in his methods to do so."

Mr. Kennaugh, India has a population some 1½ times that of the U.K. and U.S.A. put together. If the number of "ordinary people" impressed be the criterium for judging the impact of a showman—WE CAN PUT OUT 10 GELLERS FOR EVERY ONE FROM THE WEST. True—they have a less-educated following . . . and are cruder in their methods. But their objectives are identical . . . to gather a following by HOAX. I can write volumes on THE EVIL SIDE EFFECTS OF A RELIGIOUS CULT FORMED BY THESE PEOPLE.

I believe Randi—because in every respect, Geller's behaviour (his debunking of Magicians—his desire to be taken in DEAD EARNEST . . . and his vehemence against criticism) coincides with those of the "mystics" I know too well. Just because his methods are more sophisticated to cater to a more intelligent man DOES NOT MAKE HIM MORE ACCEPTABLE. I scoff at the Sai Babas here—and YOU or a few intelligent tricksters may take Geller with a pinch of salt. NOT SO THE ORDINARY PEOPLE. When a man like this starts to catch people's imagination, he must be stopped.

IF WE SAW AN ACTOR PLAY A MOST CONVINCING DOCTOR ON STAGE, WE WOULD APPLAUD HIS PERFORMANCE; IF HE STEPPED OUT INTO REAL LIFE, AND TRIED PLAYING DOCTOR, IT WOULD ONLY BE WISE TO STOP HIM. THE SAME GOES FOR SUPERMEN!

2. The statement that Randi and Bongo could start a debunking chain is of course sheer nonsense—because BOTH WARLOCK AND HARBIN HAVE BEEN PERFORMING BEFORE GELLER WAS BORN . . . WITHOUT PRO-VOKING ANY SUCH REACTIONS. This has not lessened their image or popularity. The obvious difference is that both these respected gentle-men (and hundreds of others) play SUPERMAN on stage and do NOT try it off stage.

If they play their parts VERY CONVINCINGLY and make their audi-ence BELIEVE IT'S FOR REAL . . . It's like a good story . . . which can make you laugh or cry, even if it's only fiction. Surely, Mr. Kennaugh, if Har-bin started claiming his ZIG ZAG GIRL was actual dematerialisation—and had the Stanford "Think Tank," or a panel of international doctors examine it . . . you would agree that here was some kind of nut. Even if he did fool a few guys because the illusion was made to fool . . . and some gullible people were willing to swear to it, it still would not change the crux of the matter . . . THAT A MAN IS USING TRICKERY—not TO ENTERTAIN BUT TO HOAX AND DECEIVE. If you will go back a few years in time . . . you will read endless accounts of HOUDINI's exposure of FAKE MEDIUMS. They had their champions . . . men of unquestionable integ-rity like Sir Arthur Conan Doyle . . . but men INEXPERIENCED at the business of trickery. Obviously, the best man to catch trickery is a Magi-cian . . . and not a scientist. HOUDINI did not start a debunking chain. He did not harm himself or Magic by his campaign. Why then presume that Randi or Bongo are different? Just because they have the courage to

say Geller is a HOAX? If Geller only performed for entertainment —
without INSISTING ON BEING TAKEN IN EARNEST OFF STAGE . . . I'm
quite willing to wager anything within my means that neither of these
gentlemen would have done more than praise him.

3. While balancing your "pros" and "cons" of Geller's genuineness
you have forgotten one thing: That those who fight him know more
about GELLER'S BUSINESS than the laymen who support him. As for Geller's own statement about what he calls "Controlled Conditions," these
have been described by others as "incredible sloppiness."

The correct weight of the matter is as follows:

By duplicating his feats — THE MAGICIANS HAVE ESTABLISHED A REA-
SONABLE DOUBT ABOUT THE REALITY OF HIS POWERS.

By being unable to get any results under test conditions — which will
enable the testing authorities to give him a clear certificate, Geller has
NOT YET ESTABLISHED ONE POINT IN HIS FAVOUR . . . except his personal
rantings. His tests at Stanford were "inconclusive." There is more than
one occasion when he HAS resorted to trickery. Why does a genuine
psychic need trickery in ANY FORM? And if he's only a GOOD TRICKSTER —
why the obsession with trying to be accepted as a genuine psychic?

The Magic profession is based on DECEIT FOR THE PURPOSE OF
ENTERTAINMENT. It does not encompass deceit in real life . . . or does it?
Why not start championing every confidence trickster and hoaxer that
comes along? After all — they are "far" more adept at showmanship and
selling themselves than hundreds of top-name performers.

4. I am not sure Uri has ENTERTAINED a vast audience. He may have
entertained YOU . . . because you take him with a pinch of salt and he
may have entertained me (like the Sai Baba does) . . . giving me some
ideas for new effects.

To the majority of the lay audience . . . HE IS A GENUINE PSYCHIC
WITH GENUINE POWERS. Such men can pick up a following — with very
dangerous overtones. When people tamper with gullible opinions, and
gather religious followings, they can very often create misfits and sometimes monsters. I wonder how Sharon Tate felt about mystics?

No, Mr. Kennaugh . . . I don't wish to imply the worst about Geller, because he may have only an off-beat approach towards Magic. You
may wonder what is the difference if a guy uses a hand buzzer or forges
your signature on a check . . . if it's "his idea of a practical joke!" You
may even condone his cashing the check — after all . . . it was a NOVEL
joke, that will catch far more public notice than a HAND BUZZER will!

Me — I'm an old-fashioned sort. I perform the "spirit-slates" trick but
I wouldn't charge five pounds to produce a message from someone's dead
mother! And I charge for my deceit, but not for the deceit itself, only the
ENTERTAINMENT I provide through it. The day I start selling something I
can't deliver . . . like "psychic healing" and messages from "Little Green
Men" . . . and hope to be taken in earnest all the time — I hope somewhere there will be a HOUDINI, a RANDI or a BONGO with the moral
courage and decency to stop me!

And having had my say — I'll still love reading your excellent column, and learning a hundred and one priceless things from your knowledge and experience. Thank you, Mr. Kennaugh.

SAM DALAL

This letter never appeared in *The Magigram* . . .

But now the situation has changed. We who publicly opposed Geller have become the heroes and those who failed to speak up are making the excuses, though not all the magicians think we were in the right. There are still those who think we should have let the public go right on believing in this nonsense, "because it's good for business!" I don't need that kind of business. *Some* inept magicians have even been *fooled* by Geller, then issued silly "endorsements" of his abilities!

I would point out that many of us have definite stands and declarations we make to express our code of ethics. One such is David Berglas, who has been active in England in opposition to the Geller myth and who is one of the greatest mentalist performers I have ever known. He is original, inventive, and polished in his work, and I count it as a great pleasure and privilege to consider him as a friend.

David has given me permission to publish here his statement, which is printed a full page high in his program sheet. It is headed—in big black letters—"About the Show . . ."

Mr. David Berglas would like to state that he is presenting this show strictly as ENTERTAINMENT.

Various Organisations and Societies have, in the past, made certain supernormal claims on his behalf, which have no bearing or foundation on his own views and beliefs, and which he emphatically denies.

He maintains that in his entertainments he does NOT use Psychic Phenomena, Supernatural Powers, Sixth Sense or Telepathy.

He talks of a "Trick of the Mind" as well as Sensual and Optical Illusions, which enable him to perform the seemingly impossible. Besides manipulative skill, he says, he uses deep psychological insight, acute observation and a highly trained memory.

During the war, the R.A.F. had a slogan: "The Difficult we do immediately, the Impossible takes a little longer."

David Berglas elaborated on this theme and made HIS motto: "The IMPOSSIBLE I do immediately—MIRACLES take a little longer!"

Thank you, Mr. Berglas. That says it nicely.

I call upon the conjurors of the world to take a stand on this matter. I call upon the magical organizations that place so much value upon the preservation of their trade secrets to put as much value into their concern for the public they entertain, and to insist upon certain standards of truth from their members. I urge that we devote our efforts to the entertainment of our audiences by means of subterfuge, but never the bilking or the condoning of bilking of any person or group by means of our skills. I insist that magicians of standing take action on behalf of the uninitiated to protect them against charlatans who profess divine or supernatural powers. And, most of all, I ask my fellow-magicians to preserve the dignity and integrity of this craft we hold so sacred by standing up to be counted when that craft is threatened by those who would make of it a racket.

We owe at least that much to those whom we entertain. It is they who bring us that priceless commodity, applause, without which we wither and perish. And it is they who make it possible for us to make an enjoyable living that rewards us personally in so many ways other than money.

For we are the only element that stands between the faker and his victim. Men of science and other great intellects are without that peculiar expertise that qualifies us to detect chicanery when it is practiced on a high level. We are needed, and we must respond when called. This is a challenge we must not only accept; we must lay claim to it.

Tomorrow may be too late. The charlatans are upon us.

19

Conclusion: What Geller Has Done, and Where He Can Go From Here

© 1975 United Feature Syndicate, Inc.

Here we are faced with "the perfect theory" in parapsychology. Since wonders of the mind are claimed by its advocates, we might attempt to prove whether these are genuine powers or only tricks and misconstrued experiments. But we find that the supporters of these marvels claim the scientific method cannot be applied in these cases. Also, test conditions disturb the performers, and skeptics make performance impossible. So the powers cannot be proved one way or the other.

Wild claims have been made by Geller and the Gellerites. They tell us that Geller has been retained by unnamable government officials to work magic on weapons systems. There is no proof, of course. We are told that the U.S. Department of Defense has shown an active interest in Geller and his powers — but when the department denies this claim, saying that they have found no reason to believe in his powers of magic, the Gellerites merely smile like deluded Mona Lisas and retire into mystic contemplation.*

Geller's background becomes clearer every day. Mr. Herb Zarrow, an amateur magician from New Jersey, was on holiday in Israel when his

---

* See the Appendix, letter from the Department of Defense.

tour-guide discovered his interest in conjuring and took him to see a magician named Ruckenstein in the little town of Safed. In their conversation, it developed that Ruckenstein had known Geller in the early days when the "psychic" was just a regular magician who would exchange tricks and ideas with him. Then, after a few months, Geller started to advertise that he was the real thing, and Ruckenstein showed him the door, not wanting any part of the deception.

Excerpts follow from a July 8, 1974, article in the *Montreal Gazette* concerning a "psychic" demonstration by Geller. The article, by Nigel Gibson, was entitled "He Set Watch Back an Hour."

"Do you have any keys on you?"

I fumbled in my pocket and produced three keys on a ring: two apartment keys and a front door key.

Geller picked up the keys and examined them closely. "Any preference?" he asked.

I told him if he was going to bend any of them it might as well be the front door key. Then I wouldn't have to use the fire escape to get into my apartment.

Wrong Key

He put the keys in my palm and asked me to cover them with my other hand. Placing his fist on my hand, he applied light pressure.

"Feel anything?" he said. I didn't. "OK, let's take a look." I removed my hand. One of the apartment keys was bent at a 30-degree angle.

"Oh, oh, wrong key," he said, holding them up to the light. "Cover them up again." I obliged and he repeated the procedure. This time it was the turn of the front door key—bent almost beyond repair.

. . . . . .

"Here, I'll show you what I mean. Give me your watch." I hesitated. "Come on, come on, nothing will happen to it," Geller said. I handed him the watch.

Crowd Gathered

"Check the time," he said. "I'm going to set your watch back exactly one hour." It was 4:40 P.M.

By now a crowd of about 15 had begun to gather around our table. A fat man with a huge cigar was breathing heavily over my shoulder.

Placing the watch in the palm of my hand, Geller asked me to cover it with my other hand and repeated the procedure of the keys.

"OK, look at your watch and tell me what time it is," Uri said. I looked. It said 3:40. The fat man almost swallowed his cigar. "Incroyable, incroyable," the waiter said, shaking his head.

Now, I must prove myself to be a liar, for in order to read the true story as originally printed in the *Gazette,* you must substitute "Randi" for "Geller" in these excerpts. The article describes a visit *I* made to Canada, and a demonstration *I* did for Gibson of the *Gazette.* If you read this account believing it to be a convincing proof of Geller's powers, is it any less powerful now that you know Randi is the subject rather than Uri? Think about that.

Investigate for yourself. Start with the personnel behind Geller. Harold Puthoff is said to be a Scientology "clear"—a person who has total recall of everything in his experience. Test him. Ask him on which day of the week his twenty-first birthday fell, or some question like that—simple fare for a "clear." While you're at it, you might ask him what happened to the report that was issued on that "ESP Teaching Machine" that *you* spent $80,000 to develop. Your tax money, through NASA and monitored by the Jet Propulsion Labs (JPL), went into its construction. It failed. Mind you, it *seemed* to work at first (Targ's daughter, *who was allowed to test herself and record her own results,* got wonderful scores). But when an automatic recorder was connected, scores fell to those of mathematical chance. And believe it or not, 100 out of 145 persons who tried the machine were "employees, relatives and friends"!

Want to know more about this machine? I would like to, as well, but I can't, because I wrote to SRI for a copy of the official report, as did many of my friends at my suggestion, and SRI failed to answer. If you're a taxpayer, I suggest that you write:

> Dr. C. Anderson
> Stanford Research Institute
> Menlo Park, California 94025

Ask for a copy of the NASA report on the ESP Teaching Machine, of August 1974, Project #2613. Include a stamped, self-addressed envelope. Then sit back and wait.

But don't hold your breath.

Even Targ's initial enthusiasm for Geller seems to have flagged. On December 28, 1972, he was saying to *Scientific American* magazine, re Geller: ". . . extraordinary sense perception and [his] ability to perturb physical systems have been *carefully verified* and *well documented* in this laboratory" (italics added). By March 9, 1973, Targ was saying in the "SRI Report": "We have observed certain phenomena with the subjects for which we have no scientific explanation. All we can say at this point is that further investigation is clearly warranted." There has obviously been a change of Targ's evaluation of his own tests in a little over two months!

Men of science who have tested Geller are proud of telling us about their prior accomplishments, to indicate why we should take their research seriously and believe that their observations are to be given high priority. Okay, then tell me this: If we are to take *their* past work as proof of their present reliability, why should we not take into account the past work of *Geller*? We are told that we must ignore his numerous failures, his many exposures, his court case, his refusals to be tested, and his remarkable shyness when confronted with qualified conjurors! I see a dichotomy here that I cannot accept.

Targ and Puthoff say, in a letter to *Communications Society* magazine, that, "In lengthy consultation with professional magicians, no viable conjuring explanation for these or other experiments reported in *Nature* has emerged." *What* magicians? If these gentlemen have examined this book carefully, they may now have another conclusion. I've offered *my* services, free of charge, many times, and have never even had a reply from SRI. But *I* have some explanations!

Scientists are a strange lot—those who are Gellerites. Taylor believes in nothing but metal-bending by Geller. Targ believes in most everything else, but not in metal-bending. Charles Honorton, of Maimonides Hospital, doesn't believe in Geller's metal-bending feats— *because there is no precedent in parapsychology for them!* (Then I presume Honorton does not believe in lunar landings. No precedent.)

Stanley Krippner, a leading American parapsychologist, says today, "To my way of thinking, Geller has been an embarrassment to parapsychology." And Geller merely comments, "All publicity is good publicity." I trust he still thinks so after reading this book.

One of the high-priority proofs Geller offers of his supernatural powers is the stunt he pulled in a department store in Germany. With the press present, he caused an escalator to stop dead, and the local papers were full of the wonderful event the next day.

But now to 1974, and to New York City. Geller was asked by WNEW-TV in that city to perform the same stunt. Wisely, the station's news department asked Bob McAlister, who is the host of the long-running children's television show "Wonderama" to go along with the news team. Bob is a very accomplished magician, and so a good judge of these matters. They were well aware that Geller would not have tolerated *my* "negative vibrations" and trusted that he would not know of Bob's expertise. He didn't.

Geller had suggested that Bloomingdale's department store would be ideal, since he lived near there. But WNEW decided to use Gimbel's instead, since their staff had done many projects with them in the past. When Geller heard this, just before they started out to film the stunt, he excused himself suddenly "to make a phone call." He was pretty disturbed when he got back and tried to talk them into going to Bloomingdale's as originally planned. But they proceeded to Gimbel's.

Nothing happened. Geller strove mightily, and the escalators kept going as before, in spite of the fact that there are emergency stop switches at each end of the escalators—but perhaps because McAlister had alerted the security people there to post guards at each escalator, the machinery defied Geller's every effort.

Could he have planned to have Shipi there ready to stop the escalator when needed? And was Shipi now a nervous wreck, waiting for him over at the Bloomingdale store, wondering what had gone wrong? I'd put money on it!

In the August 1973 issue of *Scientific American,* writer Martin Gardner published a tongue-in-cheek test for "clairvoyance." One of Geller's favorite gimmicks was exposed. Try this test yourself. *Think of two simple, different geometrical shapes, drawn one inside the other. (Don't think of a square; that's too easy!)*

You can try this test on your friends, wording it exactly as above, and you'll be surprised to find that the shapes they draw are a triangle and a circle arranged one of the two possible ways, though both can be called "hits." Most of the time, that is.

Dumb? Sure it is. It's obvious why it works most of the time. Would you suspect Geller of doing this? Well, he has, and he does! Colonel Austin Kibler of the U.S. Department of Defense reported that Geller had used the identical test on him. Geller tried it at the *Time* magazine office, too. In Ottawa, Canada, he did it in a press conference. At SRI, in 1972, he used it again. In England, it was the hit of the show in a BBC dressing room.

On the NBC-TV "Tomorrow" show of August 14, 1975, he used it again. Shall I go on? It's a rather limited repertoire, and now my readers can do it, too!

And how is the Israeli psychic superstar doing currently? Well, in Sweden, not so well.

That country's leading paper, *Dagens Nyheter,* has exposed Geller's claim about the SRI tests and undercut his accounts of "disinterested" scientific support. The paper told how Swedish and Norwegian scientists who investigated the Geller feats never got a chance to speak on television, though they appeared with Geller, and how six or seven people traveled there with Uri and had access to the studio and the props. In Norway, they have good reason to believe that the props were switched. It was claimed, further, that Geller saw British performer Berglas at work in Israel years ago and had copied some of his tricks. In Norway, the Magic Circle there offered Geller 50,000 kroner (about $7,000 U.S.) to produce his miracles under test conditions. He refused. In Sweden, ten out of thirteen Geller shows were canceled due to poor ticket sales. Even in New Zealand, where Geller made an initial good impression, he performed two and a half hours of nothing at all, and left a very unhappy audience; and the *New Zealand Listener* published a complete exposé of his tricks. In Australia, his first show was packed, the second had a poor house, and the third was canceled.

In the May 17, 1975, article written for the *New Zealand Listener,* two psychologists from the University of Otago, Richard Kammann and David Marks, fully exposed Geller's stunts. Said they: "To put our conclusions into a nutshell, Uri Geller's abilities are not the least bit paranormal as he claims—they are nothing more than skilful conjuring." Their 3-page write-up on Uri's feats makes the most devastating summary of his tricks that I have ever seen.

They solved his every trick, even to catching the signals from the audience. "Among Geller's retinue, his secretary, Ms. Solveg Clark, and friend Shipi Shtrang were seemingly always present among the audience— at least for the 'ESP' part of the show. This part of the show is slow-moving and rather dull, as several reviewers have observed, and even after three shows we would be reluctant to sit through another. When on two occasions one of us saw Uri glance up to Solveg Clark and simultaneously she was observed to make some rather strange hand movements, we believed Berendt and Pelz* could have a point."

Nature magazine has refused a paper dealing with Geller's purported spoon-bending powers. Now Edgar Mitchell has backed out of supporting Geller. And Professor Amos Tversky, of the University of Jerusalem, says: "I know Uri Geller, and he is a fraud . . . He manages to intimidate the skeptics and to make them appear suspicious and nontrusting . . . Some of his tricks were quite primitive, and some of his stories about himself and things he did in the past were shown to be false . . . [Allon, an amateur magician] suggested controls should be taken, and whenever these steps were taken, Uri Geller's psychic powers apparently faded away . . ."

In Stanford, Geller tried healing, as he has in Europe, and failed. But don't think that that isn't a lucrative possibility for Uri. I predict he'll be back at it. I myself am offering Geller $10,000, to wit:

This statement outlines the general rules covering James Randi's offer concerning psychic claims. Since claims will vary greatly, specific rules will be formulated for each individual claimant. However, *all claimants* must agree to the rules set forth here, before *any* agreement is entered into. Claimants will declare their agreement by sending a letter so stating to Mr. Randi. All correspondence must include a stamped, self-addressed envelope, due to the large amount of mail exchanged on this subject. Thank you.

I will pay the sum of $10,000 (U.S.) to any person who can demonstrate

---

* The Israeli psychologist and Geller's former manager, respectively, who had commented upon Shipi's signaling code.

any paranormal ability under satisfactory observing conditions. Such a demonstration must be performed under these rules and limitations:

(1) Claimant must state in advance just what powers or abilities will be demonstrated, the limits of the proposed demonstration (so far as time, location and other variables are concerned) and what will constitute a positive or a negative result.

(2) Only the actual performance of the announced nature and scope will be acceptable, done within the agreed limits.

(3) Claimant agrees that all data, photographic materials, videotape or film records and/or other material obtained, may be used by Mr. Randi in any way he chooses.

(4) Where a judging procedure is needed, such procedure will be decided upon in advance after the claim is stated. All such decisions will be arrived at by Mr. Randi and the claimant, to their mutual satisfaction, in advance of any further participation.

(5) Mr. Randi may ask that a claimant perform before an appointed representative, rather than before him, if distance and time dictate that procedure. Such performance is only for purposes of determining whether claimant is likely to be able to perform as promised.

(6) Mr. Randi will not undertake to pay for any expenses involved on the part of the claimant, such as transportation, accommodation, etc.

(7) Claimant surrenders any and all rights to legal action against Mr. Randi or any other participating agency or person, so far as may be legally done under present statutes, in regard to injury, accident, or any other damage of a physical or emotional nature, or financial or professional loss of any other kind.

(8) In the event that the claimant is successful under the agreed terms and conditions, Mr. Randi's check for the amount of $10,000 (U.S.) shall be *immediately* paid to that claimant, in full settlement.

(9) Copies of this document are available to any person who sends a stamped, self-addressed envelope to Mr. Randi requesting it.

(10) This offer is made by Mr. Randi personally, and not on behalf of any other agency or organization, though others may be involved in the examination of claims submitted.

(11) This offer is open to any and all persons in any part of the world, regardless of sex, race, educational background, etc., and will continue until the prize is awarded.

(12) CLAIMANT MUST AGREE UPON WHAT WILL CONSTITUTE A CONCLUSION THAT HE/SHE DOES *not* POSSESS THE CLAIMED ABILITY OR POWERS. This will be a major consideration in accepting or rejecting claimants.

NOTARIZED: Signed
State of New Jersey
Jane V. N. Conger   James Randi

County of Monmouth
Signed before me this 18th of June, 1981

And Geller has made no move to accept: Berglas in England is offering £5,000 for the same kind of proof, and has heard nothing. As of this writing, Geller has taken to performing "readings" for individuals for a fee of $200! Yet he has fortunes awaiting him if he will only submit to controlled tests with conjurors monitoring them!

Uri, I assure you that not *all* the world consists of fools. I know that you and Shipi must giggle yourselves silly when you think of how easily those scientists and media people have been fooled by the simple ruses you learned so well. But the vast majority of scientists, and now more and more of the media and the public, are becoming aware that the psychic superstar is depending increasingly on wild claims and hyperbole. The supporters are dropping off your slowing bandwagon.

If you have read this book carefully, you'll see that I have demonstrated: (*a*) that Geller's supposed metal-bending abilities are merely tricks accomplished by sleight of hand, (*b*) that his claims of having been tested under rigorous scientific conditions are so much hot air, (*c*) that Geller's "telepathic" abilities are demonstrated by tired old conjuring dodges that have been used for a century and which depend upon very loose control for their success, (*d*) that he has chosen to be tested by men of science who have already declared themselves believers in paranormal nonsense, (*e*) that he has made wild claims of wondrous accomplishments that never took place, (*f*) that he has been tried in a court of law and convicted on the work he did in Israel, (*g*) that media of all kinds have consistently refused—with a few notable exceptions—to publish negative accounts of his work, believing that their consumers prefer to have fanciful myths to believe in, rather than the facts, (*h*) that members of the conjuring profession themselves have, on the whole, preferred to remain silent and allow Geller to perpetuate his wild claims, in spite of their obligation to give an accurate analysis to their public, (*i*) that leading scientists who have *not* been fooled by the Gellerites have chosen to maintain a "no-comment" attitude, believing themselves to be far above such carnival affairs, while other, lesser lights of science have taken full advantage of this silence to declare idiocies in the name of science, and (*j*) that Uri Geller has perpetrated a massive fraud in denying his background as a magician and in pretending divine and supernatural powers, when he is in fact performing simple and rather trivial tricks.

Geller has announced that he will try to bring back the special lunar camera that Edgar Mitchell left on the moon—at an extravaganza to be held at the Houston Astrodome. I can't wait. Meanwhile, back at the Stanford Research Institute, they report that the original drawings Geller made during their "cheat-proof" tests are not now available. When a British television producer asked to see them, it was announced that they were "misplaced"! Dematerialized by a flying saucer, perhaps? Shades of Watergate—again!

As Roger Rapoport wrote in *Cosmopolitan,* in June 1974: ". . . in an age when rock stars can barely carry a tune, when whores can become best-selling authors and movie actors get elected to national office, it seems only reasonable that an Israeli spoon-bender with one eye on *Spectra* and the other on the box office can make it as a psychic folk hero in this terrestrial world." Yet columns in conjurors' publications like *Genii, Magick,* and *The Linking Ring* continue even now to rail against such authors as this one who try to bring sanity to a public that deserves to know the truth. I have tried in this volume to do just that, and I will defend my stand even if every conjuror in the business stands against me; I trust that this will not be the case.

Uri Geller has said, to Stefan Kanfer of *Time* magazine: ". . . Randi is jealous of me because I'm young and good-looking, and have nice wavy hair!" Well, I'm no longer as young as I'd prefer to be, and most of the hair has departed during the years, that's true.

But I sleep well, Uri.

Stand now with thine enchantments, with the multitudes of thy sorceries, wherein thou hast labored from thy youth. — Isaiah 47:12

Objections to This Book

Shortly after *The Magic of Uri Geller* was released in 1975, the parapsychology journal *Psychoenergetic Systems* published a lengthy attempt at rebuttal by Russell Targ and Harold Puthoff of what they considered to be the major errors I had committed.

Upon publication of this Targ and Puthoff blast, I immediately prepared a response. It was submitted to *Fate* magazine and to *Psychoenergetic Systems*—now defunct—but was refused. It never saw print.

Following are the 24 points I make in this book that Targ and Puthoff contended and the "facts" as they see them, together with my comments, which have heretofore been denied publication.

1. Foreword by Jaroff (p. 7): Geller convinced executives and researchers at the Stanford Research Institute (SRI) . . . that he could (among other things) distort solid metallic objects.

Fact: SRI's position on Geller's putative metal-bending ability is clearly stated in the researcher's *Nature* publication: "It has been widely reported that Geller has demonstrated the ability to bend metal by paranormal means. Although metal bending by Geller has been observed in our laboratory, we have not been able to combine such observations with adequately controlled experiments to obtain data sufficient to support the paranormal hypothesis." (*Nature* 252, No. 5476, pp. 602–607, October 18, 1974)

My Response: Leon Jaroff penned that comment, not I. However, both he and I had good reason to believe that T and P were referring to metal-bending in their glowing December 1972 letter to *Scientific American* magazine. They had already told Professor Ray Hyman, sent by the Department of Defense to SRI to evaluate T and P's claims about Geller and others, that Geller could bend metal parnormally without touching it. However, in denying that their comment to *Scientific American* referred to Geller, T and P get in even deeper trouble. They have revealed to us that they were writing about the infamous Magnetometer Experiment with Ingo Swann! This was probably the most messed-up pseudo-experiment that they ever did—incorrectly reported, badly run, loosely (if at all) controlled, and a general catastrophe. The fact that these scientists eventually reversed their opinions of Geller's ability to bend metal—by any "psychic" means—does not excuse their wild claims about the "extraordinary" powers they said they had "carefully verified and well documented" from their "highly gifted subjects."

217

2. Randi (p. 13): Few of the Geller experiments, especially the famous tests at SRI in which Geller performed apparent miracles of ESP, include in their reports the fact that one Shipi Shtrang, once claimed by Geller as his cousin and his brother, was present.

Fact: During the SRI experimentation, neither Shipi nor any other potential confederate was permitted in the target area, a pre-condition for experimentation adopted on the basis of advice by project consulting magicians.

My response: I stand by that statement. *No reports mentioned Shtrang.* It matters little whether he was "in the target area." I never said that he was! He was still *there,* and able to assist Geller. Verbal soft-shoe will not work.

3. Randi (p. 14): But scientists are loath to consult magicians.

Fact: At SRI one of the two responsible investigators is an amateur magician with over twenty years experience, a Bay Area magician who specializes in exposing fraudulent poltergeist cases is a continuing consultant from the beginning of the project, and Milbourne Christopher, a world-renowned magician and critic of psychic phenomena, was brought in to critique videotape and film of the Geller work, and to suggest protocols for further experimentation.

My response: (*a*) Arthur Hastings, the part-time magician referred to but not named here, told me that he gave T and P some rules to follow. They ignored them, and Geller insisted that Hastings not be allowed to witness the experiments. (*b*) Christopher, far from being asked to *witness* the tests, saw only selected film and tape at SRI *months after Geller had left*! He has said that there was not enough detail in the record for him to tell anything about how the tricks might have been done. Certainly none of his suggestions were later followed by T and P, who seemed willing to listen—after the event—and then chose to ignore all advice.

4. Randi (p. 14): Even while the Stanford Research Institute was involved in testing the Israeli Wonder, I wrote offering my services and never received the courtesy of a reply.

Fact: Randi's letter, dated September 6, 1973, was months after completion of the SRI work with Geller.

My response: There was more than one letter. *None* of them were answered.

5. Randi (p. 18): Then, too, there seems to be developing a public belief that science approves the trend toward parapsychological research and that most people believe in psychic marvels. It is a fact that the vast majority of scientists today have no interest, or belief, in these things.

Fact: According to a recent survey reported by Chris Evans in *New Scientist*, pp. 209, January 25, 1973, "Parapsychology—What the Questionnaire Revealed," 67 percent of nearly 1500 responding (the majority of whom are working scientists and technologists) considered ESP to be an established fact or a likely possibility, and 88 percent held the investigation of ESP to be a legitimate scientific undertaking.

My response: I stand by this statement. Chris Evans's test was not all that it might have been, and he admitted it. He failed to realize that (a) *New Scientist* is a popularized UK science magazine, read mostly by the informed layman, not full-time scientists, and (b) those who answer such polls tend to be believers, who are thus more heavily represented in the results. Other surveys have failed to support the *New Scientist* inquiry.

6. Randi (p. 31): Puthoff reprinted the *Nature* article without the page-and-a-half introduction! (Following paragraph implying editing out of material unfavorable to the paper.)

Fact: Reprint of article to which Randi refers is the standard *Nature* reprint sent to authors. The so-called Introduction Randi claims is deleted refers to an editorial at the front of the magazine, several pages earlier. *Nature* reprints standardly do not carry editorials, letters to the editor, etc.

My response: T and P had a responsibility to mention that editorial. It was an integral part, not of the scientific paper, but of the total picture *Nature* presented to its readers. Technically, T and P have a valid point; ethically, they do not. My statement is still true: Puthoff did not publish the embarrassing editorial.

7. Randi (p. 34): After reprinting *Nature* editorial Randi claims that he must give his own version of SRI paper, as SRI did not make paper available to him.

Fact: SRI paper to which he refers was in same magazine as the editorial he reprinted, a few pages later . . . a document in the public domain, available in any technical library, permission for the use of which is obtained from the magazine as was done for the editorial.

My response: I was not aware the paper was "public domain." I would rather have published the original. It was damning. I asked permission of SRI, but was never answered. That says something, I think.

8. Randi (p. 37): There was no way that I could get to see the SRI film. Only the elite of the world of science and journalism were invited (to the Columbia symposium).

Fact: The Columbia symposium was widely known to be an open symposium to which any interested individual could come and for which no invitations were required.

My response: Hearing of the film, I tried to contact Dr. Gerald Feinberg, at Columbia, who sponsored the showing. I was unable to do so, and was unaware that it was an open showing. In any case, I certainly was not invited, in spite of my known interest.

9. Randi (p. 37): Randi would have the reader believe that the compass sequence and spoon-bending sequence of the SRI film "Experiments with Uri Geller" are examples of where SRI scientists were taken in by magic tricks.

Fact: With regard to the compass sequence the film narration states: "The following is an experiment which in retrospect we consider unsatisfactory as it didn't meet our protocol standards. Here the task is to deflect the compass needle . . . However, according to our protocol, if we could in any way debunk the experiment and produce the effects by any other means, then that experiment was considered null and void even if there were no indications that anything untoward happened. In this case, we found later that these types of deflections could be produced by a small piece of metal, so small in fact that they could not be detected by the magnetometer. Therefore, even though we had no evidence of this, we still considered the experiment inconclusive and an unsatisfactory type of experiment altogether."

With regard to the spoon-bending sequence, the film states: "One of Geller's main attributes that had been reported to us was that he was able to bend metal . . . In the laboratory we did not find him able to do so . . . [It] becomes clear in watching this film that simple photo interpretation is insufficient to determine whether the metal is bent by normal or paranormal means . . . It is not clear whether the spoon is being bent because he has extraordinarily strong fingers and good control of micro-manipulatory movements, or whether, in fact, the spoon "turns to plastic" in his hands, as he claims." (Text of narration of film "Experiments with Uri Geller," shown at Columbia and elsewhere. Text released as part of SRI press release of March 6, 1973, accompanying Columbia presentation.)

My response: Yes, the film contains a disclaimer. Then why, gentlemen, were these "inconclusive and . . . unsatisfactory" sequences included in a "scientific" film at a leading university in this official unveiling of the wonders of the Psychic World discovered at Stanford Research Institute, a leading center of scientific endeavor? To add glamor and to fluff up a very poor effort, obviously. The film belongs with the Mack Sennett epics.

10. Randi (p. 48): Shipi was there, according to Hanlon, "constantly underfoot" during the tests.

Fact: Neither Shipi nor any other potential confederate was permitted in the target area during the tests. Hanlon's allegations to the contrary were refuted in Letters to the Editor, *New Scientist,* p. 443, November 1974.

My response: Again, I never said Shipi was "in the target area." But he was there, underfoot, and so was his sister—a proven confederate, as is Shipi—throughout the tests. Why? Simply because Geller wanted it that way. The mouse was running the tests—again.

11. Randi (pp. 40–50): If you made an excuse to leave the room—and could have gotten just one quick glance at Shipi Shtrang, and he was trying to signal . . . A quick glance at this target might have given Shipi an impression of a horse . . . Such a response could result from a hand signal . . . This shape, which could have been transmitted by simple hand gestures or by a verbal clue . . . They might even have been watching Shipi by now . . . etc.

Fact: As indicated above, neither Shipi nor any other potential confederate was permitted in the target area, and Geller was never permitted to change his position (i.e., enter or leave experimental room) while an experiment was in progress.

My response: Not so. The "experiments" with Geller were done largely over weekends, when SRI was deserted. Soft-drink and beer cans, food wrappers and scraps, incense sticks and general debris were evident after these sessions. I have been told that Geller *did* leave the "sealed room" during tests, and in the Faraday cage series he could see Shipi/Hannah clearly through the mesh walls.

12. Randi (p. 47): Captain Edgar Mitchell has said "I was there virtually all the time. I am a co-investigator on all that work . . . they were

so eager to keep him (Geller) around that they worked themselves into a box by meeting his every whim . . ."

Fact: Captain Mitchell was not at SRI for any of the experimentation reported in *Nature*, but rather only during early efforts to find whether it was possible to introduce strict protocols as was finally done successfully.

My response: Mitchell was there during the filming, but he was such a stickler for protocol that Geller preferred he leave during other sessions. Remember, these tests were done Geller's way or they were not done at all, or else they were done but not reported because they failed. Mitchell's comment is not less interesting just because he was subsequently shut out.

13. Randi (p. 49): Only in the tests where there was no possibility of transmission of data from a confederate did Geller refuse to try the test or just fail it. (Referring to Experiments 5–7)

Fact: Two of the three experiments (6 and 7) were carried out under the same conditions as all of the others—no potential confederates in the target area. The third experiment (Exp. 5) was a special clairvoyance experiment—again with no potential confederate in the target area.

My response: So what? When there was no way of doing the trick (and it was most often done through a confederate) Geller "passed"— or, as in the "devil" episode, resorted to tried-and-true desperation measures and succeeded. Remember, there were many "experiments" with Geller—and others at SRI—that failed and were never reported.

14. Randi (p. 49): [With regard to the Faraday cage experiments.] He could even reach his arm out of the cage. What is to prevent Shipi from signaling these three to Geller? Nothing.

Fact: The Faraday cage is entirely sealed and guarded. Only by opening the door can one reach out. With regard to Shipi acting as a confederate to signal to Geller, again, as in all experiments, neither Shipi nor any other potential confederate was permitted into the target area or knew of the target, a precaution insisted upon and followed as a result of advice from consulting magicians.

My response: I was told that the large mesh of the "cage" allowed one to reach out. I was never able to see the cage, or a photo of it, though opening the screen door is obviously not difficult. Hannah Shtrang was in the target area this time and was a general "gopher," thus being provided with an excellent opportunity to act as a confederate. Many people wandering by asked to see the target and were shown it. The control on this test was ridiculous.

15. Randi (p. 52): And is it not curious that this Geller test series was never reprinted or mentioned by any of his SRI disciples? [Referring to the 100-envelope double-blind clairvoyance test that Geller failed.]

Fact: This test, with its negative results, is also in the *Nature* paper, fourth paragraph from the end of the section on Geller.

My response: There is no way that anyone could identify the 100-envelope test reported in *Nature* with the Rebert/Otis test. T and P say, in *Nature*, "On each day he made approximately 12 recognizable drawings, which he felt were associated with the entire target pool of 100. On each of the three days, two of his drawings could reasonably be associated with two of the 20 daily targets. On the third day, two of his drawings were very close replications of two of that day's target pictures." Fact: There was never any provision for "associating" drawings with the entire pool. He was to tell the contents of *one envelope at a time*. T and P are attempting to salvage something from these failed tests, which they had to report since they were designed by others at SRI. Fact: The episode on the third day took place *after* the test was officially terminated and involved a special set of six envelopes not in the original target pool. Geller left the room several times during the tests and scored direct hits on two envelopes. Rebert solved that one; anyone could.

16. Randi (p. 59): . . . agreed to examine Geller's claims, with the arrangement that if the results were not positive no report would be issued . . . Did Geller have the same arrangement with the boys at SRI before he agreed to be tested there? I'll bet he did!

Fact: Negative results on compass deflection and metal bending are reported in the SRI film "Experiments with Uri Geller," Columbia Physics Colloquium, March 6, 1973, and negative results on metal bending and 100-envelope clairvoyance test are reported in *Nature*, October, 1974.

My response: T and P refuse to answer direct questions! Note that here they skirt the implication, never saying that they did *not* have any such arrangement with Geller. To have no negative tests—a 100 percent success—would be *too* good. (I'll *still* bet that Geller had the boys over a barrel with such an arrangement!)

17. Randi (p. 82): Now, SRI, in its great wisdom, has called in a magician briefly as consultant. Not before Geller's tests, mind you, but after. With them, the alarm system is installed after the robbery. It is interesting to note that when Geller did a subsequent series of tests there (p. 52), he failed. Any connection?

Fact: SRI called in a magician as consultant *before* any of the tests with Geller, not after. (A magician who specializes in exposing poltergeist cases as frauds.) If Randi is referring only to Milbourne Christopher, no tests, including those of page 52, were done after Christopher's consultancy, all work with Geller having been completed before Christopher's arrival.

My response: See my response to point 3.

18. Randi (p. 95): And the SRI public relations man (who has since quit the organization) called Wilhelm of *Time* to see what could be done about the story.

Fact: SRI's public relations man, Ron Deutsch, did not quit the organization over this or any other issue, and is still there.

My response: Fellows, I never said that Ron Deutsch quit "over this . . . issue"! I merely reported what I had been told, that he had left SRI. T and P are partly correct. Deutsch, at the time T and P wrote, was still at SRI; he left shortly afterward.

19. Ray Hyman quoted by Randi (p. 111): "So I asked them [Puthoff and Targ] if he could bend them without touching them (metal rings). They told me he could do it either way. I asked Puthoff if he or anyone else at SRI had seen Uri do it without touching the ring. They never did answer me. They simply assured me that he could do it either way."

Fact: The above is false reporting. It is well known that Puthoff and Targ of SRI have been agnostic on the subject of metal bending since the beginning, and reported thus both in the SRI film and in the *Nature* paper.

My response: Here we either accept Hyman's word, or call him a liar (see my point 1). He is a reputable investigator, with no reason at all to fabricate his story. He prepared a report in writing, for Washington, immediately upon his return from SRI. His visit predated the *Nature* paper by almost two years, well before T and P had abandoned all efforts to get metal-bending evidence from Geller and were forced to fall back on their poorly controlled "ESP" tests to submit as a report on what they'd done with the money.

20. Randi (p. 117): First of all, Taylor's statement about the magician is not true. Where he got that idea, I cannot tell. There was no magician present.

Fact: Taylor's statement is true; he got it from SRI researchers. A magician was present.

My response: Taylor's actual words, reported in the book (page 117) are, "Some . . . experiments were scrutinized by a magician on television monitors . . ." The account implies strongly that the magician (Christopher) watched the experiments *in progress*, not months afterwards! There was no magician there watching those experiments. Hastings had been forbidden to watch, remember? See my response to point 3.

21. Randi (p. 128): You might recall, professor, that your counterparts in America—Targ and Puthoff—obtained single-sided pulses when Uri tried to hex a sensitive weighing device. And no one thought to try testing the chart recorder then, either.

Fact: As is apparent from the SRI film: (*a*) the chart recorder was remote from Geller in the experiment, and (*b*) the chart recorder was continuously monitored by film and videotape, specifically as a guard against chicanery.

My response: T and P make my point for me! The recorder was remote from Geller, and they were watching Geller. The recorder could not have been monitored *while Geller was monitored*! Q.E.D.

22. Randi (p. 140): And, finally, as if there were not enough doubts about the procedure used to conduct this "test," *Time's* Wilhelm has reported that the set of tries with the die actually consisted of *many hundreds of throws*, the object being to get a run of consecutive wins.

Fact: There was no selection of a good run out of "hundreds of throws." There were ten throws only, as reported in the *Nature* paper, eight of which were correctly guessed by Geller, two of which were passed. All the throws were reported.

My response: (*a*) The throws were made, a few at a time, over a period of days. This is not "an experiment." It is a series of sporadic demonstrations. (*b*) There were die tests made before and after the SRI "official" tests. (*c*) Tests were also made at *Psychic* magazine. (Puthoff recently admitted these, and excepted them from the "real" tests.) (*d*) The tests were done at irregular times, when Geller felt "inspired" to do them. As usual, he was running the tests. (*e*) Pressman, the SRI photographer, reported to a scientist there that the successful tests were not done while he was present but were reported to him by Puthoff the next day. If that is the case, the filmed tests *were re-enactments*, in direct contradiction to the official text of the SRI film. Pressman now *denies* that he told anyone that. See my book *Flim-Flam!* for details.

23. Randi (p. 140): An elaborate hypothesis is put forward as to how Geller might have handled the dice box and cheated.

Fact: Film and videotape show otherwise, and magicians examining this material have failed to detect a conjuring trick.

> *My response*: "Film and videotape show otherwise"? I have asked to see this evidence, and have been denied. The *only* film we may see is of a pass! Why, if there is other film and videotape available that proves their point, did T and P choose to show a *pass*?

24. Randi (p. 211): Targ and Puthoff say, in a letter to *Communications Society* magazine, that, "In lengthy consultation with professional magicians, no viable conjuring explanation for these or other experiments reported in *Nature* has emerged." What magicians? If these gentlemen have examined this book carefully, they may now have another conclusion.

Fact: Having examined this book carefully, we find that in every instance Randi, in his efforts to fault the SRI experiments, was driven to hypothesize the existence of a loophole condition that did not, in fact, exist. If Randi believes that the conditions he hypothesized were responsible for the results of those SRI experiments with Geller that were successful, then, by their negation, Randi has provided further evidence for the genuineness of the phenomena as observed and reported.

> *My response*: I am pleased to see that whatever was presented in *The Magic of Uri Geller* as speculation has been validated in the years since. In this "Fact Sheet" Russell Targ and Harold Puthoff not only failed to rebut my book; they got themselves in deeper than ever before. All the semantic trickery and verbal obfuscation employed by T and P (and I admit they are fairly good at it) will not serve to excuse their attempt to jam the Geller "phenomenon" down the unwilling throats of science

and the public. There are those who will continue to believe that in the 1970s science validated the powers of an Israeli psychic; those who read this book and *Flim-Flam!* will know otherwise. The public can be deceived for a while, but truth is annoyingly persistent.

Appendix

UNIVERSITY OF LONDON KING'S COLLEGE

TEL: OI-836 8851   26-29 DRURY LANE LONDON WC2B 5RL

SCHOOL OF BIOLOGICAL SCIENCES   DEPARTMENT OF BIOPHYSICS

11 July, 1975

To Whom It May Concern:

Mr. James Randi appeared before us today at the Department of
Biophysics and demonstrated in a laboratory his ability to bend and
break spoons and keys that we supplied. He caused bursts on a Geiger
counter and made one of our spoons become flexible and finally break
in two while one of us held it at each end. Then Mr. Randi caused a
compass needle to deflect by about 15° and caused several watches to
advance.

We were made well aware in advance that Mr. Randi appeared before
us as a conjuror, and we watched him closely, knowing that he was doing
tricks. We gave him no advantage that might be given to a "sensitive."

After the performance, he revealed to us how some of these tricks
had been done.

We believe that in investigating phenomena of apparently paranormal nature a qualified conjuror must be closely involved.

Signed:

Maurice H. F. Wilkins FRS

Ted Richards Ph.D. (Chemistry)

Christopher Evans Ph.D. (Psychology)

David Davies Ph.D. (Geophysics)

Roger Woodham Ph.D. (Cosmic Rays)

Wait A Minute!

By Wessely Hicks

HE SEES THE FUTURE

Randall Zwinge, the man with the mind which functions like a carbon copy of your own and maybe a little ahead of it, has scored on another prediction. Mr. Zwinge foretold, a week before the Canadian National Exhibition opened, the number of people who would attend on the opneing day.

Last year, a week before the World Series started, Mr. Zwinge predicted the outcome. He named the day of the final game, the winning team and the score.

His World Series forecast was sealed in an envelope which was signed, countersigned, witnessed by a notary, and locked in a lawyer's safe. The day after the final game of the series was played, the envelope was taken out of the safe and opened. Mr Zwinge was not present.

CALLED WINNER, SCORE

His prediction was correct. He had said the New York Yankees would defeat Brooklyn Dodgers in the final game by a score of ten to six.

This year, Mr. Zwinge recorded his prediction of the number of people who would attend the Canadian National Exhibition. He made his recording on Friday, August 18, one week before the Ex opened.

Then he brought the recording into The Telegram office the following day. I took the little disc and signed my name and the date

on the seal. I scratched my name deeply on the reverse side of the record so it could not be used.

SEALED, SIGNED

Then I pasted the record in its envelope with sealing wax and pressed my house key into the wax. Finally, I signed my name across the open face of the envelope with heavy crayon so that it was scrawled across the seal, too.

The record was then locked in The Telegram safe.

Last Saturday, when the attendance figures for the first day were announced, I took the record out of the safe and checked the impressions in the sealing wax. They checked.

I carried the record in my hot little hand down to the Fairex theatre at the Canadian National Exhibition and placed it on a record player. And, while about 1,500 people sat and listened, Mr. Zwinge's voice boomed out his prediction.

A week before, he had recorded the prediction there would be 107,566 people at the Exhibition on the first day.

The published, official attendance figure was 107,500. Canadian National Exhibition officials will release no other figure though that has obviously been boosted or reduced to the nearest 100. Still, taking it as it stands, Mr. Zwinge was within one-third of one per cent. correct.

And the record was not switched, for I still have the original, doubly-

signed disc on my desk and it still predicts 107,566.

Today I had lunch with Mr. Zwinge and asked him how he had plucked 107,566 out of the misty future, especially a misty future which was fogged by a rail strike and the threat of bad weather.

"CERTAIN PERCEPTIONS"

Mr. Zwinge blinked his blue eyes behind his heavy horn-rimmed spectacles and then tapped his scholarly forehead. "Certain perceptions have been given me," he said, "and I have improved them by a deep study of the science of mental telepathy and clairvoyance."

And that's all he would say.

So when the waitress brought the bill and placed it face down on the table, I said I would make him a proposition. Placing my hand on the bill, which was still face down, I said that if he would name the figures on the bill I would pay for the lunch.

Mr. Zwinge smiled. "The total is $1.80," he said. "The table number is 22 and the waitress' number is six. She has signed her initials 'M.E.'"

It all tallied. I asked how he did it. "I remembered the prices," Mr. Zwinge said. "My scallops cost 95 cents. Your con carne cost 75 cents. You had coffee for ten cents. I had none. Total $1.80."

So I asked about the table number and the waitress' number and initials.

But Mr. Zwinge just smiled. "That's the second lesson," he said,

Toronto Evening Telegram
August 28, 1950

Wait A Minute!   By Wessely Hicks

SNOOPS ON MINDS

Randall Zwinge is a slim, bespectacled young man with a receding hair line, Extra Sensory Perception and a Psi capacity. Reduced to language we tea cup readers can understand, Mr. Zwinge can read minds. Or, as he says, he possesses a combination of telepathic, clairvoyant and prophetic senses.

Today Mr. Zwinge gave a modest, but rather disturbing exhibition of his Extra Sensory Perception and Psi capacity. At the same time, he admitted that he was one of three men in the world who can memorize a shuffled deck of cards in 3½ minutes and that his hobby is doing crossword puzzles without writing any words in the squares. He remembers.

First, Mr. Zwinge placed three cigarettes on my desk, and invited me to choose one. "I will write on a piece of paper the cigarette you will choose before you make your choice," he said. He wrote on a copy pad, tore off the sheet and placed it under the telephone on the far side of the desk.

HOBSON'S CHOICE

"Now choose a cigarette," he said. "though you have no choice. I already know which one you will choose." Being a practiced moocher, I reached for the first cigarette, changed my mind, and grabbed the third.

With a little flourish, Mr. Zwinge handed me the piece of paper from under the telephone. On it was written: "You will choose the third cigarette."

Then Mr. Zwinge picked up a copy of The Telegram. "Choose any word on that page," he said, "and encircle it with your pencil."

I retired to the far side of the room, encircled the word "door,"

tore out the fragment of paper on which it was printed, and folded the paper tightly. Mr. Zwinge tore the folded paper into bits.

"Destroy it," he said. I burned it in the ash tray.

Then Mr. Zwinge sat down with a copy pad, drew an ellipse, and wrote "Door" in the ellipse. He repeated the demonstration several times and twice I was just thinking of a word I had written on a pad across the room from him.

JUST AN OPEN BOOK

I said he was enchanted. Mr. Zwinge just shrugged modestly. "Think of a number," he said. I thought of twelve. "You're thinking of twelve," Mr. Zwinge said, almost as soon as I thought of it, and I began to feel as though I had a glass back in my head.

Mr. Zwinge said he first became aware that he possessed Extra Sensory Perception when he was nine years old. He used to answer the phone just before it rang, because he sensed that someone was dialing his number. The result was that callers were always getting busy signals. "I still sense when the phone is going to ring," he says, "but now I wait with my hands on it until it does ring."

Last year, Mr. Zwinge predicted the outcome of the World Series a week before it was played. He predicted that the New York Yankees would beat the Brooklyn Dodgers by a score of 10 to six on Sunday, October 9, to win the Series. He wrote his prediction out, sealed it in an envelope, and gave it to a lawyer, who locked it in his safe. "The lawyer was very surprised when he opened the letter and read what I had written," Mr. Zwinge says.

His World Series prediction was quite simple, really. "I just had a flash," Mr. Zwinge says. "I saw the news reel of the final game in my mind a week before it was played," he says. "Three days after the game had been played, I went to a show and saw the same news reel. I had seen it in my mind long before."

After he had prophesied the outcome of the 1949 World Series, Mr. Zwinge received more propositions than a beauty contest winner. "A man in California offered me $500 a week to call him once a day and tell him the quotations on any stock the following day," he says. "A syndicate offered to set me up in New York in the stock predicting business. People wanted to know when they should buy sweepstakes tickets. Other people wanted me to pick horses for them on any race track in the country.

"But, of course, I cant do that. I have to wait for a flash on things like that. If I could do it consistently, I'd go in business for myself."

But just to prove that his World Series forecast wasn't a fluke, Mr. Zwinge is making another prediction. "I am going to predict the number of people who will attend the opening day of the Canadian National Exhibition," he says. "I will foretell the number within one or two people and do it a week in advance.

DATE FOR THE RACES

"I will record my prediction and give you the record. When Elwood Hughes make the opening day's attendance known, you can play the record and compare my prediction with the actual figure."

If he does it, I will take no excuses. He's going to the races with me.

Toronto *Evening Telegram*
August 14, 1950

TIME

TIME & LIFE BUILDING
ROCKEFELLER CENTER
NEW YORK 10020
212 JUDSON 6-1212

June, 1975

To Whom It May Concern:

We, the undersigned persons, having read the chapter intended for "The Magic of Uri Geller" by James Randi in which the account of Uri Geller's meeting with us in the office of John Durniak is outlined, certify by our signatures that the information contained therein is essentially correct insofar as our direct experience of the event is concerned, as to the best of our individual recollection. Corrections contained herein by Mr. Randi of the version originally printed in the book, "Uri" by Andrija Puharich, are proper corrections and agree with our experience and recollection of the meeting. This we certify.

Signed,

DEFENSE ADVANCED RESEARCH PROJECTS AGENCY

1400 WILSON BOULEVARD
ARLINGTON, VIRGINIA 22209

June 18, 1975

Mr. James Randi
51 Lennox Avenue
Rumson, New Jersey   07760

Dear Mr. Randi:

Thank you for the opportunity to comment on ARPA's observations of Mr. Uri Geller's presentations. ARPA has, as a professional obligation, the duty to maintain an up-to-date knowledge of the progress and trends in world science having potential significance to the Department of Defense. To this end, ARPA personnel follow the professional literature and maintain contacts with leading research and development organizations. Thus, ARPA representatives accepted an invitation to visit the Stanford Research Institute to witness some experiments and to review data taken in earlier experiments. Neither the data presented nor their own direct observations proved adequate to convince the ARPA people either that genuine paranormal phenomena were in evidence or that this sphere of activity would be appropriate for ARPA support. ARPA has never funded or planned a research program to investigate paranormal phenomena, nor have we seen any evidence to encourage us to do so.

Sincerely yours,

T. W. Niedenfuhr
Special Assistant

Glossary

Apport: to transfer from one place to another by "psychic" means; an object so transferred. Very rare.

Clairvoyance: purported ability to see or know a fact without normal sense perception, and without the fact being known to another person.

Conjuring: art of trickery, sleight of hand, admitted jugglery.

Control: in lab tests, the system for obviating trickery or false interpretation of results from poor data-gathering. Two kinds: good and bad.

ESP: see Extrasensory perception.

Extrasensory perception: apparent perceiving of facts without use of normal senses: includes clairvoyance and woman's intuition.

Kirlian photography: process of registering high-voltage discharges on film or photographic paper. Harmless diversion.

Levitation: raising or suspension of an object without apparent means of physical support. Common conjuror's *mise en scène.*

Magic: attempt to control nature by spells or incantation or by invoking supernatural help. Often also used to denote conjuring.

Materialization: causing an object or person to assume real form or visible shape; calling up ghosts and spirits.

Medium: Person purporting to have the power or nature necessary to call up spirits or to cause supernatural events: fortune-teller.

Paranormal: term used by modern researchers to define supernatural or extrasensory abilities or events. New, fancy term.

Parapsychology: the study of paranormal events or abilities. Not a science, but an art.

PK: see Psychokinesis.

Plant communication: purported process whereby vegetables speak with one another and with humans, and react to human emotions.

Poltergeist: "mischievous spirit" that throws objects about. Not surprisingly, often found in households where neglected teenager is also found.

Precognition: purported ability to see the future.

Psi: (letter of Greek alphabet) Used to designate any supposed paranormal event or process.

Psychic: person said to have paranormal abilities. These days, not as rare as previously.

Psychokinesis: purported ability to move objects at a distance without physical means. (Not as much fun as levitation.)

Second sight: see Clairvoyance.

Sensitive: person said to be sensitive to ESP. (Also, I find, sensitive to skepticism.)

Spiritualism: religious cult devoted to calling up and communicating with dead people. Very depressing matter, with much singing.

Target: in research, the object or word decided upon to test ESP.

Telepathy: supposed process whereby thoughts are transferred from mind to mind, directly. Popular premise with conjurors.

Teleportation: claimed process whereby objects are moved instantly over any distance without physical means. Interesting, but unlikely.

UFO: Unidentified Flying Objects; flying saucer; alien spaceship; anything seen in the sky and not understood instantly.

Bibliography

A Magician Among the Spirits, by Harry Houdini, Harper & Row, New York, 1924.

Arigo: Surgeon of the Rusty Knife, by John Fuller, Thomas Y. Crowell, New York, 1974.

Cults of Unreason, by Christopher Evans, Farrar, Strauss, and Giroux, New York, 1973.

ESP: A Scientific Evaluation, by Dr. C. E. M. Hansel, New York, Charles Scribner's Sons, 1966. (Revised and expanded edition: *ESP and Parapsychology,* Prometheus Books, Buffalo, N.Y., 1980.)

ESP: The Search Beyond the Senses, by Daniel Cohen, Harcourt Brace Jovanovich, New York, 1973.

Mediums, Mystics and the Occult, by Milbourne Christopher, Thomas Y. Crowell, New York, 1975.

My Story, by Uri Geller, Praeger, New York, 1975.

Psychic Exploration, by Edgar Mitchell, G. P. Putnam's, New York, 1974.

Science: Good, Bad and Bogus, by Martin Gardner, Prometheus Books, New York, 1981.

Superminds, by John Taylor, Macmillan, London, 1975.

The Supernatural? by Lionel A. Weatherly and J. N. Maskelyne, J. W. Arrowsmith, 1891.

Test Your ESP Potential, by James Randi, Dover, New York, 1982.

Transcendental Physics, by J. C. F. Zöllner, Ballantyne Press, London, 1880.

Uri: The Journal of the Mystery of Uri Geller, by A. Puharich, Anchor Press, New York, 1974.

PAPERBACKS AVAILABLE FROM PROMETHEUS BOOKS

SCIENCE AND THE PARANORMAL

____ESP & Parapsychology: A Critical Re-evaluation   C.E.M. Hansel $9.95

____Extra-Terrestrial Intelligence   James L. Christian, editor   7.95

____Flim-Flam!   James Randi   9.95

____Objections to Astrology   L. Jerome & B. Bok   4.95

____The Psychology of the Psychic   D. Marks & R. Kammann   9.95

____Philosophy & Parapsychology   J. Ludwig, editor   9.95

____Paranormal Borderlands of Science   Kendrick Frazier, editor $13.95

____The Truth About Uri Geller   James Randi   8.95

HUMANISM

____Ethics Without God   K. Nielsen   6.95

____Humanist Alternative   Paul Kurtz, editor   5.95

____Humanist Ethics   Morris Storer, editor   9.95

____Humanist Funeral Service   Corliss Lamont   3.95

____Humanist Manifestos I & II   1.95

____Humanist Wedding Service   Corliss Lamont   2.95

____Humanistic Psychology   Welch, Tate, Richards, editors   10.95

____Moral Problems in Contemporary Society   Paul Kurtz, editor   7.95

____Secular Humanist Declaration   1.95

____Voice in the Wilderness   Corliss Lamont   5.95

____Rabbi and Minister   Carl Hermann Voss   7.95

LIBRARY OF LIBERAL RELIGION

____Facing Death and Grief   George N. Marshall   7.95

____Living Religions of the World   Carl Hermann Voss   4.95

PHILOSOPHY & ETHICS

____Animal Rights and Human Morality   Bernard Rollin   9.95

____Art of Deception   Nicholas Capaldi   6.95

____Beneficent Euthanasia   M. Kohl, editor   8.95

____Contemporary Analytic and Linguistic Philosophies   E. D. Klemke   11.95

____Esthetics Contemporary   Richard Kostelanetz, editor   11.95

____Ethics and the Search for Values   L. Navia and E. Kelly, editors   13.95

____Exuberance: A Philosophy of Happiness   Paul Kurtz   3.00

____Freedom, Anarchy, and the Law   Richard Taylor   8.95

____Freedom of Choice Affirmed   Corliss Lamont   4.95

____Fullness of Life   Paul Kurtz   5.95

____Having Love Affairs   Richard Taylor   8.95

____Humanhood: Essays in Biomedical Ethics   Joseph Fletcher   8.95

____Infanticide and the Value of Life   Marvin Kohl, editor   9.95

____Introductory Readings in the Philosophy of Science   Klemke, Hollinger, Kline, editors   12.95

____Invitation to Philosophy   Capaldi, Kelly, Navia, editors   12.95

____Journeys Through Philosophy (Revised)   N. Capaldi & L. Navia, editors   14.95

____Philosophy: An Introduction   *Antony Flew*   6.95

____Problem of God   *Peter A. Angeles*   9.95

____Psychiatry and Ethics   *Rem B. Edwards, editor*   12.95

____Responsibilities to Future Generations   *Ernest Partridge, editor*   9.95

____Reverse Discrimination   *Barry Cross, editor*   9.95

____Thinking Straight   *Antony Flew*   5.95

.. __Thomas Szasz: Primary Values and Major Contentions   9.95

____Worlds of the Early Greek Philosophers   *Wilbur & Allen, editors*   8.95

____Worlds of Hume and Kant   *Wilbur & Allen, editors*   7.95

____Worlds of Plato & Aristotle   *Wilbur & Allen, editors*   7.95

SEXOLOGY

____The Frontiers of Sex Research   *Vern Bullough, editor*   8.95

____New Bill of Sexual Rights & Responsibilities   *Lester Kirkendall*   6.95

____New Sexual Revolution   *Lester Kirkendall, editor*   6.95

____Philosophy & Sex   *Robert Baker & Fred Elliston, editors*   7.95

____Sex Without Love: A Philosophical Exploration   *Russell Vannoy*   8.95

THE SKEPTIC'S BOOKSHELF

____Atheism. The Case Against God   *George H. Smith*   7.95

____Atheist Debater's Handbook   *B.C. Johnson*   10.95

____What About Gods? (for children)   *Chris Brockman*   4.95

____Classics of Free Thought   *Paul Blanshard, editor*   6.95

____Critiques of God   *Peter Angeles, editor*   9.95

ADDITIONAL TITLES

____Age of Aging: A Reader in Social Gerontology   *Monk, editor*   9.95

____Avant-Garde Tradition in Literature   *Richard Kostelanetz, editor*   11.95

____Higher Education in American Society   *Altbach & Berdahl, editors*   9.95

____Israel's Defense Line   *I.L. Kenen*   9.95

____Pornography and Censorship   *Copp & Wendell, editors*   9.95

____Psychiatry, Mental Health Care, and Ethics   *Rem B. Edwards, editor*   9.95

The books listed above can be obtained from your book dealer
or directly from Prometheus Books.
Please check off the appropriate books.
Remittance must accompany all orders from individuals.
Please include $1.50 postage and handling for first book,
.50 for each additional book ($4.00 maximum).
(N.Y. State Residents add 7% sales tax)

Send to _____
                    (Please type or print clearly)

Address _____

City _____ State_____ Zip_____

                                    Amount Enclosed_____

Prometheus Books
700 E. Amherst St.
Buffalo, New York 14215